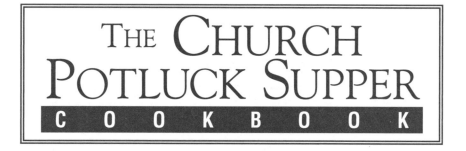

THE CHURCH POTLUCK SUPPER
COOKBOOK

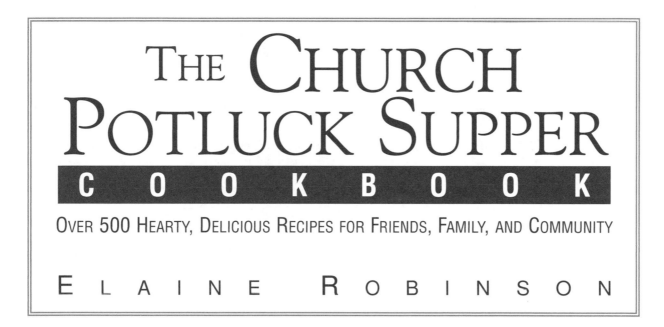

THE CHURCH
POTLUCK SUPPER
COOKBOOK

OVER 500 HEARTY, DELICIOUS RECIPES FOR FRIENDS, FAMILY, AND COMMUNITY

ELAINE ROBINSON

Adams Media Corporation
Avon, Massachusetts

Published by
Adams Media Corporation
57 Littlefield Street, Avon, MA 02322. U.S.A.
www.adamsmedia.com

ISBN: 1-58062-838-9

Printed in Canada.

J   I   H   G   F   E   D   C   B   A

Library of Congress Cataloging-in-Publication Data
Robinson, Elaine.
Church potluck supper cookbook / by Elaine Robinson.
p.   cm.
ISBN 1-58062-838-9
1. Buffets (Cookery). 2. Church dinners. 3. Church
entertainments. 4. Quantity cookery. I. Title.
TX738.5 .R63 2002
642'.4—dc21
2002011340

This publication is designed to provide accurate and authoritative information with regard to the subject matter covered. It is sold with the understanding that the publisher is not engaged in rendering legal, accounting, or other professional advice. If legal advice or other expert assistance is required, the services of a competent professional person should be sought.
—From a *Declaration of Principles* jointly adopted by a Committee of the American Bar Association and a Committee of Publishers and Associations

Many of the designations used by manufacturers and sellers to distinguish their products are claimed as trademarks. Where those designations appear in this book and Adams Media was aware of a trademark claim, the designations have been printed in initial capital letters.

Cover photograph © Michael Gadomski / Superstock.
Cover illustration by Kathie Kelleher.
Interior photographs © DigitalVision.
Interior illustration by Christopher Speakman.

*This book is available at quantity discounts for bulk purchases.
For information, call 1-800-872-5627.*

Table of Contents

Introduction

Today in America, as perhaps never before, our families and friends have become the central focus in our lives. It is ever more important to find the time for events, large or small, that bring us together. The strongest family-centered institution in our society is the church, providing not only formal worship and service opportunities for the family, but also social and fun times to be together as families. Singles can easily be a part of these fellowship times as the "church family" joins together.

There are many occasions for gathering within the church community to share a meal. As there are great varieties of people in our experience, there are great varieties of food. Picture that long table at church laid out with all kinds of food from homemade rolls to perhaps a baked striped bass, should you live near the coast or have a fisherman in your group. There are the baked beans, chicken, meatloaf, and lasagna, and then the great variety of tasty salads and delicious desserts. Oh, those whoopie pies and molasses cookies! It brings a smile as our memories roll back with enthusiasm to these events that we probably first experienced quite early in our lives. The sharing of food happens at other community events, but our emphasis will be on these activities as they take place in the life of the church.

It is not surprising that oftentimes more people will come to a meeting or event if there is food involved. People seem to enjoy meals shared in love and friendship, and we must not overlook that this does have a spiritual dimension. As in the story of the young lad who shared the loaves and fishes with Jesus, who then shared with the multitude, our sharing of food overflows into many spiritual blessings.

This book honors and remembers with affection those who for so many years cooked delicious food and always had everything ready at serving time. Lifestyles have changed, and time schedules make it difficult to work in extra responsibilities. I hope this book with its recipes and tips on planning will be helpful so that even with our time constraints these traditions can be continued. When my

husband and I were young seminarians about to be married, I was given a cookbook, inscribed with the message that "although he may be concerned with their souls, you may have to be concerned with their stomachs." Being involved in food events has never been a "have to" for me. It has always been a joy. Have you ever been asked to be on a committee for a food event and wondered how it all happens? This book has some tips for you in your planning, and planning is everything! I hope this book can help you as you "step up to the plate" and arrange for a food event. There is a strong sense of spirituality when the church family gathers to share a meal in love and friendship. These opportunities to be connected in sharing in each other's lives are a precious gift, and today Americans seem to realize that more and more. What do we have without each other?

The book, containing over 500 recipes, is divided into several areas that seem especially important to highlight. We will explore the potluck supper, the preparation of fund-raising meals, the food sale, the church picnic, entertaining at the church, and sharing food with the family in crisis. These recipes can be interchanged from chapter to chapter to fit the needs of the situation at hand.

Although this is first of all a cookbook, I hope that it will have a dimension even beyond that, for it is not meant to be simply a compilation of recipes. The spirit of the book entails more than the realm of the culinary arts, and its contents represent more than the preparation of food. It really is about people working together for a common cause in a common, yet extraordinary, spirit.

Many thanks to those people from churches around the country who have shared a recipe or two for this book. My task, a journey that has been both a challenge and a delight, has been to simply gather the fruits of other people's labor and to blend them together with my own experience. It is out of this great richness that this book has grown. ❦

Chapter One

The Potluck Supper

Potluck luncheons and suppers nourish not only our bodies, but also our souls as we come together in fellowship and community with each other. We must never take for granted "getting together for potluck."

Whatever the reason, potluck is appropriate. For example, the annual church meeting, the choir Christmas party, or the year-end Circle meeting, which celebrates the work the group has accomplished during the past year. Let us remember, also, that it is a great way to have families come together for good food, fellowship, and sometimes entertainment. One of our memorable family experiences was the Annual Birthday Potluck Supper, where everyone's birthday was celebrated! There was at least one birthday cake provided by the church for every month of the year, and everyone brought a casserole or a salad. The church also provided bread and beverages. The entertainment was special, too, usually geared to the children. It could have been a magician, or mime, chalk art, some special art form that delighted the children and caught the interest of the adults as well. What memorable occasions they were for our family, now grown, and for the children who still enjoy such evenings with their family and friends. Potluck suppers can get hectic. There may be too much macaroni, and you may even get stuck at the end of the serving line, but stop to feel and experience what is going on around you, and realize that you are a part of something special.

Even though the cooking is shared, there needs to be a coordinating committee to plan the proceedings of the event so that all runs smoothly. There are a couple of approaches to this which I will mention. You may wish to make the event truly potluck. People bring whatever they want, and if only desserts or baked beans are brought, that is what everyone eats! Another approach is to divide the group by alphabetical order and have some bring a casserole, some a dessert, and some a salad. Perhaps you would have one of the committees of the church provide all the casseroles and attendees bring salad or dessert. You may ask for casseroles and salads and the church would provide dessert. The planning committee needs to discuss how the food will be requested. Another task of the committee is to purchase the bread, butter, and beverages for the event and have them ready for serving time. Prepare a large, nicely laid-out table from which the food will be served. Provide serving spoons for each dish. Warm the ovens so that casseroles can be kept hot while people are gathering. Someone should arrange for the blessing to be said by the pastor or lay leader. It is also appropriate to have the attendees join hands around the room and sing the Doxology. It is a time to really think about "Praise God from whom all blessings flow."

Potluck may not be just for large public gatherings. Try it with your personal entertaining at home, with a few close friends or relatives. The hostess decides what the basic menu will be and does the organizing. She may wish to bake a ham and ask the guests for vegetables and salads that will complement it. When the work is divided among several people, everyone feels a part of the gathering. It is more important to share in each other's lives than to get so caught up in doing so much that you just can't fit getting together into your schedule. A meal shared in love has a spiritual dimension. Our spirits are fed by food lovingly prepared and shared.

This chapter offers a variety of recipes that can be prepared for taking to a potluck event as well as for serving as part of an everyday meal. ❦

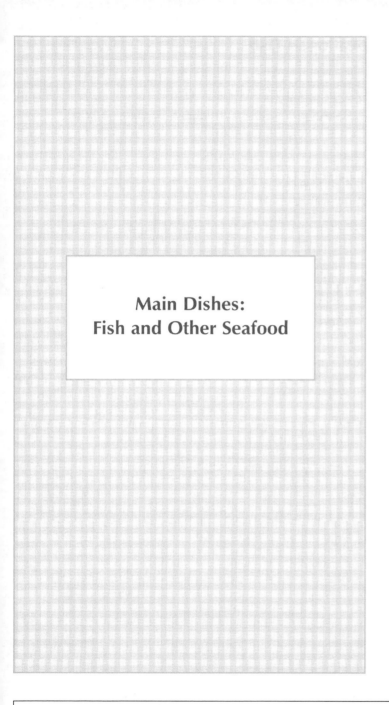

**Main Dishes:
Fish and Other Seafood**

Seafood Casserole I

Serves 6–8

2 TABLESPOONS BUTTER

2 TABLESPOONS FLOUR

2 CANS FROZEN CREAM OF SHRIMP SOUP

1/4 TEASPOON PAPRIKA

1/4 TEASPOON SALT

1/2 CUP CREAM

1 CAN CRABMEAT

1 CAN SHRIMP

1 CAN LOBSTER (OR 1 WHOLE LOBSTER)

BUTTERED BREADCRUMBS

Melt butter in top of double boiler. Blend in flour. Add soup, paprika, salt, and cream. Add seafood. Mix well, and pour into buttered casserole. Cover with breadcrumbs. Bake in 350° oven for 25–30 minutes. This may be served in patty shells.

Seafood Casserole II

Serves 4

4 SLICES OF WHITE BREAD, DICED
1 CAN OR $1/2$ POUND CRABMEAT (OTHER FISH SUCH AS TUNA,
    HADDOCK, OR BLUEFISH MAY BE USED)
$1/4$ CUP MAYONNAISE
$1/2$ CUP FINELY CHOPPED CELERY
1 TABLESPOON GRATED ONION
PIMIENTO (OPTIONAL)
$1^1/_2$ CUPS MILK
2 EGGS, BEATEN
$1/2$ CUP CREAM OF MUSHROOM SOUP
FRESHLY GRATED CHEESE
PAPRIKA (OPTIONAL)

❧ Place $1/2$ the diced bread in buttered casserole. Spread crabmeat over bread. Mix mayonnaise, celery, onion, and pimiento; spread over crabmeat. Top with remaining diced bread. Mix milk and beaten eggs with mushroom soup and pour over all. Bake at 325° for 15 minutes. Sprinkle top with grated cheese; add paprika, if you wish. Continue baking 1 hour longer.

Scalloped Fish

Serves 4

1 TEASPOON WORCESTERSHIRE SAUCE
$1^1/_2$ CUPS WHITE SAUCE
1 MEDIUM ONION, MINCED
1 GREEN PEPPER, MINCED
2 TABLESPOONS BUTTER
$1^1/_2$ POUNDS HADDOCK, COOKED IN BOILING WATER UNTIL
    FLAKY, WITH BAY LEAF AND ONION
1 CUP GRATED CHEESE
$1/2$ CUP BUTTERED BREADCRUMBS

❧ Add Worcestershire sauce to white sauce. Sauté onion and green pepper in butter until cooked, and combine with white sauce. Using a 1 quart buttered casserole, alternate layers of fish and sauce mixture. Top with cheese and $1/2$ cup buttered crumbs. Bake in a 350° oven to warm and brown.

Sole Meunière Northwest Style

Serves 2–3

1 POUND FRESH SOLE OR FLOUNDER FILLETS
SALT AND FRESHLY GROUND PEPPER TO TASTE
FRESH ROSEMARY, DILL, OR DRIED HERBS PROVENCAL
FLOUR
2–3 TABLESPOONS BUTTER, MARGARINE, OR OLIVE OIL
LEMON WEDGES

❧ Preheat oven to 450°. Dry fillets with paper towels and sprinkle with salt, ground pepper, and herbs. Sprinkle or dredge with flour, depending on how heavily you want the fish to be coated. Line a 9" × 13" glass or porcelain pan with tinfoil and add butter, margarine, or olive oil. Put in oven briefly to melt butter or margarine. Remove from oven and add fish fillets. Dot with additional butter or margarine. Bake for 10 or 15 minutes, depending on thickness of fillets and degree of flakiness or firmness desired. Garnish with lemon wedges and a sprig of fresh herbs. Serve with fresh steamed asparagus, boiled small red potatoes, and a nice, light white wine! Cleanup is easy— just throw away the tinfoil!

Variations:
• Use salmon fillets instead of sole. Cook for 20 minutes.
• Dice a fresh onion; slice several mushrooms and a clove of garlic. Add to the pan first and put the fillets on top before baking.

Maine Shrimp Casserole I

Serves 8

1 10-OUNCE CAN CREAM OF MUSHROOM SOUP
2 TABLESPOONS CHOPPED GREEN PEPPER
1 TABLESPOON CHOPPED ONION
1 TABLESPOON LEMON JUICE
2 CUPS COOKED RICE
1/2 TEASPOON WORCESTERSHIRE SAUCE
1/2 TEASPOON DRY MUSTARD
1/4 TEASPOON PEPPER
1/2 POUND CLEANED UNCOOKED SHRIMP, FRESH OR FROZEN, THAWED
1/4 CUP BREADCRUMBS
BUTTER
PAPRIKA

❧ Combine soup, green pepper, onion, lemon juice, rice, Worcestershire sauce, mustard, pepper, and shrimp. Place in a lightly greased 1½-quart casserole. Top with bread-crumbs. Dot with butter. Sprinkle with paprika. Cover and bake in 350° oven for 35 minutes.

Maine Shrimp Casserole II

Maine shrimp are quite small. If you do not have Maine shrimp, use any other smallish shrimp.

Serves 4

1 STICK BUTTER, MELTED
1 SLEEVE BUTTERY CRACKERS
1 TABLESPOON LEMON JUICE
1–2 POUNDS MAINE SHRIMP

Ɔ Melt butter and crumble crackers. Mix together and add lemon juice. Place shrimp in buttered casserole. Top with crumbs. Bake at 350° for 15 minutes.

Shrimp Casserole

Serves 6–8

1 CUP RICE, UNCOOKED
1 CUP CHOPPED ONION
3 TABLESPOONS MARGARINE
1 16-OUNCE CAN TOMATOES, DRAINED
1 CUP RICH MILK (EVAPORATED MILK MAY BE ADDED)
1 6-OUNCE CAN SHRIMP (CLEANED)

Ɔ Prepare rice according to directions on package. Sauté onion in 3 tablespoons margarine. Add to rice, along with other ingredients. Bake at 350° for 30–40 minutes.

Mother's Shrimp with Rice

Serves 2–3

1½ CUPS COOKED RICE
4 TABLESPOONS BUTTER
4 TABLESPOONS OLIVE OIL
½ MEDIUM CHOPPED ONION
2–3 CLOVES GARLIC, MINCED
2 6-OUNCE CANS SHRIMP, DRAINED
2 LEMONS
PEPPER
⅓ CUP VERMOUTH OR SAUTERNE

Ɔ You may prepare while rice is cooking. In medium-sized casserole, melt 4 tablespoons butter and 4 tablespoons olive oil. Add onion, garlic, and shrimp. Heat oven to 400° and put casserole in oven for 2 minutes. Take out and squeeze lemon juice over it, and add pepper. Do this 2 more times. The last time add the vermouth or sauterne and cook 2 more minutes. Serve over rice.

Scallops with Fettuccine

Serves 2

2–3 CLOVES GARLIC, MINCED
1 PINT BAY SCALLOPS
BUTTER
SEVERAL SPRIGS OF ITALIAN PARSLEY, CHOPPED
1/4–1/3 CUP VERMOUTH
FETTUCCINE
ROMANO CHEESE

&. Sauté garlic, then scallops, in butter just until they are tender. Add Italian parsley and vermouth. Serve over fettuccine with grated Romano cheese.

Fish Loaf with Lobster Sauce

Serves 8

1 POUND HALIBUT OR HADDOCK FILLET, COOKED AND FLAKED
2 EGGS, BEATEN
1 CUP SOFT BREADCRUMBS
2/3 CUP MILK
1/3 CUP HEAVY CREAM
SALT AND PEPPER

&. Combine all ingredients; place in buttered 9" × 5" loaf pan. Set loaf pan in a pan of hot water and bake for 30 minutes at 350°. Serve with Lobster Sauce. (Recipe follows.)

Lobster Sauce:
3 TABLESPOONS BUTTER
3 TABLESPOONS FLOUR
SALT AND PEPPER
1 CUP MILK
1/2 CUP CREAM
1 CUP LOBSTER MEAT, CUT INTO SMALL CHUNKS

&. Melt butter over medium heat and add flour, salt and pepper. Slowly add milk or cream, stirring constantly until mixture thickens. Stir in the cut-up lobster meat.

Tater Pan Fried Fish

Serves 4–6

2 POUNDS FISH FILLETS
5 TABLESPOONS FLOUR
1 EGG, BEATEN
1 TABLESPOON LEMON JUICE
SALT AND PEPPER TO TASTE
2 TABLESPOONS SESAME SEEDS
1/4 CUP INSTANT MASHED POTATO FLAKES
4 TABLESPOONS BUTTER

❧ Roll fish in flour, then in mixture of egg, lemon juice, salt, and pepper. Next, roll fillets in sesame seed and potato flakes mixture. Melt butter in skillet and place fillets into hot butter. Fry until golden brown on both sides, turning carefully. Turn heat down and cook until fish flakes easily.

Scallop Casserole

In place of the cream, cream of shrimp soup is very good. With 2 pounds of scallops, use a 2-quart casserole.

Serves 6

1 STICK BUTTER, CUT IN SMALL PIECES
1 1/2–2 POUNDS FRESH SCALLOPS
1 SLEEVE CRISP CRACKERS, CRUSHED
1 QUART ALL-PURPOSE CREAM OR HALF-AND-HALF

❧ In a large glass baking dish, put a layer of butter pieces, a layer of scallops, and a layer of crushed crackers. Repeat these layers, then pour cream over them. Bake approximately 1 hour in a 350° oven.

Clam Casserole I

Serves 4

2 EGGS
1 CAN CREAM OF MUSHROOM SOUP
1/2 CUP MILK
1/2 CUP CRACKERS, CRUSHED (ABOUT 15)
1 6-OUNCE CAN MINCED CLAMS, DRAINED
1/4 CUP BUTTER, MELTED

❧ Beat eggs slightly; add soup, milk, crackers, clams, and butter. Bake in a greased 1 1/2-quart casserole placed in a pan filled with 1/2" of hot water, at 350° for 1 hour.

Clam Casserole II

Serves 6–8

2 8-ounce cans minced clams, with liquid
2 cups coarsely crushed saltines
1 can of mushroom soup mixed with 2 cups milk
4 eggs, slightly beaten
Pepper

❧ Combine all ingredients and place in a 2-quart casserole. Bake at 375° for 45 minutes until puffed and brown. Center will be slightly moist.

Crabmeat Casserole

Serves 4

1/4 cup butter or margarine
1/4 cup flour
2 cups milk
1/2 teaspoon salt
Few grains pepper
1 cup sharp Cheddar cheese, grated
2 egg yolks
1 6-ounce can crabmeat
2 slices bread, cubed
1/4 cup breadcrumbs
2 tablespoons butter, melted

❧ Melt butter over medium heat; stir in flour and seasonings. Slowly add milk and stir until smooth. Cook until it thickens. Add grated cheese and egg yolks. Add crabmeat and bread cubes. Mix breadcrumbs and 2 tablespoons melted butter and spread on top of casserole. Bake 30 minutes in 350° oven until bubbly.

Crab Casserole

Serves 8

8 OUNCES SPAGHETTI, COOKED

1 CAN MUSHROOM SOUP

1/4 CUP DICED ONION

2 CUPS GRATED CHEESE

1 1/2 CUPS CRABMEAT (FRESH OR CANNED)

1 CUP MILK

1 TABLESPOON PIMIENTO

2 HARD-COOKED EGGS

CHOPPED OLIVES

CHOPPED CHIVES

2 TABLESPOONS BUTTER, MELTED

Combine cooked spaghetti with soup, onion, cheese, crab, and milk. Pour into buttered baking dish. Top with pimiento, chopped eggs, chopped olives, chopped chives, and melted butter. Bake at 400° for 30 minutes.

Clam-Corn Casserole

Serves 4–6

3 EGGS

1 6-OUNCE CAN BABY CLAMS

1 CUP NIBLET CORN

2/3 CUP POWDERED MILK

1 1/2 STICKS BUTTER

1 1/2 CUPS CRUMBLED CRACKERS

2 SLICES WHOLE WHEAT BREAD, CRUMBLED

PEPPER AND HERBS TO TASTE (A LITTLE TARRAGON AND OREGANO ARE SUGGESTED)

Beat eggs. Drain clams and corn, saving liquid, and add to eggs. Add powdered milk and about 2 1/4 cups liquid. (Use liquid from drained clams and corn, adding enough clam juice [canned] or milk to make up required amount.) Melt 1 1/2 sticks butter; add crackers and bread. Add pepper and herbs to taste. Combine the 2 mixtures and bake at 350° for 30–35 minutes. (If using glass cookware, reduce heat after 15 minutes to 325°.)

Golden Oyster Scallop

Serves 6

1 14-OUNCE CAN MUSHROOMS, DRAINED

1½ TEASPOONS GRATED ONION

½ TEASPOON WORCESTERSHIRE SAUCE

6 TABLESPOONS BUTTER OR MARGARINE

1 PINT OYSTERS

1 PACKAGE SODA CRACKERS (24), COARSELY CRUSHED

1 CUP CREAM, MILK, OR HALF-AND-HALF

2 TABLESPOONS BUTTER

PAPRIKA

Heat drained mushrooms, onion, Worcestershire sauce, and 6 tablespoons of butter or margarine in saucepan until butter is melted, not browned. Drain oysters and save liquid. To make the sauce, mix the oyster liquid with the cream or milk. Put ⅓ of the cracker crumbs in a 2-quart casserole. Layer ½ the oysters, ½ the mushroom mixture, ½ the sauce, and ⅓ the crumbs. Repeat, ending with the final ⅓ of the crumbs on top. Dot with remaining 2 tablespoons butter, and sprinkle with paprika. Bake at 350° for 40 minutes or until crisp and golden.

Julie's Seafood Casserole

This recipe, multiplied as needed, is popular when a group wishes to cater a meal.

Serves 6–8

1 POUND HADDOCK, HAKE, CUSK, OR COD

½ POUND ASSORTED SHELLFISH (SCALLOPS, SHRIMP, CRAB, OR LOBSTER)

1 CAN CREAM OF MUSHROOM SOUP

1 CUP BREADCRUMBS

1 CUP EVAPORATED MILK

1 CUP GRATED CHEESE

PAPRIKA

Place fish and shellfish in bottom of casserole dish. Mix remaining ingredients. Pour over fish and shellfish. Sprinkle with paprika and bake for 45 minutes at 350°.

Maryland Crab Cakes

Makes 8 cakes

1 POUND BACK-FIN LUMP CRAB OR CLAW MEAT

2 EGGS, SLIGHTLY BEATEN

2 TABLESPOONS MAYONNAISE (HOMEMADE PREFERABLE)

1 TABLESPOON HORSERADISH MUSTARD

1/2 TEASPOON SEA SALT, OR MORE TO TASTE

FRESHLY GROUND BLACK PEPPER TO TASTE

5 DROPS OF TABASCO SAUCE

1 TABLESPOON CHOPPED PARSLEY

FINE CRACKER OR BREADCRUMBS FOR COATING

FAT FOR FRYING (OLIVE OIL OR VEGETABLE SHORTENING)

❧ Carefully pick over meat. Mix eggs, mayonnaise, mustard, and other seasonings in a bowl. Add crabmeat and mix. Arrange a plate of crumbs, take a handful of crab mixture, and plop it on the crumbs. Shape into round cake. Transfer with a spatula to a sheet of waxed paper. Continue to make cakes, crumbing tops and sides. Fry in 2 batches. Fill pan 1" or so deep with oil, and heat to normal frying temperature (375°). Fry 1 side and then the other to golden brown. Drain on paper towels. Serve immediately!

Smoked Mussels with Pasta

Serves 2

1/2 CUP CHOPPED ONIONS

1 CUP MUSHROOMS, SLICED

2 3.5-OUNCE CANS SMOKED OYSTERS

1 8-OUNCE CONTAINER OF CREAM

2 TABLESPOONS BLUE CHEESE

1–2 TABLESPOONS BRANDY

ROMANO CHEESE, GRATED

2 CUPS OF COOKED PASTA

❧ Sauté onions and mushrooms together, then add oysters and cream. Reduce mixture and add blue cheese and brandy. Serve over any kind of pasta.

Cooked Shrimp Casserole

Serves 4

1 CAN CONDENSED CREAM OF MUSHROOM SOUP
1/2 CUP SOUR CREAM
1/4 CUP WATER
1 1/2 CUPS COOKED, DICED SHRIMP
1/8 TEASPOON PAPRIKA
1/4 TEASPOON TARRAGON
1 1/2 CUPS COOKED MACARONI OR NOODLES

❧ Combine ingredients. Place in a 2-quart casserole; cook about 30–45 minutes at 350° until it starts to brown on top. Grated cheese or cracker crumbs are optional.

Paella

Serves 4

1 SMALL CHICKEN, CUT INTO 8 PIECES
1/4 POUND LEAN PORK, DICED
1/4 POUND LEAN VEAL, DICED
3 TABLESPOONS SPANISH OLIVE OIL
1 CLOVE GARLIC, MINCED
2 TOMATOES, PEELED AND CHOPPED
CHOPPED ONION, OPTIONAL
1 10-OUNCE PACKAGE FROZEN PEAS
ARTICHOKE HEARTS
ARTICHOKE SPEARS
1 1/2 CUPS UNCOOKED RICE
2 1/2 CUPS WELL-SEASONED BROTH
1/4 TEASPOON SAFFRON
1/4 POUND SHELLED SHRIMP
1 7-OUNCE CAN MINCED CLAMS
WHITEFISH, OPTIONAL (COOK IN 1/2 CUP WATER UNTIL SHEEN IS OFF FISH)
LEMON SLICE

❧ Sauté chicken, pork, and veal in olive oil in a large heavy skillet. When well browned, add garlic, tomatoes, and onion (if desired). Cook 1 minute. Add peas, artichokes, rice, broth, and saffron; bring to a boil; boil 4 minutes uncovered. Separately sauté shrimp in a little olive oil; add shrimp, clams, and whitefish (if desired) to rice. Pour into large shallow casserole dish and put in a 375° oven. Bake 20 minutes or until done. Garnish with lemon slices. Enjoy!

Scalloped Clams

Serves 6

½ POUND SALTINES
1 CAN MINCED CLAMS, DRAINED
1 CAN WHOLE BABY CLAMS, DRAINED
2 EGGS, BEATEN
1 CAN CREAM OF MUSHROOM SOUP
½ STICK BUTTER, MELTED
1½–2 CUPS MILK
DASH SALT
DASH PEPPER
PAPRIKA

❧ Butter a baking dish. In a mixing bowl, break up the saltines and add remaining ingredients, mixing well. Pour into baking dish. Sprinkle top with paprika. Bake at 350° for 30–40 minutes or until firm.

Tuna Casserole I

Serves 4

1 6-OUNCE BOX STUFFING MIX
1 6-OUNCE CAN TUNA, DRAINED
1 CAN CREAM OF CHICKEN SOUP
½ CUP MILK
GRATED CHEESE

❧ Cook stuffing as directed on box. Press into a casserole dish. Flake tuna over stuffing. Add soup mixed with milk. Sprinkle grated cheese on top and cook 25–30 minutes at 350°.

Tuna Casserole II

Serves 4

2 CUPS OF COOKED NOODLES

1 6-OUNCE CAN TUNA, DRAINED

1 CAN CREAM OF MUSHROOM SOUP

1/4 CUP WATER, MILK, OR SHERRY

1/4 CUP CORNFLAKE CRUMBS

1 TABLESPOON BUTTER OR MARGARINE

GRATED CHEESE, OPTIONAL

&· Place 1/3 of the noodles in a 1-quart casserole. Cover with 1/2 of the tuna; add another layer of noodles, then another layer of tuna. Top with third layer of noodles. Mix mushroom soup with water, milk, or sherry and pour over the tuna-noodle mixture. Top with cornflake crumbs and dot with butter. Add cheese if desired. Bake at 375° until brown on top and heated through.

Salmon Loaf

This is a favorite at our house. Ingredients may be mixed ahead except for the warm milk. Add that when ready to put in oven.

Serves 6–7

1 16-OUNCE CAN OF SALMON

2 EGGS, BEATEN LIGHTLY

3 SLICES OF BREAD, BROKEN INTO SMALL CUBES

1 TEASPOON SALT

1 1/2 CUPS MILK, WARMED

1/4 CUP BUTTER, MELTED

1 ONION, CHOPPED

&· Mix together in bowl and pour into a buttered casserole dish. Bake at 350° for 1 hour.

Bubbly Bake

Serves 4

1 POUND FRESH OR FROZEN FISH FILLETS

1 CAN CREAM OF MUSHROOM SOUP OR CREAM OF
　　CELERY SOUP

1 SMALL ONION, FINELY CHOPPED

1 TABLESPOON LEMON JUICE

1/2 CUP SHREDDED SHARP CHEDDAR CHEESE

HERB-SEASONED BREADCRUMBS

☙ Cut fillets into serving-size pieces. Place in buttered casserole. Combine soup (undiluted) with onion and lemon juice. Pour over fish fillets. Top with cheese and seasoned crumbs. Bake in a hot oven, 425°, for 20–25 minutes or until fish is flaky when tested with fork.

Lutefisk

A traditional Norwegian dish consisting of codfish soaked in lye, it is purchased presoaked. It is traditionally served at Christmas time; however, some Midwestern churches continue to have lutefisk dinners even into late January and early February.

Serves 4

1 PACKAGE LUTEFISK, USUALLY ABOUT 1 POUND

3 QUARTS WATER

1/2 CUP SALT

BUTTER, MELTED

SALT AND PEPPER TO TASTE

1. Before cooking, soak lutefisk in a heavy salt solution 3–4 hours or overnight.

2. After soaking the lutefisk, bring 3 quarts of water to a boil with 1/2 cup salt. Add the fish and bring water to a boil again. When water returns to a boil, take off burner and scoop fish from the water. Serve immediately with melted butter spooned over fish and salt and pepper to taste. It is very important not to overcook or undercook the fish. It takes but a short time to cook and when done should flake easily. It should be served immediately so that it does not cool and get jellylike.

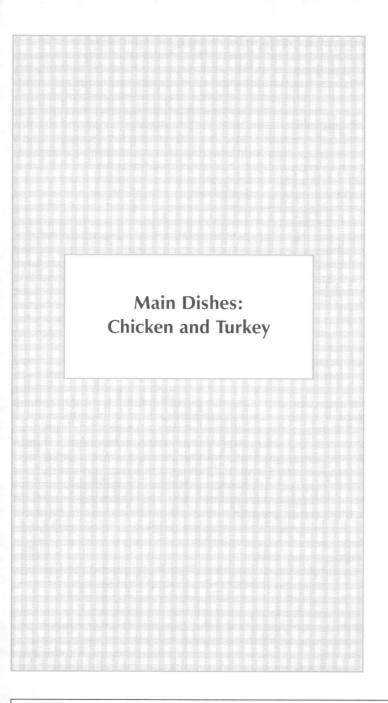

**Main Dishes:
Chicken and Turkey**

Chicken (or Turkey) Tetrazzini

Serves 6–8

1 4-OUNCE PACKAGE OF NOODLES

6 TABLESPOONS BUTTER OR MARGARINE

6 TABLESPOONS ENRICHED FLOUR

1½ TEASPOONS SALT

¼ TEASPOON PEPPER

½ TEASPOON CELERY SALT

2 CUPS CHICKEN OR TURKEY STOCK

1 CUP HEAVY CREAM, SCALDED

½ TEASPOON SHERRY OR SHERRY FLAVORING

1 6-OUNCE CAN MUSHROOMS, DRAINED

⅓ CUP SLIVERED ALMONDS, TOASTED

3 TABLESPOONS MINCED PARSLEY

2 CUPS DICED COOKED CHICKEN OR TURKEY

½ CUP GRATED PARMESAN CHEESE

Cook noodles in boiling, salted water. Drain. Melt butter or margarine; add flour and blend. Add seasonings and stock. Cook over low heat until thickened, stirring constantly. Remove from heat. Stir in cream, sherry, mushrooms, almonds, and parsley. Alternate layers of noodles, poultry, and mushroom sauce in greased 2-quart casserole. Top with cheese. Bake uncovered in 350° oven for 45–50 minutes.

Raspberry Glazed Chicken

Serves 4–6

CHICKEN, CUT UP
2/3 CUP RASPBERRY JAM
1/4 CUP VINEGAR
1/4 CUP WATER
1 TEASPOON CINNAMON
1 TEASPOON DRY MUSTARD
1/4 TEASPOON CLOVES
1/4 TEASPOON ALLSPICE

❧ Brown cut-up chicken in skillet. Transfer to baking dish. Mix remaining ingredients and cook over low heat until jam is melted and glaze is hot. Pour over chicken pieces. Bake at 350° for 45–50 minutes.

Boneless Chicken Casserole

"An old standby—terrific!"

Serves 10

10 BONELESS CHICKEN BREASTS
1/2 CUP CHOPPED CELERY
1/2 CUP CHOPPED GREEN PEPPER
2 CANS CREAM OF MUSHROOM SOUP
1/2 TEASPOON MINCED GARLIC OR 1 CLOVE GARLIC
1 CUP HALF-AND-HALF
1 1/2 CUPS GRATED SHARP CHEDDAR CHEESE
1 CUP SAUTERNE
1 CUP MAYONNAISE
PARMESAN CHEESE
ALMONDS

❧ Stew chicken with celery and green pepper until tender. Place breasts in a 9" × 13" pan. Have all ingredients at room temperature. Bring to a simmer soup, garlic, and half-and-half together. Fold in Cheddar cheese, wine, and mayonnaise. Pour over chicken; sprinkle with Parmesan cheese and almonds. Bake until hot and bubbly. Serve with rice or noodles. Freezes well!

Chicken Spectacular

Serves 8–10

2 CUPS DICED COOKED CHICKEN

1 CUP GREEN BEANS, FRENCH, DICED

1 6-OUNCE BOX MIXED WILD AND WHITE RICE, PREPARED AS
    DIRECTED

1 CAN CREAM OF CELERY SOUP

1 16-OUNCE CAN CHICKEN BROTH

1/2 CUP MAYONNAISE

1 CUP SLICED WATER CHESTNUTS

2 TABLESPOONS CHOPPED PIMIENTO

2 TABLESPOONS CHOPPED ONION

1 4-OUNCE CAN MUSHROOMS

SALT AND PEPPER

☙ Mix all ingredients together. Bake at 350° for 45 minutes in a 9" × 13" pan. Easy!

Chicken Rice Casserole

Serves 8–10

4 CHICKEN BREASTS AND 4 LEGS

1 CAN CREAM OF MUSHROOM SOUP

1 CAN CREAM OF CELERY SOUP

1 1/2 CUPS ORANGE JUICE

1 PACKAGE DRY ONION SOUP MIX

1 CUP RAW LONG GRAIN RICE

☙ Mix all ingredients except chicken together and spread in a 9" × 13" pan. Place chicken breasts and legs on top of rice mix. Sprinkle 1 package dry onion soup mix over all and cover with foil. Bake 2 hours at 300°.

Sour Cream Chicken Breasts

Serves 8–10

1/2 cup butter, melted
2 mild onions, chopped
2 1/2 cups hot water
1 16-ounce package of herb-seasoned stuffing
8 chicken breasts, skinned
Salt to taste
1 pint sour cream

Mix butter, onions, hot water, and stuffing to a moist consistency. Place 8 chicken breasts in a 9" × 13" × 2" casserole. Salt according to taste. Spread sour cream evenly over chicken breasts. Distribute stuffing mixture over chicken. Cover with foil. Bake in 325° oven for 90 minutes. Uncover last 5 minutes.

Chicken–Green Bean Casserole

Serves 10–12

2 cups hot water
6 cups seasoned croutons
1/2 cup butter or margarine
4 cups green beans (thawed, if using frozen)
1 can mushrooms, drained (optional)
2 cans cream of mushroom soup (or cream of chicken)
3 to 4 cups cut-up cooked chicken
1/2 cup milk
Slivered almonds

Combine water, croutons, and butter. Place in a greased 9" × 13" pan or large casserole dish. Mix green beans, mushrooms, soup, chicken, and milk. Pour over crouton mixture and bake at 350° for 45 minutes to 1 hour. Sprinkle with slivered almonds before serving.

Chicken Mole

Serves 6

1/4 CUP OIL

1 MEDIUM ONION, CHOPPED

1 GARLIC CLOVE, MINCED

2 POUNDS CHICKEN BREASTS

2 TEASPOONS SESAME SEEDS

1/3 CUP CHOPPED ALMONDS

1/2 CUP MILD CHILI POWDER, MORE TO TASTE

2 OUNCES UNSWEETENED CHOCOLATE, MELTED

1/4 CUP HONEY

1/4 TEASPOON WINE VINEGAR

1 TEASPOON CUMIN

1/4 CUP MESQUITE MEAL

1 CUP CHICKEN BROTH

1. Heat oil and sauté onion and garlic in large pan; set aside. In same pan, brown chicken breasts on both sides, and set aside.

2. Toast sesame seeds and almonds in dry pan.

3. Combine onions, garlic, sesame seeds, almonds, chili powder, chocolate, honey, vinegar, and cumin, stirring to blend.

4. Mix mesquite meal with 1/3 of the chicken broth and add this mixture to the sauce; then add rest of broth to sauce. Add water if sauce is too thick. Cook and stir over medium heat until sauce thickens.

5. Place chicken in ovenproof dish and cover with chili mixture. Bake at 350° for 1 hour.

Variations:
- Peanut butter can be substituted for almonds.
- Cocoa powder may be used instead of chocolate. Substitute 3 level tablespoons of cocoa and 1 tablespoon of oil for each square of chocolate.
- Flour may be substituted for mesquite meal.

Turkey Sausage

Family Size (serves 4)	Group (serves 20)
1 POUND GROUND TURKEY	5 POUNDS
3/4 TEASPOON SALT	4 TEASPOONS
3/4 TEASPOON BLACK PEPPER	5 TEASPOONS
3/4 TEASPOON DRIED SAGE	3 1/2 TEASPOONS
1/4 TEASPOON DRIED SUMMER SAVORY	1 TEASPOON
1/4 TEASPOON DRIED THYME	3/4 TEASPOON
1/4 TEASPOON ANISE	1 TEASPOON

❧ Mix ingredients. Shape into cakes. Freeze separately and use as much as needed. This is low fat, and seasonings may be varied as desired. Serve as an addition to spaghetti or as a breakfast food.

Chicken Shirley

Serves 8–10

4–5 WHOLE CHICKEN BREASTS

SALT AND PEPPER

PAPRIKA

1/2 STICK BUTTER

2 CANS CREAM OF CHICKEN SOUP

1/2 TEASPOON CURRY POWDER

2 CUPS SOUR CREAM

1 CUP SLICED MUSHROOMS, SAUTÉED

1 CUP SLIVERED ALMONDS

❧ Season chicken with salt, pepper, and paprika. Melt butter in large skillet. Add chicken and brown. Transfer to a baking dish. Combine soup and curry. Pour over chicken. Cover and bake 1 hour at 350°. Remove chicken. Stir sour cream, mushrooms, and almonds into sauce. Return chicken to dish. Spoon sauce over pieces. Bake uncovered until browned.

Searsport Chicken Pie

Serves 6

3 CUPS COOKED CHICKEN, CUT INTO LARGE PIECES
1 CAN CREAM OF MUSHROOM SOUP, UNDILUTED
1 PIMIENTO, DICED FINE
1 CAN MIXED VEGETABLES
2 CUPS SIFTED ALL-PURPOSE FLOUR
1 TEASPOON BAKING SODA
2 TEASPOONS CREAM OF TARTAR
$1/2$ TEASPOON SALT
$1/2$ CUP VEGETABLE SHORTENING
1 EGG
$1/2$ CUP MILK

1. Mix together chicken, soup, pimiento, and mixed vegetables and heat.

2. Pie Crust: Sift flour, soda, cream of tartar, and salt together. Work in the shortening, using a pastry blender or 2 knives. Beat egg and milk, add to dry ingredients, and mix together with a fork. Divide mixture in $1/2$ and roll out to desired thickness. Place 1 crust in a 10" pie plate.

3. Turn hot filling into pie and top with other crust. Cut 3 slits in center of top crust and flute edges. Bake at 400° for 18 minutes or until crust is lightly browned.

4. Cut into 6 pieces; serve hot. Delicious with mashed squash, cranberry sauce, and celery. Also good with tossed salad.

Baked Chicken with Rice

Serves 4–6

$3/4$ CUP UNWASHED RAW RICE
1 CHICKEN, CUT UP
$1/2$ PACKAGE OF DRY ONION SOUP MIX
1 CAN CREAM OF CELERY SOUP
1 CAN CREAM OF MUSHROOM SOUP
$1^1/2$ SOUP CANS OF MILK

❧ Sprinkle rice on bottom of buttered 9" × 12" pan. Place chicken on top of rice, skin side up. Sprinkle dry soup mix on chicken. Mix together celery soup, mushroom soup, and milk. Pour over chicken and bake at 300° for $2^1/2$ hours.

Variation:
Pork chops may be used instead of chicken.

Beanpot Chicken

Serves 4–6

1 STICK OR $\frac{1}{2}$ CUP MARGARINE

1 ONION, PEELED

4–5 CHICKEN BREASTS HALVES

SALT, PEPPER, AND POULTRY SEASONING TO TASTE

❧ Place margarine in bottom of bean pot. Place whole onion next. Season chicken breasts with salt, pepper, and poultry seasoning. Place on top of onion, skin side down. Put small pieces of margarine on top of breasts. Cover and bake at 350° for 3 hours.

Chicken Casserole

Serves 10

$\frac{1}{2}$ LARGE PACKAGE FROZEN BROCCOLI, COOKED

3 CUPS CUBED COOKED CHICKEN OR TURKEY

1 CAN CREAM OF CHICKEN OR MUSHROOM SOUP

1 CAN EVAPORATED MILK

3 CUPS STUFFING MIX PREPARED ACCORDING TO DIRECTIONS
    ON THE PACKAGE

2 CUPS SHREDDED CHEDDAR CHEESE

❧ Line a greased casserole dish with cooked broccoli. Top with cooked chicken. Mix soup with milk and pour over chicken. Spread stuffing over all this and top with cheese. Bake at 350° for 1 hour. This makes a large casserole.

Honey Bear Chicken

Serves 4

1 FRYER CHICKEN, CUT UP AND SKINNED
SALT AND PEPPER
1/2 CUP BUTTER OR MARGARINE, MELTED
1 CUP BROWN SUGAR
1/2 CUP PREPARED MUSTARD
2 TEASPOONS MUSTARD SEEDS

❧ Place cut-up chicken in baking dish. Season with salt and pepper. Make a sauce of melted butter or margarine, brown sugar, mustard, and mustard seeds. Pour sauce over chicken and bake uncovered at 350° for 45 minutes. Serve with rice if desired. Makes enough sauce for 2 fryers.

Succulent Seasoned Chicken

Serves 4–6

3 TABLESPOONS BUTTER OR MARGARINE
4 CHICKEN BREAST HALVES
1/2 TEASPOON DRIED SAGE
1/2 TEASPOON DRIED THYME
1/2 TEASPOON DRIED PEPPER
1/2 TEASPOON DRIED GINGER
1/2 LEMON, CUT IN WEDGES
1/2 CUP MARSALA

❧ Butter chicken breasts and sprinkle with seasonings. Squeeze lemon juice on top of seasoned chicken. Put wine in bottom of baking pan with chicken. Bake at 350° for approximately 45 minutes.

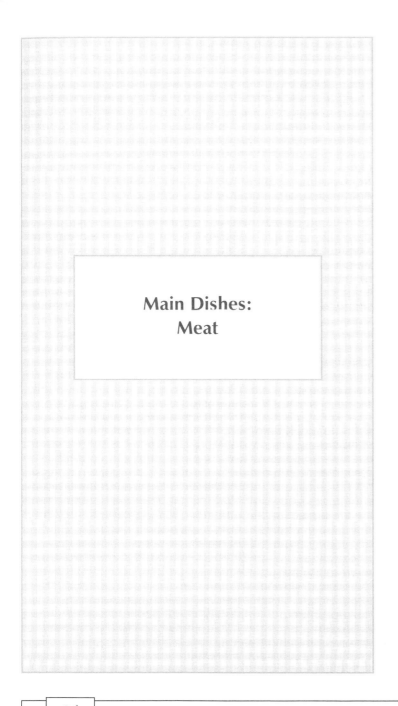

**Main Dishes:
Meat**

Fresh Vegetable and Hamburg Casserole

Serves 4–5

1/2 CUP DICED ONION

2 TABLESPOONS BUTTER OR MARGARINE

1 POUND LEAN GROUND BEEF

1 CUP DICED CELERY

1 CUP SLICED CARROTS

1/3 CUP DICED GREEN PEPPER

1 BEEF BOUILLON CUBE

3/4 CUP HOT WATER

1/2 TEASPOON SALT

1/8 TEASPOON PEPPER

4 TABLESPOONS FLOUR

1/4 CUP COLD WATER

2 CUPS MASHED POTATOES

❧ Sauté onion in butter or margarine. Add meat and cook until all pink is gone. Add celery, carrots, green pepper, beef bouillon cube, hot water, and seasonings. Cover and cook 5 minutes. Mix flour and cold water to a smooth paste and add to mixture. Turn into 1½-quart casserole. Spoon mashed potatoes around the edge of casserole. Bake in a preheated moderate oven, 350°, for 45 minutes or until golden brown over the top.

Johnny Mazette

This dish is a great crowd pleaser at a potluck supper. An empty dish always comes home. If you find that the casserole is too big to bring to the church, divide it and freeze 1/2 for later use. It only gets better!

Serves at least 12 hungry people

2 CUPS CHOPPED GREEN PEPPER

2 CUPS CHOPPED ONION

1 CUP CHOPPED CELERY

1/2 CUP BUTTER

1 POUND GROUND BEEF

1 POUND GROUND PORK*

1/2 CUP BUTTER

2 TEASPOONS SALT

1/3 CUP CHOPPED STUFFED OLIVES

1 4-OUNCE CAN SLICED MUSHROOMS WITH LIQUID

1 CAN CONDENSED TOMATO SOUP

1 8-OUNCE CAN TOMATO SAUCE

1 8-OUNCE CAN MEATLESS TOMATO MUSHROOM SAUCE**

1 POUND BROAD EGG NOODLES

2 CUPS SHREDDED CHEESE

In a large skillet, sauté pepper, onion, and celery in butter. In a separate skillet, sauté the ground meat and drain fat. Add to sautéed vegetables. Add salt and reduce heat. Cook the mixture 5 minutes. Stir in olives, mushrooms, and soups and sauces or a jar of pasta or spaghetti sauce. Cook 5 minutes. I usually turn to simmer and let the flavors meld a bit. Cook noodles and drain. Pour noodles into large casserole and add sauce, mixing well. Sprinkle shredded cheese on top. Bake at 350° for 35 minutes.

*You may use all beef.
**May use 1 28-ounce jar pasta or spaghetti sauce instead of 3 cans of soup and sauces.

Taco Hot Dish

Serves 6

1 POUND LEAN GROUND BEEF
1 PACKAGE TACO SEASONING
2 TABLESPOONS WATER
16 OUNCES SOUR CREAM
2/3 CUP SALAD DRESSING
2 TABLESPOONS CHOPPED ONION
1 PACKAGE CRESCENT ROLLS
1/2 GREEN PEPPER, CHOPPED
3 CUPS SHREDDED CHEDDAR CHEESE

❧ Cook and drain ground beef. Add taco seasoning and water. Mix sour cream, salad dressing, and onion. Set aside. Spread crescent roll dough in a 9" × 13" pan. Layer the beef and green pepper onto the crescent roll dough. Spread sour cream mixture over top. Sprinkle with cheese. Bake at 375° for 20–30 minutes.

Beef Burgundy

Serves 6–8

1 1/2–2 POUNDS STEW BEEF CUT INTO 1" CUBES
1 CAN CREAM OF MUSHROOM CONDENSED SOUP
1/2 SOUP CAN RED WINE (BURGUNDY)
1 TABLESPOON CHOPPED FRESH GARLIC OR
     1/4 TO 1/2 TEASPOON GARLIC POWDER
1 CUP FRESH MUSHROOMS, SLICED

❧ Mix ingredients together (do *not* brown meat). Bake, covered, at 325° for 3 hours. Last 20 minutes remove cover and add sliced fresh mushrooms. If not beefy enough in flavor, add bouillon. Serve over rice or noodles.

Cornish Pasties

These are traditional in the southwestern corner of Wisconsin. Miners from Cornwall settled here and brought pasties with them. Rutabagas can be used instead of carrots.

Serves 6

Pastry:

3 CUPS FLOUR
1 TEASPOON SALT
1/2 TEASPOON BAKING POWDER
1 CUP SHORTENING
2/3 CUP ICE WATER

✤ Sift together dry ingredients. Cut in shortening. Blend in enough water to hold dough together. Roll into 6 8" circles.

Filling:

2 POUNDS BEEF, CUT INTO 1/2" CUBES
2 CUPS CUBED POTATOES
2 CUPS CHOPPED CARROTS
1/2 CUP CHOPPED ONION
SALT AND PEPPER TO TASTE
BUTTER OR MARGARINE

✤ Arrange meat and veggies in layers on 1/2 of each circle. Sprinkle with salt and pepper. Top with 1 teaspoon butter. Brush edge of circles with water. Fold into semicircles and press edges together. Cut a 1/2" slit in top of each pastry. Place on heavy greased baking sheet. Bake at 425° for 15 minutes; then reduce heat to 375° for 1 hour. Remove from oven; cover with cloth and let sit for 15 minutes.

Norwegian Meatballs (adapted by a Dutch cook)

Serves 8–10

1/4 CUP CHOPPED ONION
1 POUND GROUND CHUCK
1/4 CUP PORK SAUSAGE
1/2 CUP DRY BREADCRUMBS
3/4 CUP MILK
1 EGG, BEATEN
2 TEASPOONS SUGAR
2 TEASPOONS SALT
1/2 TEASPOON NUTMEG
1/4 TEASPOON ALLSPICE
OIL FOR BROWNING, ENOUGH TO COVER THE BOTTOM OF PAN LIGHTLY

Gravy (Sauce):

3 TABLESPOONS FLOUR
1/4 TEASPOON PEPPER
1/2 TEASPOON SALT
2 CUPS LIGHT CREAM, MILK, OR BROTH

✤ Mix all meatball ingredients together thoroughly. Shape into 1" to 1 1/2" balls. Brown in hot fat, turning often to retain shape. Remove from heat and pour off all but thin film of fat. To make gravy, add flour and stir in quickly the cream, milk, or broth, scraping up all browned pieces from pan. Boil sauce over medium heat for 2 or 3 minutes, stirring constantly until thick and smooth. Mix well so that all of the meatballs are well covered with sauce. Continue cooking meatballs in gravy for at least an hour.

Lefse—Served with Norwegian Meatballs

Serves 6–8

4 POUNDS RUSSET POTATOES

6 TABLESPOONS MARGARINE OR BUTTER, MELTED

3 TABLESPOONS HALF-AND-HALF OR LIGHT CREAM

2 TEASPOONS SUGAR

2 CUPS (OR SO) FLOUR

1. Peel and cook about 4 pounds of russet potatoes in salted water just until done. They should still have a little "backbone" in them. Overcooking will make them mushier, and they will need more flour. Twice rice the potatoes or mash them very thoroughly so that there are no lumps.

2. Measure out 6 cups of mashed potatoes. Add melted butter, cream, and sugar. Mix well and cool thoroughly, several hours or overnight.

3. Add about 2 cups of flour and mix well. Use an ice cream scoop to form balls of dough and keep the balls refrigerated. Work a little extra flour into each dough ball and knead it a little before rolling out on a floured pastry cloth. Roll out as thin as possible, using a grooved lefse rolling pin if possible. Bake each piece on a lefse griddle at 450° to 475°. Turn as soon as underside shows brown marks.

Chinese Hamburger Casserole

Serves 8

1 POUND GROUND BEEF

2 ONIONS, CHOPPED FINE

$1/2$ CUP CELERY, CHOPPED

1 CAN CREAM OF MUSHROOM SOUP

1 CAN CREAM OF CHICKEN SOUP

$1 1/2$ CUPS WARM WATER

$1/2$ CUP UNCOOKED RICE

$1/4$ CUP SOY SAUCE

$1/4$ TEASPOON PEPPER

1 3-OUNCE CAN CHOW MEIN NOODLES

❦ Brown meat, onions, and celery until meat is crumbly. *Do not add salt.* Add soups; fill cans with $1 1/2$ cups warm water and add to meat mixture. Stir in rice, soy sauce, and pepper. Turn into large, lightly greased casserole. Cover and bake 30 minutes at 350°. Remove cover and bake 30 minutes. Cover with noodles and bake 10 more minutes.

Enchilada Casserole (Mexico)

Serves 8–10

1 LARGE ONION
1½ POUNDS GROUND BEEF
1 CAN TOMATO PASTE
1 CUP WATER
1 LARGE CAN RED CHILI SAUCE OR ENCHILADA SAUCE
12 CORN TORTILLAS
1 POUND GRATED MONTEREY JACK OR MILD CHEDDAR CHEESE
1 LARGE CAN RIPE OLIVES, SLICED
1 CAN CHILI AND BEANS

➲ Brown onion and ground beef. Combine tomato paste, water, and chili sauce. Add to meat mixture and bring to a boil. Layer ¼ of the meat mixture in a 2-quart casserole. Cover with 3 tortillas. Cover tortillas with ¼ of the cheese and olives. Alternate remaining ingredients in layers, making 4 layers each. Pour on chili and beans before adding top layer of cheese and olives. Bake at 325° for 1 hour. Let sit for 15 minutes before serving.

Mexican Casserole

Serves 8

1 POUND HAMBURGER
½ CUP ONION, DICED
½ TEASPOON GARLIC SALT
1 8-OUNCE CAN TOMATO SAUCE
1 CUP SLICED RIPE OLIVES
1 CUP COTTAGE CHEESE
1 CUP SOUR CREAM
1 CAN CHILIES
1 6½-OUNCE PACKAGE CORN CHIPS
2 CUPS MILD WHITE CHEESE, SHREDDED

➲ Cook hamburger, onion, garlic salt, and tomato sauce in frying pan. Add olives. Mix cottage cheese, sour cream, and chilies. Crush corn chips. Layer in casserole: chips, meat filling, sour cream mixture, cheese; repeat layers. Bake at 350° for 30–40 minutes.

International Casserole

This is even better as leftovers!

Serves 8–10

6 Italian sausages
1 pound ground beef or turkey
1 7-ounce box macaroni
2 16-ounce cans stewed tomatoes
1 8-ounce can tomato sauce with onion
1 6-ounce can tomato paste
1 tablespoon garlic salt
1 tablespoon dried basil
1 tablespoon dried oregano
2½ cups water
1 pound of Muenster cheese, shredded

❧ Brown sausages and ground beef or turkey. Cut sausages into small pieces; drain. Add uncooked macaroni and all other ingredients, except cheese. Bake covered in large casserole at 350° for 1–1½ hours. Uncover; top with shredded cheese and bake until cheese is melted.

Martha's Company Casserole

Serves 6–8

½ pound noodles
1 tablespoon butter
1 pound ground beef
2 8-ounce cans tomato sauce
1 8-ounce package cream cheese, softened
½ pound cottage cheese
¼ cup sour cream
⅓ cup minced onion
1 tablespoon minced green pepper
2 tablespoons butter, melted

❧ Cook and drain noodles. Melt butter in a skillet and sauté the ground beef. Stir in the tomato sauce. Remove from heat. Combine the cream cheese, cottage cheese, sour cream, onion, and green pepper. In an oblong casserole dish, spread ½ the noodles; cover with the cheese mixture, then the rest of the noodles. Top with 2 tablespoons melted butter and then the meat sauce. Bake at 375° for 45 minutes.

Meat Loaf I

Serves 6

1½ POUNDS HAMBURGER

1 CUP OATMEAL

1 TEASPOON SALT

2 EGGS

¼ CUP CHOPPED ONION

1 CUP TOMATO JUICE

2 TABLESPOONS KETCHUP

3 TABLESPOONS BROWN SUGAR

1 TABLESPOON VINEGAR

❧ Mix first 6 ingredients. Put in loaf pan. Bake at 350° for 45–50 minutes. Mix last 3 ingredients and add during baking.

Meat Loaf II

This is a wonderful meat loaf, moist and delicate. It slices perfectly.

Serves 10

4 SLICES BREAD

1 POUND GROUND BEEF

½ POUND EACH GROUND VEAL AND PORK

1¼ TEASPOONS SALT

1 ONION, CHOPPED FINE

2 TABLESPOONS PREPARED MUSTARD

½ CUP MINUTE TAPIOCA

2 CUPS CANNED TOMATOES

1 CUP MILK

1 CUP WATER

❧ Soak bread in water and press dry. Add bread to remaining ingredients and mix well. Pour into greased loaf pan. Bake in 450° oven for 15 minutes; then turn oven to 350°. Bake an additional 45 minutes.

Gerry's Meat Loaf

Serves 4–6

4 SLICES WHITE BREAD, CRUMBLED
1 POUND GROUND BEEF
1 MEDIUM ONION, CHOPPED
1 TABLESPOON PARSLEY FLAKES
1 CAN TOMATO SOUP, UNDILUTED
1 EGG
SALT AND PEPPER TO TASTE

❧ Combine ingredients in order given and mix until well blended. Turn into an 8" × 4" × 2" loaf pan and bake for 1 hour at 400°.

Variation:
Instead of parsley, ¹/₂ cup chopped green olives or green peppers may be substituted.

Swedish Meat Loaf

Serves 8

1¹/₂ POUNDS GROUND BEEF
1 EGG
¹/₂ CUP HERB-SEASONED STUFFING MIX
1 CAN CREAM OF MUSHROOM SOUP
¹/₂ CUP SOUR CREAM
¹/₄ TEASPOON NUTMEG

❧ Mix beef, egg, stuffing mix, and ¹/₃ can of soup. Bake 1 hour at 350°. Blend remaining soup and sour cream with nutmeg. Heat in double boiler and serve over loaf.

Swedish Meatballs I

Serves 6–8

1¹/₂ POUNDS GROUND BEEF
1 CUP BREADCRUMBS OR CRUSHED SODA CRACKERS
1 EGG, UNBEATEN
¹/₂ CUP MILK
2 TABLESPOONS CHOPPED ONION
1 TEASPOON SALT
¹/₈ TEASPOON PEPPER
¹/₈ TEASPOON NUTMEG

❧ Combine all ingredients and mix well. Make into balls (about 1"–1¹/₂"). Brown well in frying pan with hot oil. Add about ¹/₂ cup water. Cover and simmer for 20 minutes.

Gravy:
PAN DRIPPINGS PLUS ENOUGH WATER TO MAKE 2 CUPS
1–2 BEEF BOUILLON CUBES
¹/₂ CUP FLOUR
1 CUP COLD WATER

❧ Remove meatballs from pan and scrape pan for drippings. Add enough water to make about 2 cups of liquid. Add 1 or 2 beef bouillon cubes as needed for flavor. Mix ¹/₂ cup flour and 1 cup cold water until smooth; add to drippings. Bring to a rolling boil, turn down heat, and let boil for 3 or 4 minutes. Add more water if too thick. Season to taste.

Swedish Meatballs II

Serves 12–15

4 SLICES SOFT BREAD

1 CUP MILK

2 TEASPOONS SALT

1/2 TEASPOON NUTMEG

2 EGGS

1/8 TEASPOON PEPPER

3 POUNDS GROUND BEEF

2 LARGE ONIONS, CHOPPED

2 GREEN PEPPERS, CHOPPED

2 TABLESPOONS BUTTER

2 CANS CONDENSED CHICKEN-WITH-RICE SOUP

2 CUPS TOMATO SOUP

❧ Soften bread in milk. Add salt, nutmeg, eggs, pepper, and beef. Shape into golf ball–sized meatballs. Sauté onions and green peppers in butter. Remove from skillet and brown the meatballs a few at a time. Add sautéed vegetables and soups. Cover and simmer for 40 minutes.

Porcupine Meat Balls

Serves 4

1 POUND GROUND BEEF

1/2 CUP RICE, UNCOOKED

1/2 CUP WATER

1 TEASPOON SALT

1/2 TEASPOON PEPPER

1 ONION, CHOPPED

1 TEASPOON WORCESTERSHIRE SAUCE

1 CAN TOMATO SOUP

❧ Mix all ingredients except tomato soup and form into balls. Place in casserole. Pour over meatballs 1 can tomato soup mixed with 1 can of water. Bake at 350° for 45 minutes.

Mary's Chili

Serves 2–4

1 LARGE ONION, SLICED
3 TABLESPOONS OIL
1 POUND GROUND BEEF
1 GREEN PEPPER, CHOPPED
1½ CUPS (15-OUNCE CAN) COOKED KIDNEY BEANS
     WITH LIQUID
2½ CUPS (28-OUNCE CAN) TOMATOES WITH LIQUID
1½ TEASPOONS SALT
⅛ TEASPOON CAYENNE PEPPER
3 WHOLE CLOVES
1 BAY LEAF
½ TABLESPOON CHILI POWDER

❧ Sauté onion in oil. In a separate pan, brown the meat and drain. Add drained meat to onion in pan along with rest of ingredients. Cover and simmer 45 minutes, adding water if necessary.

Chilly-Night Chili

Serves 6–8

1 LARGE ONION, CHOPPED
BUTTER
1 POUND HAMBURGER
1 OR 2 (15-OUNCE) CANS KIDNEY BEANS
1 CAN TOMATO SOUP, UNDILUTED
1 TEASPOON SALT
1 TABLESPOON CHILI POWDER
½ CUP SLICED RIPE OLIVES

❧ Sauté onion in 2–3 tablespoons butter. In a separate pan, brown meat and drain. Add to sautéed onion along with rest of ingredients. Let simmer for 30 minutes. Before serving sprinkle with sliced ripe olives.

Beef and Corn Casserole

Serves 6–8

1 GREEN PEPPER, CHOPPED

2 ONIONS, CHOPPED

2 TABLESPOONS OIL

2 POUNDS GROUND BEEF

2 LARGE CANS CREAMED-STYLE CORN

SLICED TOMATOES

BUTTERED CRUMBS, WHEAT GERM, OR CRUSHED BUTTERY
CRACKERS

❧ Sauté green pepper and onions in oil. Cook until onions are golden. Add ground beef. Cook and stir until browned. Place in a buttered baking dish (3-quart rectangle is good). Layer the corn on top of meat mixture. Layer tomatoes over corn. Sprinkle with buttered crumbs, wheat germ, or crushed crackers. Serve with a green salad, vinegar and oil dressing, crusty French bread, fresh fruit, and a beverage.

Inside-out Ravioli

Serves 6–8

1 POUND GROUND BEEF

1/2 CUP CHOPPED ONION

1 CLOVE GARLIC, MINCED

1 10-OUNCE PACKAGE FROZEN SPINACH

16 OUNCES SPAGHETTI SAUCE WITH MUSHROOMS

8 OUNCES TOMATO SAUCE

6 OUNCES TOMATO PASTE

1/2 TEASPOON SALT

DASH OF PEPPER

2 CUPS SHELL OR ELBOW MACARONI, COOKED AND DRAINED

1 CUP SHREDDED SHARP CHEDDAR CHEESE

1/2 CUP SOFT BREADCRUMBS

2 EGGS, WELL BEATEN

1/4 CUP SALAD OIL

❧ Brown first 3 ingredients in large skillet. Cook spinach using package directions; drain, reserving liquid; add water to make 1 cup. Add spinach liquid and next 5 ingredients to meat mixture. Simmer 10 minutes. Combine spinach with macaroni and remaining ingredients and spread in a 13" × 9" × 2" baking dish. Top with meat sauce. Bake at 350° for 30 minutes. Let stand 10 minutes before serving.

Dynamites

Serves 6–8

1 BUNCH CELERY

1 POUND GREEN PEPPERS

1 POUND ONIONS

1 LARGE (28-OUNCE) CAN TOMATO PURÉE

1 6-OUNCE CAN TOMATO PASTE

2 8-OUNCE CANS TOMATO SAUCE

GARLIC AND SUGAR TO TASTE

SMALL AMOUNTS OF OREGANO AND RED PEPPER

SALT AND PEPPER TO TASTE

$1/4$ CUP OIL

1 POUND HAMBURGER

HOT DOG ROLLS

GRATED CHEESE

❧ Cut vegetables into large skillet; add purée, paste, and sauce. Add 2 cans of water with the paste. Add oregano, a little red pepper, salt and pepper, $1/4$ cup oil, garlic, and sugar to taste. Brown 1 pound hamburger and add to mix. Cook slowly until vegetables are done. Serve over hot dog roll, sprinkled with grated cheese.

Luau Ribs

Serves 5–6

2 ($4^{1}/_{2}$-OUNCE) JARS PEACH BABY FOOD*

$1/3$ CUP CATSUP

2 TABLESPOONS SOY SAUCE

$1/3$ CUP VINEGAR

2 CLOVES GARLIC, MINCED

$1/2$ CUP BROWN SUGAR

1 TEASPOON SALT

2 TEASPOONS GINGER

DASH OF PEPPER

4 POUNDS MEATY SPARERIBS

❧ For sauce, mix all ingredients except ribs. Rub ribs on both sides with salt and pepper. Place ribs, meat side up, in a shallow foil-lined pan. Bake for 15 minutes at 450°. Spoon off fat. Pour sauce over ribs. Continue baking in a moderate oven, 350°, for $1^{1}/_{2}$ hours or until done. The oven may be turned down to 300° and the ribs cooked longer, about 2 hours.

*You may use regular canned peaches or canned tropical fruit and purée in food processor.

Roast Leg of Lamb

Serves 6–8

1 5-POUND LEG OF LAMB

1 TEASPOON SALT

2 CLOVES GARLIC, CHOPPED FINE

1/4 TEASPOON PEPPER

1/4 BAY LEAF, CRUSHED

1/4 TEASPOON DRIED MARJORAM

1/4 TEASPOON SUGAR

1/4 TEASPOON GINGER

1/4 TEASPOON THYME

1 TABLESPOON OLIVE OIL

❧ Wipe lamb with a damp cloth. Cut gashes in the roast and rub all over with olive oil. Combine all of the remaining ingredients and fill the gashes with the mixture. Roast at 500° for 15 minutes. Reduce heat to 350° and continue to roast for 1 1/2 hours.

Six-Layer Dinner

This is easy, good, inexpensive, and nutritious!

Serves 6–8

2 CUPS SHREDDED CARROTS

1 GREEN PEPPER, SEEDED AND CHOPPED

1 CUP CHOPPED CELERY

2 CUPS SLICED RAW POTATOES

1/2 CUP RAW BROWN RICE

1 CUP SLICED ONIONS

1 1/2 POUNDS GROUND BEEF ROUND, BROWNED

1/2 CUP WHEAT GERM

1 QUART TOMATO JUICE

SALT AND PEPPER

❧ Preheat oven to 325°. Combine carrots, green pepper, and celery. Place potatoes in bottom of buttered casserole. Sprinkle with rice and cover in layers with onions, browned beef, vegetables, and wheat germ. Pour tomato juice over all. Cover tightly and bake 2 1/2 hours. May be halved. A little grated cheese is good sprinkled on top just before removing from oven.

Peachy Pork Potato Dish

Serves 6

1 (16-ounce) can cling peach slices
6 pork chops
Salt and pepper
6 medium-sized sweet potatoes, cooked and peeled*
4 tablespoons maple syrup

 Drain peaches. Brown chops well on both sides. Season with salt and pepper. Arrange thick slices of sweet potato in greased casserole. Cover with peaches and drizzle with maple syrup. Place browned chops on top. Bake covered, in 350° oven, 45 minutes.

*Canned sweet potatoes may be used to avoid boiling and peeling.

Hawaiian Sausage Casserole

Serves 4–6

1 20-ounce can pineapple chunks, undrained
1 16-ounce can whole sweet potatoes, drained and cut into 1/2" pieces
3/4 pound smoked sausage, sliced
3 tablespoons brown sugar
2 tablespoons cornstarch
1/4 teaspoon salt
1 tablespoon butter or margarine
Marshmallows, optional

 Drain the pineapple chunks, reserving the juice. Add enough water to the juice to measure 1 1/4 cups. Set this aside. Place pineapple chunks, sweet potatoes, and sausage in a 10" × 6" × 2" baking pan. Set this aside. Combine sugar, cornstarch, and salt in a saucepan. Gradually add pineapple juice mixture, stirring constantly until mixture thickens and comes to a boil. Boil 1 minute, stirring constantly. Remove from heat and add butter, stirring until melted. Pour over sausage and pineapple mixture. Cover and bake at 350° for 35 minutes. Casserole can be uncovered for the last few minutes and marshmallows added to the top. Bake a few more minutes until marshmallows are browned.

Chinese Chop Suey

Serves 4–6

1/4 CUP BUTTER

3 CUPS DICED PORK

2 CUPS ONIONS, THINLY SLICED

2 CUPS CELERY, THINLY SLICED

2 TEASPOONS SALT

1/2 TEASPOON PEPPER

2 CUPS HOT WATER OR CHICKEN BROTH

2 CANS BEAN SPROUTS (DRAIN AND RINSE)

CHOW MEIN NOODLES

Thickening/Flavoring:

2/3 CUP COLD WATER

4 TABLESPOONS CORNSTARCH

4 TEASPOONS SOY SAUCE

2 TEASPOONS SUGAR

☙ Melt butter in skillet. Add meat and stir to sear. Add onions and cook 5 minutes. Add celery, salt, pepper, and hot water or broth. Cover and cook 5 minutes. Add sprouts, mix, and heat to boiling point. In a small bowl, combine thickening and flavoring ingredients. Add to meat mixture. Stir lightly and cook 5 minutes. Serve hot with chow mein noodles.

Hot Bar-B-Q Sauce

Yields 1 1/2 cups

1 CUP KETCHUP

1/4 CUP LEMON JUICE

1/4 CUP WATER

3 TABLESPOONS VINEGAR

2 TABLESPOONS OIL

1/2 TEASPOON HOT PEPPER

1 TABLESPOON BROWN SUGAR

1 TEASPOON SALT

1 TEASPOON DRY MUSTARD

1 TEASPOON PAPRIKA

1/2 TEASPOON BLACK PEPPER

1/2 TEASPOON ONION POWDER

1/2 TEASPOON GARLIC POWDER

☙ Mix ingredients and bring to a boil; simmer 10 minutes. Use to dress pork, beef, or fowl when barbecuing.

Barbecued Ribs

Serves 4

1 TABLESPOON VINEGAR

1/2 CUP WATER

1 TABLESPOON WORCESTERSHIRE SAUCE

1/2 TEASPOON SALT

1/2 TEASPOON CHILI POWDER

1/2 CUP KETCHUP

3 POUNDS SPARERIBS

❧ Combine first 6 ingredients and pour over ribs in a baking pan. Bake 2 hours at 325°. Baste often.

Old Favorite Ham Loaf

Serves 6

1/2 POUND GROUND PORK

1 1/2 POUNDS GROUND CURED HAM

1 EGG, BEATEN

1 CUP BREADCRUMBS

1/2 CUP MILK

3 TABLESPOONS CANNED TOMATO SOUP

1/2 TEASPOON PAPRIKA

1/3 TEASPOON SALT

1 MEDIUM ONION, SLICED

❧ Mix the above ingredients, except the onion slices, together. Transfer to a loaf pan. Lay onion slices over top. Bake at 350° for 1–1 1/2 hours, basting occasionally with a few tablespoons of hot water. Serve with Mustard Sauce (recipe follows).

Mustard Sauce:

1/2 CUP TOMATO SOUP

1/2 CUP PREPARED MUSTARD

1/2 CUP VINEGAR

1/2 CUP SUGAR

1/2 CUP MARGARINE

3 EGG YOLKS, BEATEN

❧ Combine all ingredients and cook in double boiler until thick. This sauce will keep indefinitely in a cool place.

Sylta (Swedish Jellied Meat)

Serves 8–10

4 POUNDS GOOD BEEF

2 POUNDS PORK ROAST

2 POUNDS CHICKEN BREASTS, WASHED

SALT TO TASTE

2 OR 3 WHOLE BAY LEAVES

UNFLAVORED GELATIN

WHOLE PEPPERCORNS TO TASTE

1. Put beef and pork in large kettle and chicken in separate kettle. Add salt to taste. Put 2 bay leaves into beef/pork pot and 1 bay leaf into chicken pot. Barely cover both with lukewarm water. Bring both to a boil and simmer on very low heat for 2–3 hours (beef and pork), 1½ hours for chicken.

2. Drain meat and chicken, saving stock. Remove bay leaves. Chop meat and chicken into cubes. Put cubed meat and chicken together in a large kettle. Measure stock in which both meat and chicken were cooked. Pour over meat and chicken in large kettle.

3. For each 2 cups of stock used, dissolve 2 envelopes of unflavored gelatin in 4 tablespoons of cold water. Add to stock and cubed meat after bringing meat and stock mixture to a bubbly boil. Stir well. Season with whole peppercorns and extra salt if needed. Pour into molds and chill. Slice and eat cold with vinegar and Swedish Rye bread—a traditional Christmas breakfast. Also very nice sliced cold on Limpa bread for Christmas Eve.

Saucy Noodles

Serves 8

1 12-OUNCE PACKAGE NOODLES

½ POUND POLISH KIELBASA

1 32-OUNCE JAR SPAGHETTI SAUCE

1 6-OUNCE CAN TOMATO PASTE

1 TABLESPOON ITALIAN SEASONING

❧ Cook noodles according to package directions. Quarter kielbasa lengthwise and slice thinly. Place under broiler until crisp and lightly browned. Remove from pan with slotted spoon, draining excess fat. Blend spaghetti sauce, tomato paste, and Italian seasoning in saucepan; add cooked kielbasa and heat through over medium heat. Drain noodles and top each serving with sauce.

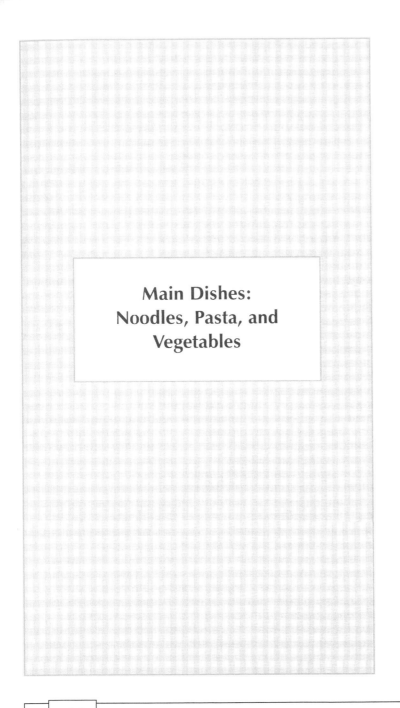

**Main Dishes:
Noodles, Pasta, and
Vegetables**

Noodle Pudding

Very nice served with ham.

Serves 8–10

1 8-OUNCE PACKAGE OF MEDIUM-WIDE EGG NOODLES,
    COOKED
6–8 OUNCES SOFTENED CREAM CHEESE
6 TABLESPOONS BUTTER
3 LARGE EGGS
1/2 CUP SUGAR
1 CUP MILK
1 CUP APRICOT NECTAR

❧ Place cooked noodles in casserole. Add cream cheese
and butter. Toss. Mix together eggs, sugar, milk, and apricot
nectar. Pour over noodles. Bake at 350° for 40 minutes.

Quick Rice Casserole

This dish keeps well and is easily doubled.

Serves 4–5

1 CUP UNCOOKED RICE

1 CAN BEEF CONSOMMÉ

1 CUP WATER

½ STICK BUTTER

1 TEASPOON DRIED BASIL

1 TEASPOON DRIED THYME

1 TEASPOON DRIED MARJORAM

SALT AND PEPPER

⁑ Combine all ingredients; pour into a well-buttered casserole dish. Bake, covered, 1 hour and 15 minutes at 375°. Stir after 20 minutes.

Vegetable Soufflé

Serves 6–8

2 CUPS CUBED SOFT WHITE BREAD

1 CUP CUBED AMERICAN CHEESE

6 TABLESPOONS BUTTER OR MARGARINE

2 CUPS CANNED EVAPORATED MILK

4 EGGS, BEATEN

1 17-OUNCE CAN MIXED VEGETABLES, DRAINED

⁑ Grease casserole dish with margarine. Add bread, cheese, and butter. Heat milk and pour over the above ingredients and stir. Stir in eggs. Stir in vegetables. Bake at 350° for 45 minutes. If using a glass casserole, bake at 325°.

Corn and Carrot Casserole

Serves 6

1 cup white sauce
1/4 cup grated Cheddar cheese
1 egg
1 pound carrots, cooked and mashed
1 can whole kernel corn
1 teaspoon sugar

Make white sauce and add sugar and cheese. Beat egg and add white sauce gradually. Mix vegetables and add to sauce. Sprinkle crumbs on top. Bake in 8" × 12" pan at 350° for 30 minutes.

Terrific Vegetable Casserole

Serves 8

1 cup cooked rice
3 pounds zucchini, cooked, drained, and mashed
2 cups shredded Cheddar cheese
1/2 cup chopped green onions
1/4 cup chopped fresh parsley
3 eggs, beaten
1/2 cup butter or margarine, melted
Salt and pepper, to taste
Paprika

Combine first 5 ingredients. Stir in eggs, butter, and salt and pepper. Spoon into baking dish. Sprinkle with paprika. Bake at 350° for 1 hour.

Summer Squash Casserole

Serves 6–8

2 pounds yellow or zucchini squash
1/4 cup finely chopped onion
1 cup condensed cream of chicken or mushroom soup
1 cup sour cream
1 cup shredded carrots
1 8-ounce package herb stuffing
1/2 cup margarine, melted

Cook squash and onion in boiling water for 5 minutes. Drain. Combine soup and sour cream. Stir in carrots. Fold in squash and onion. Combine stuffing mix and margarine. Spread 1/2 of stuffing mixture on bottom of 12" × 7" × 2" casserole dish. Spoon vegetable mixture over it. Sprinkle remaining stuffing on top. Bake at 350° for 25–30 minutes.

Green Vegetable Casserole

Serves 8–10

2 10-ounce packages of frozen spinach or broccoli*
1 stick butter or margarine, melted
1 8-ounce package cream cheese
Lemon juice
1/4–1/2 package seasoned stuffing mix

❧ Cook frozen spinach or broccoli according to package directions. Place drained vegetable in casserole dish. Add the melted butter to the softened cream cheese. Add a splash of lemon juice to cream cheese mixture. Layer over the vegetable. Crush 1/4–1/2 package dry seasoned stuffing mix. Layer stuffing crumbs over cream cheese mixture. Bake at 350° uncovered for 30 minutes.

*You may use fresh vegetables if you prefer.

Scalloped Tomatoes

Serves 8

1 cup diced celery
1/2 cup chopped onion
2 tablespoons butter
2 tablespoons flour
3 slices bread, toasted and buttered
1 29-ounce can tomatoes
1 tablespoon sugar
1 teaspoon salt
Dash pepper
2 teaspoons prepared mustard

❧ Cook celery and onion in butter until just tender; blend in flour. Cut toast into 1/2" cubes. In a 1 1/2-quart casserole, combine the onion and celery mixture with the tomatoes, 1/2 the toast cubes, sugar, salt, pepper, and mustard. Bake at 350° for 30 minutes. Top casserole with remaining toast cubes and bake 20 minutes longer.

Vegetable Quiche

Serves 6 for main dish or 12 for appetizer

1/2 PACKAGE PIE CRUST MIX

1 POUND FRESH SPINACH, COOKED AND WELL DRAINED

1/2 CUP CHOPPED GREEN ONIONS

1 CLOVE GARLIC, MINCED

2 TABLESPOONS BUTTER OR MARGARINE

1 1/2 CUPS (6 OUNCES) SHREDDED SWISS CHEESE

3 EGGS, LIGHTLY BEATEN

3/4 CUP MILK

1 TEASPOON SALT

1 TEASPOON DRIED BASIL

1/2 TEASPOON CELERY SALT

2 MEDIUM-SIZED TOMATOES, THINLY SLICED

1 TABLESPOON PACKAGED BREADCRUMBS

1 TABLESPOON PARMESAN CHEESE

1. Prepare pie crust mix, following package directions, or make your own single pie crust recipe. Roll out to a 12" round on a lightly floured surface; fit into a 9" pie plate. Trim overhang to 1/2"; turn under and flute to make a stand-up edge.

2. Press excess water out of spinach; chop finely.

3. Sauté green onions and garlic in butter in a medium-sized skillet until golden. Add spinach; cook over medium heat, stirring constantly until excess moisture evaporates.

4. Combine spinach mixture, Swiss cheese, eggs, milk, salt, basil, and celery salt in a large bowl; stir well to mix.

5. Turn into a prepared pastry shell. Arrange thinly sliced tomatoes around outer edge of quiche. Bake in a hot oven, 425°, for 15 minutes; lower oven temperature to moderate, 350°, and bake 10 minutes longer. Combine breadcrumbs and Parmesan cheese in a small bowl; sprinkle over tomato slices. Bake quiche 10 minutes longer or until top is puffy.

Cauliflower Casserole

Serves 8 as a side dish

1 HEAD CAULIFLOWER
1/4 CUP BUTTER OR MARGARINE
1/4 CUP DICED GREEN PEPPER
1/4 CUP CHOPPED ONION
1/4 CUP FLOUR
2 CUPS MILK
SALT AND PEPPER TO TASTE
1/2 CUP GRATED CHEDDAR CHEESE

❧ Break cauliflower into florets and boil 10 minutes. Drain. Melt butter in heavy pan and lightly brown green pepper and onion. Blend in flour and milk gradually, stirring constantly until thickened. Season with salt and pepper. Place 1/2 of the cauliflower in a greased casserole; cover with 1/2 the sauce and 1/2 the cheese. Repeat layers. Bake 15–20 minutes in 350° oven.

Zucchini Casserole I

Serves 8

3 CUPS GRATED ZUCCHINI
1 MEDIUM ONION, GRATED
4 EGGS
1 CUP PREPARED BISCUIT MIX
1/2 TEASPOON SALT
1/3 CUP OIL
1/2 CUP GRATED PARMESAN CHEESE

❧ Mix first 6 ingredients together. Put in buttered casserole; sprinkle with Parmesan cheese. Bake at 350° for 45 minutes. This is as good cold as hot.

Zucchini Casserole II

Serves 8 as a side dish

6 CUPS SLICED ZUCCHINI

1/4 CUP CHOPPED ONION

1 CAN CREAM OF MUSHROOM OR CREAM OF CHICKEN SOUP

1 CUP SOUR CREAM

1 CUP SHREDDED CARROTS

1 8-OUNCE PACKAGE STUFFING MIX

GRATED CHEESE, OPTIONAL

🥢 Cook zucchini and onion for 5 minutes. Drain. Combine soup and sour cream. Fold in drained zucchini mixture and raw carrots. Spread stuffing on bottom of 2-quart pan. Spoon vegetable mixture on top, adding cheese. Bake at 350° for 25–30 minutes.

Eggplant-Cheese Casserole

Serves 4–6

1 LARGE EGGPLANT, PEELED AND SLICED

1 EGG, BEATEN

2 TABLESPOONS WATER

3 TABLESPOONS VEGETABLE OIL

1 POUND GROUND BEEF

2 MEDIUM ONIONS, CHOPPED

2 8-OUNCE CANS TOMATO SAUCE

1 TEASPOON SALT, OPTIONAL

1/2 TEASPOON PEPPER

1/4 TEASPOON DRIED BASIL

1/4 TEASPOON DRIED OREGANO

1 CLOVE GARLIC, CRUSHED (GARLIC SALT MAY BE SUBSTITUTED)

1/2 POUND MOZZARELLA CHEESE, SLICED

🥢 Dip eggplant slices in mixture of egg and water. Sauté in oil until lightly browned and drain; remove from pan and set aside. Cook beef and onions in remaining oil until onion is golden. Remove fat. Add tomato sauce and seasonings. Layer eggplant, meat sauce, and cheese in 2-quart casserole, ending with cheese. Bake in 350° oven 45–50 minutes.

Stuffed Green Peppers

Serves 6

3 LARGE GREEN PEPPERS

1 15-OUNCE CAN CORNED BEEF HASH

1/2 CUP KETCHUP

1/2 CUP GRATED PARMESAN CHEESE

✣ Cut peppers in 1/2 and remove seeds. Blanch in hot water. Mix corned beef hash with ketchup and Parmesan cheese. Put small amount of water in bottom of baking dish. Fill the pepper halves and place in the baking dish, cut side up. Bake at 350° for 30 minutes.

Sweet and Sour Carrots

Serves 8

1 CAN TOMATO SOUP

1 TEASPOON DRY MUSTARD

1/2 CUP COOKING OIL

3/4 CUP SUGAR

1 10-OUNCE JAR SWEET PICKLED ONIONS

VINEGAR

2 LARGE GREEN PEPPERS, DICED AND COOKED UNTIL JUST TENDER

2 POUNDS CARROTS, DICED AND COOKED

✣ Mix tomato soup, dry mustard, oil, and sugar. Simmer 5 minutes. Drain and reserve juice from pickled onions; add enough vinegar to juice to make 3/4 cup. Add to tomato mixture and simmer 5 minutes. Remove from heat. Add onions, green peppers, and carrots. Mix well and store for 12 hours in refrigerator. Reheat and serve. May also be served cold.

Corn Casserole

Makes 10 side-dish servings

1 15-OUNCE CAN CREAM-STYLE CORN
1 SMALL CAN REGULAR CORN
1 CAN MUSHROOM SOUP
2 EGGS, BEATEN SLIGHTLY
3 SLICES OF BUTTERED BREAD, CRUMBLED
2 CUPS MILK
1 SMALL ONION, CHOPPED FINE
2 TABLESPOONS BUTTER, MELTED
2 TABLESPOONS FLOUR

✺ Combine all ingredients and place in a 2-quart casserole at 375° for 45 minutes.

Broccoli Casserole

Makes 6 side-dish servings

2 PACKAGES FROZEN CHOPPED BROCCOLI
2 CUPS BREAD STUFFING
1 STICK MARGARINE, MELTED
1 CAN CREAM OF CELERY SOUP

✺ Cook broccoli in water for 3 minutes. Drain. Mix the stuffing and margarine together. In a casserole dish spread ½ of the broccoli. Top with ½ of the soup. Add ½ of the stuffing. Repeat. Bake at 350° for 30 minutes.

Creamed Broccoli Pudding

Makes 8 side-dish servings

2 10-OUNCE PACKAGES FROZEN CHOPPED BROCCOLI
1 CUP SALAD DRESSING
1 CUP GRATED SHARP CHEDDAR CHEESE
2 EGGS, SLIGHTLY BEATEN
1 CUP CONDENSED CREAM OF CELERY SOUP
2 TABLESPOONS MINCED ONION
CRACKER CRUMBS
BUTTER, MELTED

✺ Cook broccoli using package directions and drain well. Make a mixture of salad dressing, cheese, eggs, soup, and onion. Add the broccoli and mix well. Pour into greased casserole. Cover with cracker crumbs that have been mixed with melted butter. Bake at 350° for 45 minutes.

Baked Cabbage, Tomato, and Cheese

Makes 6–8 side-dish servings

3 CUPS FINELY SHREDDED CABBAGE
1½ CUPS DICED TOMATOES
3/4 TEASPOON SALT
1/8 TEASPOON PEPPER
1/8 TEASPOON PAPRIKA
2 TEASPOONS LIGHT BROWN SUGAR
1 CUP SHREDDED CHEESE
1 CUP DRY BREADCRUMBS
2 TABLESPOONS BUTTER OR MARGARINE

❧ Cook cabbage in boiling salted water for 5 minutes; drain. Combine tomatoes, salt, pepper, paprika, and sugar. Bring just to boiling point. Arrange ½ of tomato mixture in buttered baking dish. Cover with ½ of cabbage, then ½ of cheese and breadcrumbs. Repeat layers. Dot top with butter. Bake at 325° for about 30 minutes, or until browned.

Baked Lima Beans

Serves 10 as a side dish

1 LARGE ONION
1 CLOVE GARLIC
3 TABLESPOONS MARGARINE
4 10-OUNCE PACKAGES FROZEN LIMA BEANS, DEFROSTED
1 LARGE CAN TOMATO SAUCE
1 15-OUNCE CAN STEWED TOMATOES
1 TABLESPOON BROWN SUGAR
1 TEASPOON SALT
1 TEASPOON DRY MUSTARD
1/4 TEASPOON PEPPER
STRIPS OF UNCOOKED BACON

❧ Sauté onion and garlic in margarine. Add to rest of ingredients, except for bacon, and mix. Put into a 2-quart baking dish with bacon strips on top. Bake uncovered at 300° for about 40 minutes.

Winter Squash Quiche

Serves 6–8

10" PASTRY SHELL, BAKED

4 SLICES BACON, FRIED, OR 1/4 CUP BACON BITS

2 TABLESPOONS CHOPPED ONION

1 CUP SHREDDED SWISS CHEESE

3 EGGS, BEATEN

1 1/2 CUPS MILK

1 CUP COOKED AND MASHED WINTER SQUASH

1/4 TEASPOON SALT

1/8 TEASPOON NUTMEG

1/8 TEASPOON PEPPER

&. Combine in bowl and pour into pastry shell. Bake at 350° for 50–60 minutes. Let stand 5 minutes.

Macaroni Casserole

Serves 6

2 CUPS UNCOOKED MACARONI

2 CUPS MILK

2 CANS MUSHROOM SOUP

1 SMALL JAR CHIPPED BEEF

4 HARD-COOKED EGGS

2 CUPS SHREDDED CHEDDAR CHEESE

&. Mix all ingredients and place in refrigerator overnight. Bake next day at 350° for 1 hour.

Easy Quiche

Serves 6–8

3 EGGS, BEATEN

1/3 CUP BUTTER OR MARGARINE, MELTED

1/2 CUP PREPARED BISCUIT MIX

1 1/2 CUPS MILK

1 CUP GRATED CHEESE, PREFERABLY CHEDDAR

1 CUP CHOPPED HAM

&. Mix ingredients together thoroughly. Pour into greased 10" pie plate. Bake at 350° for 40–45 minutes. Let stand a few minutes before cutting.

Bean Casserole

Makes 8 side-dish servings

2 15-ounce cans French-style green beans

1 cup condensed mushroom soup

3/4 cup milk

1 2.8-ounce can dried fried onions, divided

 Mix green beans, soup, milk, and 1/2 can onions in casserole. Bake 30 minutes at 350°. Sprinkle remaining onions on top and bake 5 minutes longer.

Slow-Cooker Baked Beans

Serves 8–10

4 cups dried beans

Small piece lean salt pork

1/2 teaspoon onion powder

6 tablespoons brown sugar

1/4 teaspoon pepper

1/2 cup molasses

2 teaspoons mustard

1 teaspoon salt

Put beans in kettle with 2 quarts of water and soak overnight. In the morning, drain beans and add fresh water. Bring to a boil; boil 15 minutes. Drain beans and put in slow cooker. Add remaining ingredients. Add 4–6 cups of water, making sure beans are covered with water. Cook on high for 1 hour and then on medium for 4 hours.

Cheese Dreams

Serves 8, or can be cut in small wedges and served as an appetizer

1/2 pound bacon

2 cups grated sharp Cheddar cheese

1 cup diced green pepper

1/2 cup mayonnaise

1 tablespoon (plus) mustard

1 package of 8 hamburger buns

Onions (optional)

Fry onions (optional) and bacon until crisp. Crumble and add to cheese and pepper, mayonnaise and mustard. Mix thoroughly and spread on buns. Broil until cheese is bubbly and brown.

Sweet Potato Casserole

This recipe is easily halved or multiplied.

Serves 12

6–8 cups boiled and mashed sweet potatoes
Scant 1/2 cup sugar
2 eggs
1 teaspoon vanilla
1/4 cup butter, melted (optional)
Dash each of cinnamon and clove

Mix together and put in a greased 2-quart or larger casserole dish.

Topping:
1 cup brown sugar (packed)
1 cup chopped nuts, preferably pecans
1/3 cup flour
1/3 cup butter (not melted)

Mix with a fork to crumb consistency. Sprinkle on top of potatoes. Bake 30 minutes at 350° or until bubbly.

Scalloped Potatoes in Cheese Sauce

Serves 8

6 potatoes
2 tablespoons cornstarch
2 cups milk
4 tablespoons margarine
Salt and pepper to taste
6 ounces American cheese, shredded
30 buttery crackers
1 4-ounce jar pimiento, drained and chopped
3/4 cup chopped green pepper
1 stick margarine, melted
Paprika

1. Preheat oven to 350°. Butter sides and bottom of an 11" × 8" × 2" baking dish.

2. Peel and slice potatoes into a medium-sized pot. Cover with water and bring to a boil. Boil for approximately 3 minutes, just to ensure tenderness. Do not completely cook.

3. Meanwhile, make cheese sauce as follows: Dissolve cornstarch in milk, stirring until smooth. Add margarine, salt, and pepper. Stirring constantly, bring to a boil over medium heat. After sauce thickens, add cheese, beating with whisk until smooth.

4. Spread potatoes on bottom of baking dish. Pour sauce over all. Crush buttery crackers coarsely, adding drained pimiento, chopped green pepper, and melted margarine. Mix well. Cover casserole with cracker-crumb mixture. Dust with paprika. Bake at 350° approximately 30–35 minutes or until golden brown.

Pot Luck Potatoes

Serves 8

1 32-ounce bag of frozen hash brown potatoes*
1/2 cup chopped raw onions
1/8 teaspoon black pepper
1 can cream of chicken or cream of mushroom soup
8 ounces sour cream or whole milk yogurt
2 cups grated Cheddar cheese
1/2 cup small curd cottage cheese
1/4 cup butter or margarine, melted
1 cup crushed cornflakes or breadcrumbs

🐚 If using frozen potatoes, be sure to thaw them completely before adding onions, pepper, soup, sour cream, cheese, and cottage cheese. Place mixture in a 2-quart casserole. Make a topping of butter or margarine and cornflakes or breadcrumbs. Bake at 350° for 30 minutes or until bubbly and brown on top. A layer of Chinese noodles is also good on top.

*You may cook fresh potatoes, peel, and cut into small cubes.

Sweet Potato and Cranberry Casserole

Serves 8

4 large sweet potatoes
1/2 cup brown sugar
2 tablespoons margarine
1 cup cranberries
1/2 cup orange juice

Topping:
1/2 cup chopped walnuts
1 tablespoon brown sugar
2 tablespoons margarine
1/2 teaspoon cinnamon

🐚 Boil potatoes 30–40 minutes. Peel and cut into 1/4" slices. Arrange 1/2 in greased 2-quart casserole. Sprinkle with 1/4 cup brown sugar. Dot with margarine. Sprinkle with 1/2 cup cranberries. Repeat, using remaining cranberries. Pour orange juice over. Bake covered in 350° oven for 45 minutes. Uncover and put topping on. Bake another 10 minutes.

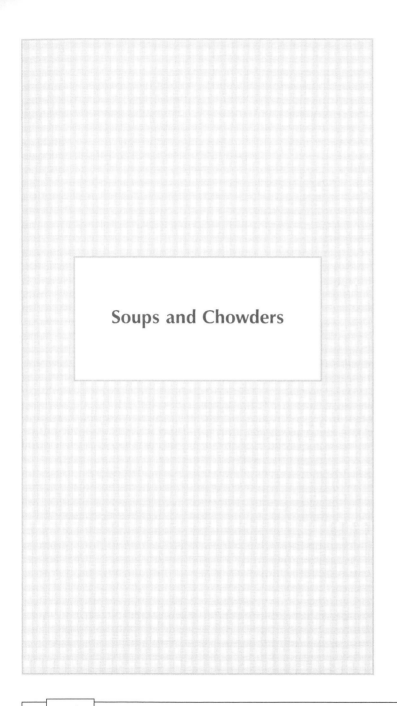

Soups and Chowders

Tomato and Rice Soup

Serves 10

1$\frac{1}{2}$ POUNDS TOP ROUND, CUT INTO 1" CUBES

2 QUARTS WATER

1 CAN (35 OUNCES) TOMATOES

3 BEEF BOUILLON CUBES

$\frac{1}{2}$ TEASPOON PEPPER

$\frac{1}{2}$ TEASPOON THYME, CRUMBLED

$\frac{1}{4}$ TEASPOON LEAF MARJORAM, CRUMBLED

5 CARROTS, PARED AND SLICED $\frac{1}{2}$" THICK

5 STALKS CELERY, SLICED $\frac{1}{2}$" THICK

1 ONION, COARSELY CHOPPED

$\frac{1}{2}$ CUP UNCOOKED WHITE RICE

❧ Brown beef in large saucepan. Add water. Bring to boiling. Lower heat and simmer 20 minutes or until meat is almost tender. Stir in tomatoes and their liquid, breaking up chunks with a spoon. Add bouillon, pepper, thyme, and marjoram. Simmer 1 hour. Add carrots, celery, onion, and rice for last 30 minutes of cooking.

Spinach Mushroom Soup

Makes 6 cups

4–6 TABLESPOONS CHOPPED ONION

4 TABLESPOONS BUTTER

1 6-OUNCE CAN SLICED MUSHROOMS

4 TABLESPOONS FLOUR

2 CUPS VEGETABLE BROTH

JUICE FROM 1/8 OF A LEMON

1 10-OUNCE PACKAGE FROZEN CHOPPED SPINACH, DRAINED
AND SQUEEZED DRY

1 CAN EVAPORATED MILK

1–2 TEASPOONS SHERRY

WHITE PEPPER AND SALT TO TASTE

CRISP, CRUMBLED BACON (OPTIONAL)

❧ Sauté onion briefly in butter. Add mushrooms and sauté briefly. Add flour and stir to absorb; cook 1 minute. Add broth and lemon juice. Stir in spinach. Bring to a boil, stirring. Remove from heat. Stir in evaporated milk, sherry, and seasonings to taste. May garnish with crisp, crumbled bacon.

Stewed Escarole and Cannellini Beans

Serves 4

1 HEAD ESCAROLE

1 TEASPOON SALT

2 TABLESPOONS OLIVE OIL

1 CLOVE GARLIC, MINCED

1 28-OUNCE CAN TOMATOES, CHOPPED*

1 15-OUNCE CAN CANNELLINI BEANS

SALT AND FRESHLY GROUND PEPPER TO TASTE

PARMESAN CHEESE

❧ Discard the discolored and tough outer leaves of the escarole. Remove core and wash leaves under cold running water until clean. Place in a large kettle with salt and cover with water. Bring to a boil, cover, and lower heat. Boil gently for 10–15 minutes. Drain and leave in colander. In same kettle, heat oil and sauté garlic for 3 minutes. Add tomatoes and cannellini beans with all of the liquid and simmer for 5 minutes. Add escarole and simmer until escarole is tender, about 8–10 minutes. Serve soup garnished with grated Parmesan cheese.

*You may use stewed tomatoes. Use 2 14.5-ounce cans.

Wedding Soup

Serves 2–3

2 15-OUNCE CANS CHICKEN BROTH

1/2 HEAD ESCAROLE, CLEANED AND CHOPPED

1–2 CUPS SMALL PIECES OF COOKED CHICKEN OR SMALL
COOKED MEATBALLS

SMALL RING PASTA

GRATED PARMESAN OR CHEDDAR CHEESE

✍ Heat chicken broth in a medium-sized pan. Add escarole, chicken or meatballs, and whatever amount of ring pasta you wish. Serve hot with grated cheese.

Fish Chowder

Serves 6

6 POTATOES, DICED

3 ONIONS, DICED

SALT AND PEPPER TO TASTE

1 1/2 POUNDS HADDOCK, CUT IN PIECES

1 PINT MILK

1/2 CAN EVAPORATED MILK

1 STICK BUTTER

✍ Put potatoes, onions, salt, and pepper in a saucepan* and just barely cover with water. Boil until tender. Add fish and turn heat to lowest point on stove and simmer until done, about 5 minutes. At this point, set pan over hot water. Add milk and butter. Serve when ready to eat. Will reheat nicely.

*You may use a double boiler instead of a saucepan. Have hot water ready in bottom pan.

Minestrone Soup

Serves 8

$^1/_3$ cup olive or canola oil

1 cup celery, chopped

1 onion, chopped

2 cups cabbage, sliced

2 beef bouillon cubes

1 15-ounce can yellow eye beans

2 quarts water

Dash of garlic salt

$^1/_2$ tablespoon dried parsley

$^1/_4$ teaspoon each of dried basil, pepper, and oregano

1 28-ounce jar spaghetti sauce

Potatoes, peeled and cut up (as many as people you are serving)

❧ Heat oil. Sauté celery, onion, and cabbage. Add bouillon cubes, beans, water, garlic salt, and spices. Add spaghetti sauce and potatoes. Cook, covered, for 2 hours on medium-low heat.

Lamb Stew

Serves 4–6

1 pound boned lamb shoulder

$^1/_4$ cup flour

Pepper

2–3 tablespoons olive oil

1$^1/_2$ quarts boiling water

Garlic salt

2 carrots, quartered

1 onion, quartered

2 large potatoes, pared and quartered

$^1/_2$ turnip, cut into small pieces

$^1/_4$ cup celery, chopped

4 beef bouillon cubes

$^1/_3$ cup flour

$^2/_3$ cup water

❧ Cut lamb into 1" cubes; place flour and a dash of pepper in paper bag with lamb. Shake until meat is well covered. Brown meat well in olive oil in a deep kettle. Add boiling water and a dash of garlic salt. Cover and simmer for 30 minutes. Add carrots, onion, potatoes, turnip, celery, bouillon cubes, and a dash of pepper. Simmer 1$^1/_2$ hours. Make a paste of $^1/_3$ cup flour mixed with $^2/_3$ cup water. Add flour paste to stew. Heat for 10 minutes longer.

Joann's Portuguese Vegetable Soup

Serves 10–12

1–1½ POUNDS BEEF SHANK

1 CUP DRY SPLIT PEAS

1 TABLESPOON SALT

3 CLOVES GARLIC, MINCED

8 CUPS WATER

1 POUND CHORIZO OR ITALIAN SAUSAGE, REMOVED FROM
　　CASING

1 LARGE (28-OUNCE) CAN TOMATOES, COARSELY CHOPPED

2 MEDIUM CARROTS, FINELY CHOPPED

1 MEDIUM ONION, CHOPPED

1 MEDIUM GREEN PEPPER, CHOPPED

¼ CUP BARLEY

❧ In a large kettle, combine beef, split peas, salt, garlic, and water. Bring to a boil. Reduce heat; simmer, covered, 1 hour. Remove beef shank. Cool meat, cut off bone, and dice. Return to kettle. Add sausage, forming into small balls, tomatoes, carrots, onion, and green pepper. Simmer, covered, 40 minutes. Add barley; simmer another 45 minutes or until barley is tender. Best if cooked the day before serving.

Minestrone Soup

Serves 4

½ CUP CHOPPED ONION

½ CUP CHOPPED CELERY

1 16-OUNCE CAN WHOLE TOMATOES, UNDRAINED

1 CUP SHREDDED GREEN CABBAGE

2 MEDIUM-SIZED CARROTS, SLICED (1 CUP)

¼ TEASPOON SALT

⅛ TEASPOON PEPPER

½ CUP ELBOW MACARONI (COOKED)

1 16-OUNCE CAN RED KIDNEY BEANS

1 CUP WATER

❧ Prepare all vegetables and precook in microwave until tender. In a large saucepan, put onion and celery. Add tomatoes on low heat. Add cabbage, carrots, salt, and pepper. Mix macaroni and kidney beans. Add water if needed. Cook on medium until heated. Soup will be thick. Ladle into soup cups and serve.

Cheesy Brat Stew

Serves 4–6

6 BRATWURST LINKS, CUT INTO $1/2$" PIECES

4 MEDIUM POTATOES, CUBED

1 15-OUNCE CAN GREEN BEANS, DRAINED

1 SMALL ONION, CHOPPED

1 CUP GRATED CHEDDAR OR AMERICAN CHEESE

1 CAN CREAM OF MUSHROOM SOUP

1 CUP WATER

❧ Mix all of the above ingredients in a large skillet. Cover and simmer over medium heat for 30 minutes or until potatoes are done.

Marilou's Vegetable Cheese Chowder

Serves 6–8

2 CUPS POTATOES, CUT INTO $1/4$" CUBES

1 CUP CHOPPED CELERY

1 CUP DICED ONION

2 CUPS WATER

5 TABLESPOONS BUTTER OR MARGARINE

6 TABLESPOONS FLOUR

1 TEASPOON DRY MUSTARD

2 CUPS MILK

1 LARGE (28-OUNCE) CAN DICED TOMATOES

3 TEASPOONS DRIED PARSLEY

SALT AND PEPPER TO TASTE

1 8-OUNCE PACKAGE OF CHEESE SLICES, CUT INTO STRIPS
   (DO NOT USE CHEDDAR; IT WILL CREATE A POOR
   CONSISTENCY)

❧ Boil potatoes, celery, and onion in water until soft. In a saucepan, melt the butter over low heat; add flour and mustard. Slowly stir the milk into the butter mixture and heat until thickened. Add to the potato mixture. Add remaining ingredients, adding the cheese last.

Cheese Potato Soup

Serves 6–8

3 TABLESPOONS BUTTER

1 CUP DICED CARROTS

1 CUP DICED ONION

1/2 CUP DICED CELERY

3 CUPS WATER

3 CHICKEN BOUILLON CUBES

4 CUPS CUBED POTATOES

2 CUPS MILK

3/4 CUP SHREDDED GRUYERE CHEESE

1 1/2 CUPS SHREDDED SHARP CHEDDAR CHEESE

SALT AND PEPPER TO TASTE

ᔰ Melt butter; add carrots, onion, and celery. Cook until tender. Add water, bouillon cubes, and potatoes; cook until potatoes are tender. Add milk and heat. Stir in cheese. Season with salt and pepper.

Hamburg Stew

Serves 4–5

1 POUND HAMBURG

1 TABLESPOON MARGARINE

1 1/2 CUPS DICED CARROTS

1/2 CUP DICED CELERY

1 CUP DICED POTATOES

1/2 CUP TOMATO JUICE WITH PULP*

1 MEDIUM ONION, CHOPPED

3 1/2 CUPS WATER

2 TEASPOONS SALT

1/8 TEASPOON PEPPER

1 BEEF BOUILLON CUBE

2 TABLESPOONS FLOUR

2 TABLESPOONS WATER

ᔰ Shape meat into walnut-sized balls and brown in margarine. Drain fat from meatballs and put in a saucepan. Add all other ingredients, except for flour, and simmer about 45 minutes. Thicken with 2 tablespoons flour and water mixed together well before adding to stew. Add dumplings if desired.

*Instead of tomato juice, you could put in a can of regular or stewed tomatoes.

Vegetarian Chili

Serves 8

3/4 cup chopped onion

2 cloves garlic, minced

3 tablespoons olive oil

2 tablespoons chili powder

1/4 teaspoon dried basil

1/4 teaspoon dried oregano

1/4 teaspoon cumin

2 cups finely chopped zucchini

1 cup finely chopped carrots

1 28-ounce can tomatoes

1 14.5-ounce can tomatoes, drained and chopped

1 15-ounce can kidney beans, undrained

2 15-ounce cans kidney beans, drained and
    thoroughly rinsed*

Chopped onions, tomatoes, lettuce, green peppers,
    and Parmesan cheese to garnish

In a large kettle, sauté onion and garlic in olive oil until soft. Mix in chili powder, basil, oregano, and cumin. Stir in zucchini and carrots until well blended and cook for 1 minute over low heat, stirring occasionally. Stir in tomatoes and the drained and undrained beans. Bring to a boil and then simmer for 30–40 minutes. Even better the next day!

You may also add broccoli and green pepper if desired.
* Instead of 3 cans of kidney beans, use 2 cans kidney beans and 1 can chickpeas.

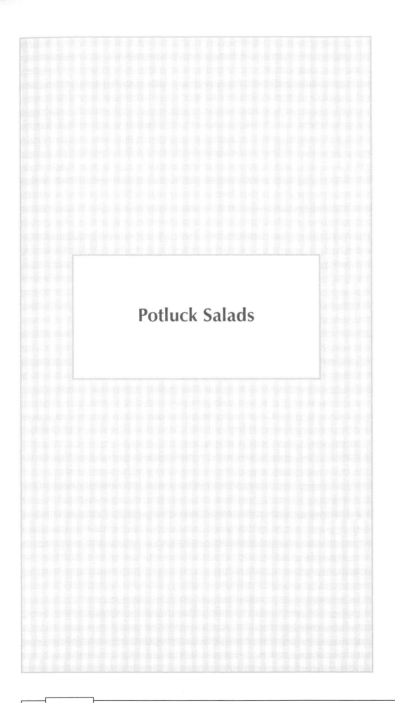

Potluck Salads

24-Hour Fruit Salad

Serves 6–8

2 CUPS CANNED PITTED WHITE CHERRIES, DRAINED

2 CUPS PINEAPPLE TIDBITS, DRAINED

2 CUPS MANDARIN ORANGES, DRAINED

16 LARGE MARSHMALLOWS, CUT INTO EIGHTHS

1 CUP HEAVY CREAM, WHIPPED

Dressing:

3 EGG YOLKS, BEATEN

2 TABLESPOONS SUGAR

2 TABLESPOONS VINEGAR

2 TABLESPOONS PINEAPPLE SYRUP

1 TABLESPOON BUTTER

DASH SALT

❧ Combine dressing ingredients in top of double boiler. Cook over hot (not boiling) water until thick, stirring constantly. Cool. Stir in fruits and marshmallows. Fold in whipped cream. Spoon gently into serving bowl. Chill 24 hours in refrigerator, so flavors can blend to fruity perfection.

Cranberry Orange Salad

Makes about 5 cups or 10 side salads
or 14 relish servings

2 3-OUNCE (OR 1 6-OUNCE) PACKAGES GELATIN, ANY FLAVOR
1/4 TEASPOON SALT
1 CUP BOILING WATER
1 CUP ORANGE JUICE
1/4 TEASPOON CINNAMON
DASH OF GROUND CLOVES
1 16-OUNCE CAN WHOLE BERRY OR JELLIED CRANBERRY SAUCE
1 CUP DICED ORANGE SECTIONS
1 CUP CHOPPED APPLE
1/2 CUP CHOPPED CELERY

❧ Dissolve gelatin and salt in boiling water. Add orange juice. Add spices and cranberry sauce. Chill until thickened. Fold in fruit and celery. Pour into 6-cup mold or bowl. Chill until firm, about 3 hours. Serve as salad or relish. You may sprinkle some chopped walnuts over the top, before salad is firm. You cannot do this if you plan to turn salad out from a mold.

Raisin Sunshine Salad

Serves about 6

2/3 CUP SEEDLESS RAISINS
1 3-OUNCE PACKAGE LEMON-FLAVORED GELATIN
1 1/4 CUPS HOT WATER
2 TABLESPOONS FRESH LEMON JUICE
1 CUP UNDRAINED CRUSHED PINEAPPLE
1/4 TEASPOON SALT
1 1/2 CUPS GRATED CARROT
SALAD GREENS

❧ Rinse raisins, cover with water, and boil 5 minutes. Cool and drain. Dissolve gelatin in hot water. Blend in lemon juice, pineapple, and salt. Cool until slightly thickened. Fold in raisins and carrot. Turn into individual molds or 8" square pan and chill until firm. Unmold or cut into rectangles, and serve on salad greens.

Fruit Salad

Serves 6

1 8-OUNCE CONTAINER OF WHIPPED TOPPING

1 3-OUNCE PACKAGE OF GELATIN, DRY

1 8-OUNCE CONTAINER OF COTTAGE CHEESE

8 OUNCES OF ANY CANNED FRUIT, DRAINED

❧ Mix well and chill.

Holiday Fruit Salad

Serves 6

1 16-OUNCE CAN FRUIT COCKTAIL, DRAINED

1 16-OUNCE CONTAINER WHIPPED TOPPING

1 4-OUNCE CAN MANDARIN ORANGES, DRAINED

1 10-OUNCE PACKAGE MINI MARSHMALLOWS

❧ Mix all ingredients together in medium-sized bowl. Top of salad may be garnished with cherries.

Pear Salad

Serves 4

1 LARGE (29-OUNCE) CAN PEARS, MASHED AND DRAINED, JUICE RESERVED

1 3-OUNCE PACKAGE LIME-FLAVORED GELATIN

1 8-OUNCE PACKAGE CREAM CHEESE

1/2 CUP DRY WHIPPED TOPPING MIX (USE 1 PACKAGE)

❧ Boil 1 cup pear juice (use all juice in can). Dissolve gelatin in it. Add mashed pears, cream cheese, and topping. Beat with eggbeater and chill to set.

Pretzel Salad

Serves 12–15

3/4 CUP MARGARINE

3 TABLESPOONS SUGAR

2 2/3 CUPS COARSELY CRUSHED PRETZELS (NOT THE
STICK PRETZELS)

1 8-OUNCE PACKAGE CREAM CHEESE

3/4 CUP SUGAR

1 8-OUNCE CONTAINER WHIPPED TOPPING

2 SMALL OR 1 LARGE PACKAGE STRAWBERRY GELATIN

2 CUPS BOILING WATER

1 16-OUNCE PACKAGE FROZEN SLICED STRAWBERRIES

❧ Cream margarine, 3 tablespoons sugar, and crushed pretzels. Press into a 9" × 13" pan. Bake in 350° oven for 10 minutes. Let cool. Mix cream cheese, 3/4 cup sugar, and whipped topping. Spread over pretzel mixture. Seal sides well. Combine gelatin and boiling water, dropping in frozen strawberries while water is hot. Allow gelatin to thicken a little and then fold over cheese mixture. Refrigerate overnight.

Lime Jellied Salad

Serves 4–6

1 3-OUNCE PACKAGE LIME GELATIN

1 2/3 CUPS BOILING WATER

1 8-OUNCE PACKAGE CREAM CHEESE

1 CUP ALL-PURPOSE CREAM

1 CUP CRUSHED PINEAPPLE, DRAINED

1/2 CUP EACH OF WALNUTS AND CHERRIES, OPTIONAL

❧ Mix gelatin with 1 2/3 cups boiling water. Allow to set. Blend with cream cheese and cream. Add pineapple, walnuts, and cherries.

All Souls Salad

Serves 10–12

1 3-ounce package lemon gelatin

1 package lime gelatin

2 cups hot water

1 cup mayonnaise

1 cup evaporated milk

1 pound cottage cheese

1 20-ounce can crushed pineapple with juice

1 cup broken nuts

❧ Mix gelatin and water and chill. Blend thoroughly mayonnaise, milk, and cottage cheese. Add to gelatin mixture with pineapple and nuts. Place in mold that has been rinsed in cold water. Chill.

Heavenly Salad

Serves 6

1 8-ounce can crushed pineapple

2 3-ounce packages lemon gelatin

2 cups hot water

1 cup cold water

1 3-ounce package cream cheese

2/3 cup vanilla ice cream

❧ Put pineapple in strainer to drain, reserving juice. Dissolve gelatin in hot water; add cold water. Chill in freezer until mixture begins to thicken. In the meantime, cream the cheese, gradually adding the juice from the pineapple. When gelatin mixture is slightly thickened, whip it with an electric beater until fluffy. Beat in cream cheese mixture, ice cream, and crushed pineapple. Pour into mold and chill until firm, approximately 2 hours.

Strawberry Salad

Serves 10–12

2 3-ounce packages strawberry gelatin
1½ cups boiling water
1 16-ounce package frozen strawberries, slightly thawed
1 13.25-ounce can crushed pineapple, undrained
2 mashed bananas
2 cups sour cream or whipped topping

❧ Combine gelatin and boiling water. When completely dissolved, add strawberries and stir. Add pineapple and mashed bananas. Pour ½ the mixture into a 6½-cup mold. Chill until partly set and then spread sour cream over it. Add remaining gelatin mixture. Chill until set. If desired, 1 cup of chopped nuts may also be added to the gelatin with fruit.

Strawberry Shimmer

Serves 4–6

1 3-ounce package strawberry gelatin
1 cup boiling water
1 10-ounce package frozen strawberries, partially thawed
1 8-ounce container of strawberry yogurt

❧ In a large bowl, dissolve gelatin in boiling water. Stir in strawberries until thawed and gelatin is partially set. Stir in yogurt until creamy and well blended. Pour carefully into gelatin mold. This recipe is easy to double or triple. Other flavors may be substituted.

~

Cranberry Salad

Serves 4–6

1 3-ounce package lemon gelatin
1 cup boiling water
1 can whole cranberry sauce
1 cup crushed pineapple, drained
Chopped walnuts

❧ Dissolve gelatin in boiling water. Add cranberry sauce; mix into gelatin. Add crushed pineapple and walnuts. Pour into mold and refrigerate.

Cranberry Chutney

6–8 cups

16 OUNCES FRESH OR FROZEN CRANBERRIES
2 CUPS SUGAR
1 CUP ORANGE JUICE
1 CUP RAISINS
1 CUP CHOPPED WALNUTS
1 CUP CHOPPED CELERY
1 MEDIUM CORTLAND APPLE, CHOPPED
1 TABLESPOON GRATED ORANGE PEEL (OPTIONAL)
1 TEASPOON GROUND GINGER OR GINGER MARMALADE

Heat berries, sugar, and orange juice to boiling. Simmer 15 minutes. Stir frequently. Stir in remaining ingredients. Cover and refrigerate. Keeps very well and easy to make. Nice complement to most meats. Use as a relish.

Lime Sour Cream Gelatin

Serves 8–10

1 LARGE PACKAGE LIME GELATIN
1 CUP BOILING WATER
2 CUPS COLD WATER
1 SMALL (8-OUNCE) CAN CRUSHED PINEAPPLE
1/2 CUP CHOPPED NUTS
1 CUP SOUR CREAM
1 CUP FINELY CHOPPED CELERY
1/2 CUP CHOPPED MARASCHINO CHERRIES

Dissolve gelatin in boiling water. Add cold water. Add remaining ingredients. Mix well. Pour into a mold and chill until set.

Mohave Fruit Salad

Serves 6–8

2 CUPS CHOPPED APPLES
6 OUNCES SHARP CHEDDAR CHEESE, CUBED
1/2 TEASPOON GRATED ORANGE RIND
1 CUP FRESH ORANGE SECTIONS
1/2 CUP CHOPPED WALNUTS
1/2 CUP SALAD DRESSING OR MAYONNAISE
1 TEASPOON LEMON JUICE

Mix all ingredients lightly in a medium bowl. Chill. Raisins might be nice added also!

Apricot-Pineapple Salad

Serves 6–8

1 3-OUNCE PACKAGE LEMON GELATIN
1 CUP HOT WATER
1 CUP MAYONNAISE
1 CUP CREAM, WHIPPED
1 20-OUNCE CAN APRICOTS, DRAINED AND CHOPPED
1 SMALL (8-OUNCE) CAN CRUSHED PINEAPPLE, DRAINED
1/2 CUP CHOPPED PECANS

Mix gelatin into hot water. Let set until it starts to thicken but is still rather soft. Beat gelatin until fluffy. Add 1 cup mayonnaise and 1 cup whipped cream. Blend well. Add chopped apricots along with the crushed pineapple and pecans.

Tangy Fruit Salad

Serves 10–12 as a side dish

1 CUP PINEAPPLE JUICE
1/3 CUP DRY ORANGE-FLAVORED DRINK MIX
1 SMALL PACKAGE VANILLA INSTANT PUDDING
1 15-OUNCE CAN MANDARIN ORANGES, DRAINED
1 15-OUNCE CAN FRUIT COCKTAIL, DRAINED
1 20-OUNCE CAN PINEAPPLE CHUNKS, DRAINED
2–3 APPLES, SLICED
2–3 BANANAS, SLICED

Mix pineapple juice, orange-flavored drink mix, and pudding mix together. Add fruit, except for bananas, and stir well. Add bananas just before serving.

Apple and Cranberry Salad

Serves 8–10

1 3-OUNCE PACKAGE STRAWBERRY GELATIN
1 CUP HOT WATER
2 RED APPLES, CORED BUT NOT PEELED
1 POUND CRANBERRIES
3/4–1 CUP SUGAR

Dissolve strawberry gelatin in 1 cup of hot water. Chop apples and cranberries finely in a food processor. Add the apples and cranberries together with the sugar to the gelatin. Refrigerate until set.

Cream Cheese and Gelatin Salad

Serves 6

1 PACKAGE CHERRY GELATIN

1 CUP HOT WATER

1 8-OUNCE PACKAGE CREAM CHEESE

1 8-OUNCE CAN CRUSHED PINEAPPLE, UNDRAINED

1 CUP NUTS

❧ Dissolve gelatin in hot water. Add cream cheese and beat until foamy. Add pineapple and nuts. Refrigerate.

Apple Crunch Salad

Serves 10–12

2 CUPS WATER

1/2 CUP CINNAMON CANDIES

2 3-OUNCE PACKAGES CHERRY GELATIN

3 CUPS APPLESAUCE

1 8-OUNCE PACKAGE CREAM CHEESE

1/2 CUP CELERY, CHOPPED

1/2 CUP CHOPPED PECANS

1/2 CUP SALAD DRESSING

❧ Boil water; stir in candy and gelatin until dissolved. Add applesauce. Pour into mold or cake pan. Chill until set. Mix other ingredients. Spread over gelatin mixture in cake pan or you may "frost" the set gelatin when you unmold the salad.

Tangy Shrimp Mold

Serves 6

1 3-OUNCE PACKAGE LEMON GELATIN

1 CUP BOILING WATER

1 CAN TOMATO SOUP

1 CUP MAYONNAISE

1 8-OUNCE PACKAGE CREAM CHEESE

1 TABLESPOON HORSERADISH

1 CUP MINCED CELERY

1 TABLESPOON GRATED ONION

2 TABLESPOONS MINCED GREEN PEPPER

2 CUPS SHRIMP

❧ Dissolve gelatin in boiling water; add soup and other soft ingredients. Chill. When partially thickened, add celery, onion, green pepper, and shrimp. Chill in a 6 1/2-cup mold until set.

Chicken Soufflé Salad

Serves 6

1 3-OUNCE PACKAGE LEMON GELATIN
1 CUP HOT WATER
1/2 CUP COLD WATER
1/2 CUP MAYONNAISE
2 TABLESPOONS LEMON JUICE
1/4 TEASPOON SALT
DASH OF PEPPER
1 1/2 CUPS DICED COOKED CHICKEN
1/2 CUP DICED CELERY
1/3 CUP TOASTED SLIVERED ALMONDS
1/4 CUP DICED PIMIENTO
1/4 CUP DICED GREEN PEPPER
1 TEASPOON GRATED ONION

Dissolve gelatin in hot water; add cold water. Add mayonnaise, lemon juice, salt, and pepper. Pour into tray and chill in freezer 15–20 minutes or until fairly thick. Turn into bowl and beat until fluffy. Fold in remaining ingredients. Chill until firm in an 8 1/2" × 4 1/4" × 2 1/2" loaf pan.

Hot Chicken Salad I

Serves 8–10

3 CUPS DICED COOKED CHICKEN
2 CUPS THINLY SLICED CELERY
1/2 CUP SLIVERED SALTED ALMONDS
1/4 CUP PIMIENTO
1 1/4 CUPS MAYONNAISE
3 TABLESPOONS LEMON JUICE
2 TABLESPOONS GRATED ONION
1 TEASPOON SALT
1/4 TEASPOON PEPPER
1 CUP BREADCRUMBS
2 TABLESPOONS MARGARINE, MELTED

Place first 4 ingredients in a large bowl. Blend mayonnaise, lemon juice, onion, salt, and pepper; add to chicken and toss gently with a fork. Place in a shallow oiled casserole. Toss breadcrumbs with melted margarine and sprinkle over salad. Bake in 375° oven approximately 30 minutes, until heated and browned.

Hot Chicken Salad II

Serves 12

4 CUPS CUBED COLD COOKED CHICKEN
2 CUPS CHOPPED CELERY
1–2 HARD-BOILED EGGS, SLICED
1 CAN WATER CHESTNUTS, SLICED
1 CUP MAYONNAISE
1 TEASPOON SALT
1 CAN CREAM OF CHICKEN SOUP
1 TABLESPOON ONION, MINCED
1 CUP GRATED CHEESE
CROUTONS

❧ Combine all ingredients except cheese and croutons. Pack into a 9" × 13" × 2" pan. Cover with cheese and croutons. Refrigerate overnight. Bake at 375° for 25–30 minutes.

Broccoli Salad

Serves 6

1 HEAD OF BROCCOLI, BROKEN INTO SMALL FLORETS
1 8-OUNCE CAN SLICED WATER CHESTNUTS
1 4-OUNCE CAN MUSHROOMS
1 2.5-OUNCE CAN BLACK OLIVES

❧ Place all above ingredients in a tightly "zipped" plastic bag. Add an 8-ounce bottle of Italian dressing. Close bag tightly and refrigerate 6 hours before serving.

Broccoli-Cranberry Salad

Serves 8–10

1$\frac{1}{4}$ CUPS COARSELY CHOPPED CRANBERRIES
$\frac{1}{3}$ CUP SUGAR
1 BUNCH BROCCOLI, 1$\frac{1}{4}$–1$\frac{1}{2}$ POUNDS
$\frac{1}{2}$ CUP CHOPPED CELERY
$\frac{1}{2}$ CUP CHOPPED ONION
$\frac{1}{2}$ CUP RAISINS
$\frac{1}{2}$ CUP CHOPPED NUTS
1 CUP MAYONNAISE
$\frac{1}{2}$ CUP SUGAR
$\frac{1}{4}$ CUP VINEGAR

❧ Coat cranberries with $\frac{1}{3}$ cup sugar. Use tops only of broccoli, and cut into florets. Mix cranberries, broccoli, celery, onion, raisins, and nuts. Blend mayonnaise, sugar, and vinegar. Toss this dressing with salad and chill 1$\frac{1}{2}$ hours before serving.

Mexican Chef Salad

Serves 6

1 POUND LEAN GROUND BEEF
1 CAN KIDNEY BEANS, DRAINED
1/4 TEASPOON SALT
1 LARGE ONION
4 TOMATOES
1/4 HEAD OF LETTUCE
4 OUNCES CHEDDAR CHEESE, GRATED
8 OUNCES TORTILLA CHIPS, PLAIN OR TACO, CRUMBLED
1 LARGE AVOCADO
8 OUNCES FRENCH OR THOUSAND ISLAND DRESSING

❧ Brown ground beef; add kidney beans and salt. Simmer 10 minutes. Keep warm. Chop onion, tomatoes, and lettuce. Add Cheddar cheese. Add meat, beans, and chips. Slice and add a large avocado and French or Thousand Island dressing and toss.

Copper Pennies

Makes 15 side-dish servings

2 POUNDS CARROTS, CUT IN CIRCLES
1/2 CUP SALAD OIL
3/4 CUP VINEGAR
1 CUP SUGAR
1 CAN TOMATO SOUP
1 TEASPOON DRY MUSTARD
1 TEASPOON WORCESTERSHIRE SAUCE
1 SMALL GREEN PEPPER, CHOPPED
1 SMALL ONION, CHOPPED
1 7-OUNCE CAN MUSHROOM PIECES
1/2 CUP CELERY, CHOPPED

❧ Cook carrots until just tender. Mix salad oil, vinegar, sugar, tomato soup, dry mustard, and Worcestershire sauce and simmer 5 minutes. Pour dressing on vegetables. Let marinate for 12 hours. To serve, remove carrots with slotted spoon. Keeps well. Can be made ahead.

Pea and Bean Salad

Makes 12–15 side-dish servings

2 CANS RED KIDNEY BEANS
2 10-OUNCE PACKAGES FROZEN PEAS
1 LARGE ONION, FINELY CHOPPED
1 CUP FINELY CHOPPED CELERY
MAYONNAISE
SALT AND PEPPER

❧ Drain kidney beans. Rinse frozen peas under hot tap water. Mix together kidney beans, peas, onion, and celery. Mix in mayonnaise to coat and salt and pepper to taste. Best made in morning for evening serving.

Sweet and Sour Beet Salad

Serves 8

2 3-OUNCE PACKAGES LEMON-FLAVORED GELATIN
3 CUPS BOILING WATER
1/2 CUP BEET LIQUID
2 TABLESPOONS LEMON JUICE
2 TABLESPOONS VINEGAR
1 TABLESPOON HORSERADISH
1 1/2 TEASPOONS ONION SALT
2 CUPS SLICED BEETS
1/2 CUP DICED CELERY
COTTAGE CHEESE

❧ Dissolve gelatin in 3 cups boiling water. Add beet liquid, lemon juice, vinegar, horseradish, and onion salt. Chill until slightly thickened. Fold in beets and celery. Chill in 5-cup mold. Unmold and garnish with cottage cheese.

Cottage Cheese Salad

Serves 8–10

2 POUNDS COTTAGE CHEESE
1 LARGE PACKAGE WILD STRAWBERRY GELATIN
1 SMALL (8-OUNCE) CAN CRUSHED PINEAPPLE, JUICE AND ALL
1 11-OUNCE CAN MANDARIN ORANGES, DRAINED
1 9.5-OUNCE CONTAINER WHIPPED TOPPING

❧ Mix cheese and dry gelatin. Add fruit. Fold in whipped topping and chill.

Kraut Salad

Makes 8–10 side-dish servings

1 27-OUNCE CAN SAUERKRAUT
1 LARGE SWEET ONION
1 GREEN PEPPER
1 CUP CELERY
1 CUP SUGAR
1/2 CUP SALAD OIL
1/2 CUP WHITE VINEGAR

⊷ Drain and wash kraut with cold water. Chop onion, pepper, and celery. Mix kraut and chopped vegetables with sugar, oil, and vinegar. Keep covered in refrigerator.

~

Three-Bean Salad

Makes 8–10 side-dish servings

1 15-OUNCE CAN CUT GREEN BEANS, DRAINED

1 15-OUNCE CAN CUT YELLOW BEANS, DRAINED

1 15-OUNCE CAN KIDNEY BEANS, DRAINED

1 ONION, SLICED

1 GREEN PEPPER, SLICED

3/4 CUP SUGAR

2/3 CUP VINEGAR

1/3 CUP SALAD OIL

1 TEASPOON SALT

1 TEASPOON BLACK PEPPER

DASH GARLIC POWDER

⊷ Combine all ingredients. Best if made the day before serving and refrigerated. Recipe may be doubled.

Superb Potato Salad

Serves 8–10

1 ENVELOPE UNFLAVORED GELATIN

1/4 CUP COLD WATER

1 CUP BOILING WATER

1/4 CUP LEMON JUICE

2 TABLESPOONS SUGAR

1 TEASPOON SALT

1/2 CUP WHIPPING CREAM, WHIPPED

1 CUP MAYONNAISE

2 HARD-BOILED EGGS, CHOPPED

4 CUPS DICED COOKED POTATOES

1 CUP DICED CELERY

1/4 CUP DICED GREEN PEPPER

1/4 CUP DICED PIMIENTO

1/4 CUP CHOPPED ONION

1/4 CUP CHOPPED FRESH PARSLEY

1 1/2 TEASPOONS SALT

8 STUFFED GREEN OLIVES, SLICED

⊷ Soften gelatin in cold water. Add boiling water and stir until dissolved. Add lemon juice, sugar, and salt. Chill until mixture is partially set. Fold whipped cream into mayonnaise. Combine remaining ingredients; add whipped cream mixture. Fold potato mixture into partially set gelatin. Pour into oiled 6 1/2-cup mold. Chill until firm.

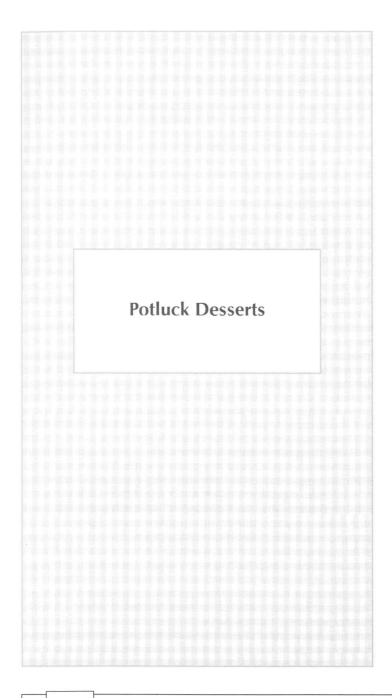

Potluck Desserts

Strawberry Angel Dessert

Serves 12–15

1 6-OUNCE PACKAGE STRAWBERRY GELATIN
2½ CUPS BOILING WATER
1 POUND FROZEN SLICED STRAWBERRIES, THAWED
2 TABLESPOONS SUGAR
2 CUPS WHIPPED TOPPING
10" ANGEL CAKE, TORN IN PIECES

❧ Dissolve gelatin in boiling water. Stir in strawberries and sugar. Chill. Fold in whipped topping. Cover bottom of pan with cake pieces. Pour strawberry and whipped topping mix over cake pieces. Refrigerate 4–5 hours. Cover with glaze and refrigerate until ready to use.

Glaze:

1 3-OUNCE PACKAGE OF STRAWBERRY GELATIN
1¾ CUPS HOT WATER

❧ Dissolve gelatin in water and chill. Use when slightly thick by pouring over cake mixture.

Coconut-Pineapple Cake

Serves 12

1 PACKAGE YELLOW CAKE MIX

1 20-OUNCE CAN CRUSHED PINEAPPLE

1 CUP SUGAR

1 LARGE PACKAGE VANILLA PUDDING MIX, NOT INSTANT

1 CUP WHIPPING CREAM, WHIPPED

1 CUP CHOPPED PECANS

FLAKED COCONUT

ᏚᎧ Make yellow cake mix according to directions on package. Bake in 9" × 13" pan. Cook undrained pineapple and sugar until sugar is well dissolved. Cook vanilla pudding mix as directed on package. After baking cake, poke holes with handle of wooden spoon into cake. Pour pineapple mixture over top, then pudding. Put whipped cream on top. Sprinkle nuts and coconut. Refrigerate overnight. Even better two days later.

Velvet Lunch Cupcakes

Makes 10–12 cupcakes

1 CUP SUGAR

1/2 CUP SHORTENING

1 EGG, NOT BEATEN

3 TABLESPOONS MOLASSES

1 CUP SOUR MILK*

1 CUP SEEDLESS RAISINS

2 CUPS FLOUR

1 TEASPOON BAKING SODA

1 TEASPOON SALT

1 TEASPOON CINNAMON

3/4 TEASPOON NUTMEG

1/2 TEASPOON GROUND CLOVES

ᏚᎧ Cream sugar and shortening. Add egg, molasses, sour milk, and raisins. Sift together flour, soda, salt, and spices. Add to first mixture. Bake in cupcake pans for 20 minutes at 350°.

*To make sweet milk sour, mix 2 tablespoons vinegar into sweet milk.

Pumpkin Pie Dessert

Serves 15

1 PACKAGE YELLOW CAKE MIX (RESERVE 1 CUP)

1/2 CUP BUTTER OR MARGARINE, MELTED

1 EGG

3 CUPS (1 POUND, 14 OUNCES) PUMPKIN PIE FILLING MIX OR

1 POUND SOLID PUMPKIN MIXED WITH 1/2 CUP BROWN SUGAR FIRMLY PACKED AND 2 1/2 TEASPOONS PUMPKIN PIE SPICE

1/4 CUP SUGAR

1/4 CUP BUTTER OR MARGARINE

Mix together cake mix, melted butter or margarine, and egg. Press into a 13" × 9" pan. (Grease bottom of pan only.) Spread pumpkin pie mix over bottom layer. Mix reserved cake mix with sugar and cut in unmelted butter or margarine. Sprinkle topping over pumpkin. Bake at 350° for 45–50 minutes, or until knife comes out clean when tested. Serve with whipped topping or ice cream.

Blueberry Cake

Serves 9

2 EGGS, SEPARATED

1 CUP SUGAR

1/2 CUP SHORTENING OR 1 STICK MARGARINE

1/2 TEASPOON SALT

1 1/2 CUPS SIFTED ALL-PURPOSE FLOUR

1 TEASPOON BAKING POWDER

1/3 CUP MILK

1 1/2 CUPS FLOURED BLUEBERRIES

Beat egg whites and add 1/2 cup sugar to keep stiff. Set aside. Cream shortening; add salt and remaining sugar. Add unbeaten egg yolks. Beat until creamy. Sift flour. Measure and sift together with baking powder. Add to creamed mixture alternately with milk. Fold in floured blueberries. Fold in beaten egg whites and sugar mixture. Turn into a well-greased 8" × 8" pan. Sprinkle top with sugar. Bake at 350° for 50 minutes.

Pineapple Cake

Serves 12–16

2 CUPS FLOUR

2 CUPS WHITE SUGAR

2 TEASPOONS BAKING SODA

1 LARGE CAN CRUSHED PINEAPPLE, WITH JUICE

2 EGGS

1 TEASPOON VANILLA

1 CUP NUTS

❧ Combine flour, sugar, and baking soda. Mix pineapple with beaten eggs and vanilla. Gradually add flour mixture and 1 cup nuts. Bake in a greased and floured 13" × 9" pan at 350° for 35 minutes.

Crème de Menthe Cake

Serves 20

1 PACKAGE WHITE CAKE MIX

1/2 CUP CRÈME DE MENTHE

1 16-OUNCE CAN FUDGE TOPPING

1 9-OUNCE CONTAINER WHIPPED TOPPING

❧ Prepare cake mix according to package directions. Stir in 1/4 cup crème de menthe. Spread in 9" × 13" pan. Bake at 350° for 30 minutes or until cake tests done. Cool thoroughly. Spread with fudge topping. Combine whipped topping and 1/4 cup crème de menthe. Mix well and spread over fudge topping. Chill until serving time. This makes a colorful holiday dessert.

Crème Brûlée

Serves 6

1 QUART HEAVY CREAM
2 TABLESPOONS SUGAR
8 EGG YOLKS, BEATEN WELL
1 TEASPOON VANILLA EXTRACT
3/4–1 CUP LIGHT BROWN SUGAR

1. Preheat oven to 350°.

2. In the top of a double boiler, combine cream and sugar. Cook and stir until sugar has dissolved and the mixture is hot. Pour over the beaten egg yolks. Add vanilla and blend thoroughly.

3. Pour the mixture into 6 individual custard dishes or into 1 9" × 2" round baking dish. Set the cups, or the dish, into a larger pan and surround with hot water to the depth of about 1". Bake for 1 hour.

4. Let stand to cool and refrigerate covered with plastic wrap, overnight.

5. Remove from refrigerator and cover the top with 1/4" of finely sifted light brown sugar. Place the custard(s) under the broiler approximately 4"–6" from flame. Leaving the oven door open, watch carefully until the sugar has melted.

6. Remove the custard, cover with plastic wrap, and return to the refrigerator to chill. The sugar will harden into a glaze. If moisture collects under the wrap when chilled, take a paper towel and gently blot the moisture.

Gram's Gingerbread

Serves 12–16

1/2 CUP SUGAR
1/2 CUP SHORTENING, MELTED
1 EGG, BEATEN
1 CUP MOLASSES
1 CUP HOT COFFEE
2 1/2 CUPS FLOUR
1 1/2 TEASPOONS BAKING SODA
1 TEASPOON CREAM OF TARTAR
1/2 TEASPOON SALT
1 TEASPOON GINGER
CINNAMON SUGAR

Cream together sugar and shortening. Stir together with egg, molasses, and hot coffee. Add flour, soda, cream of tartar, salt, and ginger. Mix well and pour into a 9" × 13" pan and sprinkle top with cinnamon sugar. Bake at 350° for 35 minutes.

Lightning Cake

Serves 8

1 2/3 CUPS FLOUR

1 CUP SUGAR

2 TEASPOONS BAKING POWDER

1/4 TEASPOON SALT

1 EGG

MILK

1 TEASPOON VANILLA

3 TABLESPOONS MELTED SHORTENING OR VEGETABLE OIL

ஃ Sift flour, sugar, baking powder, and salt into bowl. Break egg in a cup. Fill cup to top with milk. Mix with dry ingredients. Add vanilla and melted shortening. Mix well. Bake at 350° for 30 minutes in a 7" × 9" pan. Blueberries or other fruit may be added to the dry mix if desired before adding milk, egg, and shortening. Blueberries won't settle to bottom if coated with dry mix. Flavor with lemon and frost with chocolate frosting. Exceptionally good.

One-Pan Chocolate Cake

Serves 10–12

1 1/2 CUPS FLOUR

1 CUP SUGAR

1 TEASPOON BAKING SODA

3 TABLESPOONS COCOA

6 TABLESPOONS CANOLA OIL

1 TABLESPOON VINEGAR

1 CUP WATER

ஃ In a 9" × 13" pan, put flour, sugar, soda, cocoa, oil, and vinegar. Pour water over all and stir with a fork until smooth. Bake at 350° oven for 30 minutes or until toothpick comes out clean.

Applesauce Cake

Serves 8

1 CUP SUGAR

1/4 CUP BUTTER OR MARGARINE

1 2/3 CUPS SWEETENED APPLESAUCE

2 CUPS FLOUR

1 HEAPING TEASPOON BAKING SODA

1 TEASPOON CINNAMON

1/2 TEASPOON GINGER

1/2 TEASPOON NUTMEG

1 CUP RAISINS

❧ Cream together sugar with butter or margarine. Add applesauce. Sift together flour, soda, cinnamon, ginger, and nutmeg. Add to creamed mixture. Add raisins and mix them well with dry ingredients so all raisins are covered with flour mix. (This prevents raisins from going to the bottom.) Mix all together. Bake in 2 loaf pans at 350° for 45 minutes. This recipe has no salt and no eggs.

Hot Milk Sponge Cake

Serves 8

2 EGGS	1 TEASPOON BAKING POWDER
1 CUP SUGAR	DASH SALT
1 TEASPOON VANILLA	1/2 CUP MILK
1 CUP SIFTED FLOUR	1 TABLESPOON BUTTER

❧ Beat eggs until foamy. Add sugar and vanilla gradually and beat until thick and light, for 5 minutes. Sift together flour, baking powder, and salt. Add all at once and mix well. Heat milk and butter just until bubbles start to form at the edge. Butter may not be melted. Add to flour mixture and stir in quickly. Pour into an 8" square greased and floured pan and quickly put pan in a 350° oven. Bake until top springs back when lightly touched, about 25–30 minutes. Frost with topping (recipe follows).

Topping:

5 TABLESPOONS CREAM

3 TABLESPOONS BUTTER

1/2 CUP BROWN SUGAR

1/2 CUP COCONUT

1/4 CUP CHOPPED NUTS

❧ Mix ingredients together and heat to boiling in small saucepan. Spread over hot cake and place under broiler just until it bubbles. Watch closely as it burns quickly.

Basic Bars

Makes 20–24 bars

1 18-OUNCE PACKAGE YELLOW CAKE MIX

1/2 CUP BROWN SUGAR

1/2 CUP COOKING OIL

2 TABLESPOONS WATER

2 EGGS, BEATEN

1 CUP (IN ALL) OF YOUR CHOICE: NUTS, CHOCOLATE BITS,
    COCONUT, RAISINS, DATES

🍃 Mix cake mix with sugar, oil, water, and eggs. Add any or a combination of your choice of nuts, coconut, etc. (Chocolate bits and nuts are a nice choice.) Spread into greased 9" × 13" pan. Bake at 350° for 20 minutes. Cool and cut into squares.

Top-of-the-Stove Chocolate/ Oatmeal Cookies

2–3 dozen cookies

1 STICK BUTTER OR MARGARINE

2 CUPS SUGAR

1/2 CUP MILK

2 1/2 SQUARES UNSWEETENED CHOCOLATE

3 CUPS QUICK OATMEAL*

1 TEASPOON VANILLA

🍃 Bring first 4 ingredients to a boil over medium heat, stirring to mix sugar in thoroughly and help with melting of chocolate. Boil hard for 1 minute. Remove from heat. Add oatmeal and mix thoroughly. Drop by teaspoon onto waxed paper and cool. May be trimmed with candy if desired.

*You may instead use 2 1/2 cups quick oats and 1/2 cup shredded coconut.

Raisin Bars

Makes 2 dozen bars

1 CUP SEEDLESS RAISINS

1 CUP WATER

1/2 CUP OIL OR BUTTER OR MARGARINE

1 EGG, SLIGHTLY BEATEN

1 CUP SUGAR

1 3/4 CUPS SIFTED FLOUR

1/4 TEASPOON SALT

1 TEASPOON BAKING SODA

1 TEASPOON CINNAMON

1 TEASPOON NUTMEG

1 TEASPOON ALLSPICE

1/2 TEASPOON GROUND CLOVES

1/2 CUP WALNUTS

🍴 Combine raisins and water in large saucepan. Bring to boil. Remove from heat and stir in oil or butter. Cool to lukewarm. Stir in egg and sugar. Sift together dry ingredients. Beat into raisin mixture. Stir in nuts. Pour into greased 9" × 13" × 2" pan. Bake at 375° for 20 minutes or until done. When cool, cut into bars. If desired, dust with confectioners' sugar before serving.

Cherry Coconut Squares

Makes 20–24 bars

2 CUPS FLOUR

1 CUP BUTTER

6 TABLESPOONS CONFECTIONERS' SUGAR

1 TEASPOON SALT

🍴 Mix all 4 ingredients well. Press into a 9" × 13" pan. Bake for 25 minutes at 350°. (Filling recipe follows.)

Filling:

2 CUPS SUGAR

1/2 CUP FLOUR

1 TEASPOON BAKING POWDER

1/2 TEASPOON SALT

1 TEASPOON VANILLA

1 CUP COCONUT

1 CUP CHOPPED WALNUTS

1 CUP MARASCHINO CHERRIES, CHOPPED

4 EGGS, BEATEN LIGHTLY

🍴 Mix all ingredients together, except the eggs. Add the eggs; mix well. Pour over crust and bake for 25 more minutes at 350°.

Apple Squares

Serves 16

6 TABLESPOONS BUTTER
2 EGGS
1 CUP WHITE SUGAR
1 TEASPOON BAKING SODA
1/2 TEASPOON SALT
1 TEASPOON VANILLA
1/4 TEASPOON CINNAMON
1 CUP FLOUR
2 CUPS APPLES, CHOPPED
1/2 CUP WALNUTS, CHOPPED

Combine butter, eggs, and sugar. Beat until well mixed. Add baking soda, salt, vanilla, cinnamon, and flour. Mix well. Add apples and walnuts. Use a 9" × 9" pan. Bake at 350° for 40–50 minutes. Sprinkle with confectioners' sugar when taking them out of the oven.

Apple Brownies

Serves 8

1 STICK MARGARINE
1 CUP SUGAR
1 EGG, LIGHTLY BEATEN
2 MEDIUM APPLES, PARED, CORED, AND CHOPPED FINE
1/2 CUP CHOPPED NUTS
1 CUP SIFTED FLOUR
1/2 TEASPOON BAKING POWDER
1/2 TEASPOON BAKING SODA
1/4 TEASPOON SALT
1/2 TEASPOON CINNAMON
1 CUP CHOCOLATE BITS

Cream margarine with sugar. Add egg. Mix in apples and nuts. Blend dry ingredients and stir lightly into apple mixture. Add chocolate bits. Pour into a well-greased pan, 7" × 11". Bake at 350° oven about 40 minutes. Place on rack to cool. Cut into squares.

Apple Crisp

Very good!

Serves 8

6–8 APPLES PEELED, CORED, AND SLICED

4 TEASPOONS LEMON JUICE

$^1/_4$ CUP WHITE SUGAR

$^1/_2$ TEASPOON CINNAMON

$^1/_2$ TEASPOON GROUND NUTMEG

$^1/_3$ CUP FLOUR

1 CUP UNCOOKED "OLD FASHIONED OATS" (NOT INSTANT)

$^1/_2$ TEASPOON SALT

$^1/_2$ CUP BROWN SUGAR, PACKED

$^1/_4$ POUND BUTTER, MELTED

🍴 Fill pan with apples about 2" deep. Pour lemon juice over apples. Mix sugar, cinnamon, and nutmeg. Stir into apples. In a bowl, combine flour, oats, salt, brown sugar, and butter. Spread over apples. Bake for 30 minutes at 350°.

Apple Cobbler

Serves 6

$^3/_4$ CUP SUGAR

1 TABLESPOON CORNSTARCH

$^1/_8$ TEASPOON SALT

$^1/_2$ TEASPOON CINNAMON

$^3/_4$ CUP WATER

$1^1/_2$ TEASPOONS LEMON JUICE

2 TABLESPOONS BUTTER OR MARGARINE

$4^1/_2$ CUPS SLICED, PEELED APPLES

SWEET BISCUIT DOUGH (RECIPE FOLLOWS)

🍴 In a large pan, combine the first 5 ingredients. Bring to a boil, stirring constantly, and add the lemon juice, butter, and apples. Cook for 2 minutes and place in a shallow 2-quart baking dish. Top with Sweet Biscuit Dough and bake at 400° for 25 minutes or until golden brown. Serve hot.

Sweet Biscuit Dough:

$1^1/_4$ CUPS FLOUR	$^1/_4$ CUP BUTTER OR
$1^1/_2$ TEASPOONS BAKING POWDER	MARGARINE
$1^1/_2$ TABLESPOONS SUGAR	$^1/_4$ CUP MILK
$^1/_4$ TEASPOON SALT	1 EGG, SLIGHTLY BEATEN

🍴 Mix dry ingredients. Cut in butter to resemble coarse crumbs. Combine milk and egg. Add to above mixture, stirring with a fork until dough forms a ball. Knead 7 times on a floured board. Roll out to $^1/_4$" thickness, cut out with a 2" cutter, and place on cobbler. This recipe doubles or triples very well.

Blueberry Buckle

Serves 9

Batter:

2 CUPS SIFTED FLOUR

3 TEASPOONS BAKING POWDER

$1/2$ TEASPOON SALT

$1/2$ CUP SOFT BUTTER

$1/2$ CUP SUGAR

2 EGGS

$3/4$ CUP MILK

2 CUPS BLUEBERRIES, WASHED AND DRAINED

Topping:

$1/3$ CUP FLOUR

$1/4$ CUP BUTTER

$3/4$ CUP BROWN SUGAR

2 TEASPOONS CINNAMON

Preheat oven to 375°. Grease 9" × 9" × 2" baking pan. Sift flour, baking powder, and salt together. In a large bowl combine butter, sugar, and eggs; beat at high speed with electric mixer until fluffy. At low speed, add dry ingredients alternately with milk. Fold in blueberries. Pour into prepared pan and sprinkle with combined topping ingredients. Bake 35 minutes or until done.

Chocolate Crème de Menthe Dessert

Serves 16–20

24 CHOCOLATE SANDWICH COOKIES, CRUSHED (2 CUPS)

$1/4$ CUP BUTTER, MELTED

1 PINT HEAVY CREAM

1 7.5-OUNCE JAR MARSHMALLOW CRÈME

$1/4$ CUP CRÈME DE MENTHE (GREEN)

Mix cookies with melted butter. Spread $1/2$ in 9" × 13" pan. (Keep $1/2$ for topping.) Whip cream; add marshmallow and crème de menthe. Pour mixture over cookie crumbs and cover with remaining crumbs. Put in freezer. Serve slightly thawed.

Jessie's Secret Recipe

Serves 4

1 PACKAGE MINIATURE MARSHMALLOWS

4 TABLESPOONS PORT WINE

$1/2$ PINT CREAM, WHIPPED

NUTS

DESSERT TOPPING AND MARASCHINO CHERRIES

Mix marshmallows and port wine. Marinate, stirring several times, overnight. (If mixture forms solid ball, break up with spoon.) Before serving, mix in whipped cream. Top with chopped nuts or dessert topping and cherries.

Fruit Compote

Serves 10–12

1 LARGE (29-OUNCE) CAN PEAR HALVES WITH JUICE
1 LARGE CAN PEACH HALVES WITH JUICE
1 LARGE PACKAGE MIXED FRUIT (FROZEN)
1 CUP STRAWBERRIES, CUT UP
1 TEASPOON BRANDY FLAVORING
2 TABLESPOONS LEMON JUICE

 Cut fruit into bite-size pieces. Cover with juice. Add strawberries, flavoring, and lemon juice. Chill before serving.

Rhubarb Bread Pudding

Serves 6

2 CUPS DICED RHUBARB
3/4 CUP SUGAR
1 TABLESPOON GRATED LEMON RIND
1 1/2 TABLESPOONS LEMON JUICE
1 CUP BREADCRUMBS
1 CUP MILK
1 EGG, BEATEN

 Mix all together and put into buttered casserole. Dot with butter. Bake, covered, 1 hour at 375°.

Beignet Cake (or Pudding Cake)

Serves 6–8

1 CUP BROWN SUGAR
1 CUP HOT WATER
1/2 STICK MARGARINE
1 CUP FLOUR

3/4 CUP SUGAR
3/4 CUP MILK
1 TEASPOON BAKING POWDER

 Mix first 3 ingredients in a 9" × 9" pan. Put in oven at 350° until margarine melts. Combine the rest of the ingredients. Put in pan and bake 20 minutes at 350°.

Squash Pudding

Serves 6–8

2 CUPS COOKED SQUASH
2 CUPS MILK
1 CUP SUGAR
PINCH SALT
1 TEASPOON CINNAMON
1/2 TEASPOON GROUND CLOVES
1/2 TEASPOON GINGER
2 EGGS

 Place all ingredients in a large bowl. Beat with mixer until blended. Pour into greased 2-quart casserole. Bake at 350° for 1 hour. Top with whipped cream.

Rice Pudding

Serves 8–10

1 CUP RICE (NOT INSTANT), COOKED

2/3 CUP SUGAR

1/3 CUP MARGARINE

2 TEASPOONS VANILLA

1/2 TEASPOON SALT (OPTIONAL)

3 EGGS, BEATEN

5 CUPS MILK

1 TEASPOON NUTMEG

❧ Mix all ingredients and put in a Pyrex casserole dish. Place casserole dish in a 1/2" water bath (just as you would a custard). Bake in 350° oven for approximately 60–70 minutes. Serve with strawberries and whipped cream or lemon pudding.

Crow's Nest (Apple Pudding)

Serves 4

1 1/2 CUPS FLOUR

1/2 TEASPOON SALT

1 1/2 TEASPOONS BAKING POWDER

1/3 CUP BUTTER OR MARGARINE

MILK

1 EGG, WELL BEATEN

6–8 APPLES, PEELED AND SLICED

BUTTER

1 TEASPOON CINNAMON

3/4 CUP SUGAR

❧ Sift flour, salt, and baking powder. Work butter or margarine into the flour mixture using fingers or pastry cutter until well blended. Add milk to make soft dough, and then add egg. Fill 8" or 9" pie pan with sliced apples and spread batter on apples. Bake in 375° oven for 45 minutes or until apples are tender. When done turn upside down onto another plate and dot with butter, cinnamon, and sugar. Serve warm with whipped cream.

Bread Pudding

Serves 16–20

5 CUPS BREAD, BROKEN INTO PIECES
8 EGGS, BEATEN
1½ TEASPOONS CINNAMON
1½ TEASPOONS NUTMEG
½ TEASPOON SALT
1 CUP SUGAR
8 CUPS HOT MILK
2 TABLESPOONS BUTTER

✍ Mix all together and bake in a greased 9" × 13" × 2" pan at 350° for 1 hour.

Baked Lemon Pudding

Serves 4

1 CUP SUGAR
BUTTER, SIZE OF WALNUT
1 HEAPING TABLESPOON FLOUR
2 EGG YOLKS, BEATEN
JUICE OF 2 LEMONS
1 CUP MILK
2 EGG WHITES, BEATEN

✍ Cream sugar and butter together. Add flour and egg yolks. Mix together. Add lemon juice, milk, and egg whites. Spread in unbuttered 1-quart casserole. Bake uncovered for 30 minutes in preheated 350° oven. Serve warm, either plain or with cream.

Pineapple Fluff Torte

Serves 16–20

1 3-OUNCE PACKAGE LEMON GELATIN
1 CUP BOILING WATER
2 CUPS GRAHAM CRACKER CRUMBS
½ CUP BUTTER OR MARGARINE, MELTED
¼ CUP CHOPPED NUTS (OPTIONAL)
½ CUP SUGAR
1 8-OUNCE PACKAGE CREAM CHEESE (ROOM TEMPERATURE)
1 12-OUNCE CAN EVAPORATED MILK, CHILLED
1 LARGE (20-OUNCE) CAN CRUSHED PINEAPPLE, DRAINED
1 TEASPOON VANILLA

✍ Dissolve lemon gelatin in 1 cup boiling water. Mix graham cracker crumbs, butter or margarine, and nuts. Press into a 13" × 9" × 2" pan to make a firm bottom layer. Bake crust at 350° for 20 minutes. Set aside and let cool. Add sugar to cream cheese and mix well. Add this mixture to the gelatin mixture. Beat 2 mixtures together. Whip evaporated milk, which has been thoroughly chilled. Fold gelatin/cheese mixture, plus pineapple and vanilla, into whipped milk. Pour over graham cracker crust. Chill overnight.

Flan

Serves 8

4 EGGS

1 CAN SWEETENED CONDENSED MILK

1 CAN REGULAR MILK (USE CONDENSED MILK CAN TO
   MEASURE)

2 TABLESPOONS VANILLA

3–4 TABLESPOONS SUGAR

❧ Beat first 4 ingredients together thoroughly using an electric mixer. Melt 3–4 tablespoons sugar in a small, heavy saucepan over medium heat until sugar turns brown and liquid. Using a turning motion, coat the sides of bowl. Add egg mixture. Set in a pan of water and bake in a 350° oven 45 minutes to an hour. When a knife inserted in middle comes out clean, the flan is done. Time will vary from flan to flan. The flan should look quite firm. Let cool in refrigerator several hours. Invert over plate before serving. It should fall out easily. Slice in small slices because it is very rich!

Czechoslovakian Bars

Makes 24 bars

2 CUPS MARGARINE

2 CUPS SUGAR

4 EGG YOLKS

2 CUPS CHOPPED WALNUTS

4 CUPS FLOUR

1 18-OUNCE JAR OF YOUR FAVORITE PRESERVES

❧ Cream butter, sugar, and egg yolks. Add nuts and flour and mix well. Press 1/2 of mixture into 9" × 13" pan. Spread preserves over mix. Top with remaining dough. Bake at 325° for 1 hour. Bars will be quite thick. If you prefer a thinner bar, use a jelly roll pan with lip. Cut to size desired.

Cream Puff Ring

Serves 10

1 CUP WATER
1/2 CUP BUTTER
1 CUP SIFTED FLOUR
4 EGGS
1 10-OUNCE PACKAGE FROZEN STRAWBERRIES, DRAINED
CONFECTIONERS' SUGAR
CREAM FILLING (RECIPE FOLLOWS)

❧ Grease a pizza pan. Bring water and butter to a boil. Reduce heat and add flour. Stir until mixture forms a ball. Remove from heat. Beat in eggs 1 at a time. Mixture will be smooth. Drop by teaspoonfuls to form a large circle on pan. Bake in 400° oven for 45 minutes. Cool. Cut off top. Fill shell with Cream Filling. Top with strawberries (raspberries would be tasty, too). Replace top. Arrange strawberries on top of cover and dust with confectioners' sugar.

Cream Filling:

1 3.25-OUNCE PACKAGE REGULAR VANILLA PUDDING AND
  PIE MIX, NOT INSTANT
1 1/2 CUPS MILK
1 CUP HEAVY CREAM, WHIPPED
1 TEASPOON VANILLA

❧ Combine pudding mix and milk. Cook, stirring constantly, to full, rolling boil. Remove from heat. Cover with waxed paper. Cool. Fold in whipped cream and vanilla. Fill cream puff shell.

Lemon Curd

Makes about 1 1/2 cups

GRATED RIND AND JUICE OF 4 LEMONS
4 EGGS, BEATEN
4 OUNCES BUTTER
1 POUND SUGAR

❧ Put all ingredients into the top of a double boiler, or in a basin standing in a pan of simmering water. Stir until the sugar has dissolved. Continue heating, stirring from time to time, until the curd thickens. Strain into a sterilized jar and cover tightly. Store in refrigerator. May be served with Old-Fashioned Pound Cake (recipe follows).

Old-Fashioned Pound Cake

Serves 12–16

1 CUP BUTTER, SOFTENED
1/2 CUP VEGETABLE SHORTENING
3 CUPS SUGAR
5 EGGS
3 CUPS ALL-PURPOSE FLOUR
1 TEASPOON BAKING POWDER
1 CUP MILK
1 TEASPOON VANILLA EXTRACT
1 TEASPOON LEMON EXTRACT

🍮 Cream butter and shortening. Add sugar, beating until light and fluffy. Add eggs, 1 at a time, beating well after each addition. Combine flour and baking powder. Add to creamed mixture alternately with milk. Mix well after each addition. Stir in vanilla and lemon extracts. Pour into greased and floured 10" tube pan. Bake at 350° for 1 hour and 15 minutes or until cake tests done. Cool in pan 10–15 minutes and then remove from pan and cool completely.

Marshmallow Delight

Serves 6

1 1/2 CUPS WHIPPING CREAM
1/2 CUP SUGAR
1 TEASPOON VANILLA
1 CUP CRUSHED PINEAPPLE, DRAINED
1/2 POUND LARGE MARSHMALLOWS, CUT UP*
1 CUP CHOPPED WALNUTS

🍮 Whip the cream, and when nearly whipped add sugar and vanilla. With a large spoon slowly stir in the pineapple, cut marshmallows, and walnuts. Put in refrigerator for an hour and serve in sherbet glasses.

*Cut marshmallows with scissors that have been dipped in hot water.

Sugar Pie Sauce

Serves 4–6

2 CUPS BROWN SUGAR

6 TABLESPOONS FLOUR

1/4 CUP BUTTER

1 1/2 CUPS WARM MILK

❧ Mix brown sugar and flour in a saucepan. Add butter and cook on low heat, stirring to melt the sugar. Add the warm milk. Let it cook slowly until the mixture thickens. Put in an uncooked pie crust and add another crust on top. Bake at 450° until the pie crust is well done.

Ben's No-Salt, Low-Cholesterol Pie Crust

2 crusts

3/4–1 CUP SAFFLOWER OIL

4–5 TABLESPOONS COLD WATER

2 3/4 CUPS ALL-PURPOSE FLOUR

❧ Mix these ingredients with a fork. Roll out 1 crust between 2 sheets of waxed paper on countertop that has been dampened. The dampness helps prevent slipping when rolling dough. Repeat for second crust after filling pie plate. This recipe is suitable for 6", 8", and 9" pie crusts.

Ben's Favorite Apple Pie

Serves 6

1/4 CUP LIGHT BROWN SUGAR

1/2 CUP WHITE SUGAR

2 TABLESPOONS FLOUR

1 1/2 TEASPOONS CINNAMON

1/4 TEASPOON NUTMEG

7 CUPS SLICED, PEELED APPLES (SLICED 1/4" THICK)

PIE CRUST (RECIPE FACING) FOR 2-CRUST PIE

1 1/2 TABLESPOONS VANILLA

1 TABLESPOON LEMON JUICE

2 TABLESPOONS BUTTER OR MARGARINE

❧ Combine sugars, flour, cinnamon, and nutmeg. Mix lightly through apples. Place mix in pastry-lined 9" pie plate. Add vanilla and lemon juice and dot with butter. Cover with top crust. Flute edges and cut vents in top. Bake at 425° oven for 50–60 minutes or until crust is brown.

Fresh Blueberry Pie

Serves 8

3/4 CUP WATER

3 CUPS FRESH BLUEBERRIES

1 TABLESPOON BUTTER

1 CUP SUGAR

3 TABLESPOONS CORNSTARCH

DASH OF SALT

1 TEASPOON LEMON JUICE

9" PIE CRUST (EITHER PASTRY OR GRAHAM CRACKER), BAKED

1. Bring 3/4 cup water and 1 cup of blueberries to a boil. Cook gently for about 4 minutes. Add 1 tablespoon butter.

2. Mix together 1 cup sugar, 3 tablespoons cornstarch, and a dash of salt. Add this mixture to the hot blueberry mixture. Cook slowly until thick and clear.

3. Remove from heat and add 1 teaspoon lemon juice. Put 2 cups of blueberries in bottom of a 9" baked pie shell. Pour hot blueberry mix over and mix gently.

4. Refrigerate or leave at room temperature. Serve with sweetened whipped cream. *Delicious!*

Ultimate Blueberry Pie

Serves 8

4 CUPS BLUEBERRIES

9" PIE CRUST (EITHER PASTRY OR GRAHAM CRACKER), BAKED

3 TABLESPOONS CORNSTARCH

3/4–1 CUP SUGAR

DASH OF SALT

1/4 CUP WATER

1 TABLESPOON LEMON JUICE

2 TABLESPOONS BUTTER

❧ Pour 2 cups of fresh berries into cooled pie shell. Heat remaining 2 cups of berries in saucepan with cornstarch blended well with sugar, salt, and water. Remove from heat when mixture has thickened; add lemon juice and butter, stirring until dissolved. Pour mixture over berries in pie plate. Chill for several hours. May be served with whipped cream.

Mouthwatering Strawberry Pie

This tastes even better if you have picked the berries yourself on a warm summer's day!

Serves 6–8

4 CUPS FRESH STRAWBERRIES

9" PIE SHELL, BAKED

1 CUP SUGAR

3 HEAPING TABLESPOONS CORNSTARCH

1/4 TEASPOON SALT

1/2 CUP COLD WATER

WHIPPED CREAM AND VANILLA, IF DESIRED

❧ Hull and wash 1 quart of strawberries. Select 2 cups of the best berries and slice in 1/2. Place the strawberries in the bottom of a baked and cooled pie shell. Mash the remaining 1/2 of the berries, place in a saucepan, and bring to a boil. Add sugar, cornstarch, salt, and 1/2 cup cold water. Cook about 15 minutes or until thickened. Pour over the uncooked berries in the pie shell. Refrigerate until well chilled. Serve with sweetened whipped cream, with a few drops of vanilla added, if desired.

Peanut Butter–Cream Cheese Pie

Serves 8

2 3-OUNCE PACKAGES CREAM CHEESE, SOFTENED

3/4 CUP SIFTED CONFECTIONERS' SUGAR

1/2 CUP PEANUT BUTTER

2 TABLESPOONS MILK

1 ENVELOPE WHIPPED TOPPING MIX

COARSELY CHOPPED PEANUTS

8" PIE SHELL, BAKED

❧ In mixer bowl, beat cream cheese and sugar until creamy. Add peanut butter and milk, beating until smooth and creamy. Prepare dessert topping according to directions on package. Fold into peanut butter mixture. Pour into baked pie shell. Chill in refrigerator 5 hours or overnight. Garnish top with coarsely chopped peanuts.

Raspberry Cream Pie

This pie was always the dessert at the annual lobster bake held either in Peg's large field or down at Turbats Creek at Mabel's cottage. What wonderful occasions those years ago! I remember the laughter, strong and lasting friendships, wonderful food, and this great pie. In later years my husband's secretary used to make it for his birthday present.

Serves 6–8

9" BAKED PIE SHELL (USE A DEEP PIE PLATE)

Raspberry Mix:

1 3-OUNCE PACKAGE BLACK RASPBERRY GELATIN

1/4 CUP SUGAR

DASH SALT

1 1/4 CUPS BOILING WATER

1 TEASPOON LEMON JUICE

1 10-OUNCE PACKAGE FROZEN RASPBERRIES

1 CUP HEAVY CREAM

1/3 CUP CONFECTIONERS' SUGAR

1 3-OUNCE PACKAGE CREAM CHEESE

DASH SALT

1 TEASPOON VANILLA

Combine gelatin, sugar, salt, boiling water, lemon juice, and frozen raspberries (separate with fork). Let set until jelly firm. Whip cream. Refrigerate. Add confectioners' sugar gradually to softened cream cheese. Add salt and vanilla. Beat well and fold into whipped cream. In baked pie shell, put 1/2 of whipped cream mixture, coating well the sides of the pie shell to keep it crisp. Then add 1/2 of gelatin mixture, then whipped cream mixture, and finish with gelatin mixture. Chill several hours. *The best!*

Breads

No-Fail Popovers

Serves 8

1 CUP FLOUR
1 CUP MILK
1/2 TEASPOON SALT
2 EGGS (IF SMALL, USE 3)

1. Put all in a bowl and mix. Do *not* beat out the lumps. Pour into greased muffin cups, filling them 1/2 full.

2. Put in *cold* 400° oven and bake 35–40 minutes undisturbed. If necessary, reduce heat to dry out, and cook 10 more minutes.

Note: If using the large popover/muffin tins, put 1/2 cup mixture in each muffin cup.

Bubble Rolls

Serves 16–20

2 CUPS SCALDED MILK

2 TABLESPOONS BUTTER OR MARGARINE

2 TABLESPOONS SUGAR

1 TABLESPOON SALT

1 YEAST CAKE

1/4 CUP LUKEWARM WATER

1 EGG

5–6 CUPS FLOUR

1 1/2 STICKS BUTTER OR MARGARINE

BROWN SUGAR, CHERRIES, CRUSHED WALNUTS, CINNAMON

❧ Pour scalded milk over butter, sugar, and salt. Dissolve 1 yeast cake in 1/4 cup lukewarm water; add 1 egg. Combine with scalded milk mixture. Add 5 or 6 cups flour. Knead. Let rise. Melt 1 1/2 sticks butter or margarine. Put 1/2 of melted butter in 10" angel food pan. Sprinkle brown sugar, cherries, crushed walnuts, and cinnamon. Add 1 layer of rolls. (Take pieces of dough and roll into balls.) Add remainder of butter, brown sugar, cherries, etc., and then another layer of rolls. Let rise. Bake at 375° for 35 minutes.

55-Minute Dinner Rolls

Makes 12 to 18 rolls

1 CUP WARM MILK

2 TABLESPOONS SHORTENING, MELTED

3 CUPS FLOUR

1/4 TEASPOON SALT

2 TABLESPOONS SUGAR

2 SMALL YEAST CAKES DISSOLVED IN A LITTLE WATER.

❧ Mix in large bowl and let rise 15 minutes. Take out on bread board, knead, and then roll. Cut dough with biscuit cutter, brush with butter, fold over, and brush with butter again. Let rise 40 minutes. Bake 15 minutes in a biscuit oven.

Cheddar Olive Bread

Serves 8–10

LOAF OF FRENCH BREAD
1 CUP SHREDDED CHEDDAR CHEESE
1/4 CUP MAYONNAISE
3 TABLESPOONS GREEN ONIONS
1/2 TEASPOON CHILI POWDER
2 TABLESPOONS SLICED RIPE OLIVES

ଶ Slice bread in 1/2 lengthwise. Mix together Cheddar, mayonnaise, onions, and chili powder. Spread on bread. Sprinkle with ripe olives. Wrap each 1/2 in foil. Bake at 350° for 15 minutes. Unwrap and continue baking until brown and bubbly.

Margaret Meloney Swenson's Irish Soda Bread

Makes 1 large loaf

3 1/2 CUPS FLOUR
1 TABLESPOON BAKING POWDER
1 TEASPOON BAKING SODA
1 TEASPOON SALT
1/3 CUP SUGAR
1 CUP RAISINS
1/4 CUP BUTTER, MELTED AND COOLED
1 EGG, LIGHTLY BEATEN
1 1/2 CUPS BUTTERMILK
1 TEASPOON CARAWAY SEEDS (OPTIONAL)

ଶ Sift flour, baking powder, soda, and salt into a large bowl. Stir in remaining ingredients. Use extra flour to shape; knead gently. Bake at 400° for 30 minutes. Delicious.

Chapter Two

Fund-Raising Suppers

There comes a time in most churches for the need to raise funds. There is a benefit to these fund-raising tasks beyond the financial considerations. Community is built while the planning, preparation, and "delivery" of the event is being carried out. Working together in a sociable environment is important so that people find enjoyment in the experience.

Here are a few tips that may be helpful in preparation for a fund-raising event. These are offered primarily for those who may have never done a fund-raiser, but they may be helpful even to those who are experienced. The example will be a turkey dinner, but do keep in mind that the same principles would probably apply to any large dinner. A large dinner is one that is larger than your family! These recipes can be multiplied or reduced to suit your needs.

Appoint a committee, whose responsibility will be to plan, produce, and deliver the event to its successful conclusion. The committee should meet and decide on a date for the event, if one has not yet been determined. The next important decision is the menu. Decide in detail what the menu will be, and write it all down. Planning is so important. Once the meal is planned on paper, the first giant step has been taken.

Will all ingredients for the meal be purchased, or will some items be solicited from people in the church? Discussing this issue will not only help you determine the cost of putting on the supper, but will assist you in your time-management planning as well. If, for example, you will solicit pies for dessert, you do not have to think about shopping for or preparing dessert. Members of the committee or someone they delegate will need to do the soliciting. However, you will have to plan who will be cutting the pies and when, as well as space to hold them before serving.

Think through, as closely as you can, the cost of putting on this meal. This helps in determining what the cost of the tickets will have to be in order to make a profit. It is discouraging when an event costs more to put on than is realized from ticket sales. For some meals you may wish to accept monetary donations instead of selling tickets. In certain situations, this can result in more profit than selling tickets would have.

Asking for donations of food for an event once in a while is a good thing, but if you do meals on a very regular basis, people can get tired of always making a pie or a salad. Judge for yourself how your church family feels about this and go from there. Times change, and with today's busy lifestyle, it is not always doable for people to cook and donate.

Careful food preparation is very important. Planning on how to go about the actual preparation of the food must be thought through. If using frozen turkeys, or any other frozen meat, allow time for these turkeys to be thawed in a refrigerator. Depending on the size of the birds and the number that will be thawing in the refrigerator at one time, it may take several days. It could be as long as eight days. These birds should not be thawed on the kitchen counters! Determine what time these birds should start to cook on the day of the meal, allowing time for them to be carved in time for serving. Do not have them done too early, so that they sit around too long before serving. Do not plan to stuff the birds. Two reasons: (1) The risk of bacteria is too great, and (2) it is difficult to determine serving amounts when you stuff the birds. Make the dressing separately and bake it in pans or in a large electric roaster oven. The large electric roaster is a good way to go. You can mix the dressing fairly early in the day (mid- to late morning), and it will cook slowly and thoroughly until serving time. Your ovens are free for the turkeys and then the heating of rolls and/or baking of desserts, if that will be necessary.

Do what you can the day before. Potatoes can be peeled and covered with cold water. The next day, drain the water off; put on fresh water and cook. Know your stove! Allow time for a stove that takes a long time to heat, and be aware that a large quantity of food will take longer to cook than you may realize. You want the potatoes done for serving time. It is so frustrating to watch the clock and wait for them to cook. (Please note in the recipe section the instructions for mashing potatoes—they really do work!)

Think through the rest of the menu, keeping the time schedule in mind. If serving rolls, someone needs to wrap them in foil for heating. If serving jellied salads, make them a day ahead to allow plenty of time for jelling. All the celery, et cetera, can be chopped the day ahead, saving precious time and creating less mess on meal day. If serving tossed salad, wash and refrigerate the greens the day before. The same can be done with preparation of dressing if you are doing a turkey dinner. Shred the bread (see Turkey Dressing recipe on page 114), chop the onions and celery, and, if possible, cook the turkey necks and giblets for the turkey stock the day before. If that is not possible, put these items on to cook very early the day of the meal so that the turkey stock can be used to moisten the stuffing mixture. The onions and celery can be sautéed and refrigerated the day before and put into the dressing on the day of the meal. Time has a way of flying by on the day of the event. Cooking in larger quantities takes more preparation time; therefore, it is important to do some of the prep work ahead. Lettuce for five people washes up fairly quickly, but lettuce for twenty-five people takes a bit longer.

How the meal will be served needs to be discussed. Will it be family style or buffet? If it will be family style, you will need to decide how many tables you will have. Count the number of items being served and determine how many serving dishes, large serving spoons, and meat platters, et cetera, you will need. If serving buffet style, determine what equipment you will need to serve the meal from one long serving table. Serving buffet style certainly has its merits. You will need less wait-staff. You can keep the food warmer by either serving from a roaster oven or putting lesser amounts of food in the serving dishes and keeping the rest warm in the kitchen. Always prepare enough for those who wish to have seconds, but when

food is served family style, sometimes people's eyes are bigger than their tummies and the food doesn't go quite far enough. It is simpler all around to serve buffet style, but some events may require family-style serving. Always have enough servers to pour the coffee, and if you have people who are unable physically to go to a buffet table, have these servers wait on these people.

Arrange to have the tables and chairs set up in advance of the day of the event, if possible. If you don't have a roll of white table paper, try to get one. Tablecloths are not practical for this type of event, and white table paper looks nice. At paper supply stores, you can get paper placemats in several colors. Pick the color you want and get a box of placemats. Have one for each place setting. Placemats are especially helpful if people are going to be straggling in at different times. As guests finish their meal and leave, clear away their place settings and put down a clean placemat and clean utensils. It looks so unappealing to seat people where the table paper has become soiled and you do not have placemats. It is always nice to have several people come to the church in the morning to set the tables. If serving family style, dinner plates must be set at each place. If serving buffet style, put the dinner plates on the serving table. For either type of serving procedure, the flatware, napkins, and cups and saucers must be placed. Put salt and pepper shakers and sugar bowls at each end of the table. Nearer serving time, the cream pitchers, butter dishes, and baskets of rolls can be placed. A tiny vase with one or two blossoms in the center of each table adds a very nice touch. Although the food should be nicely prepared, there is always more to eating at a church supper than just the food. It has a special atmosphere of community and fellowship.

About $1^1/_2$ hours before serving time, make the coffee. If using a large pot, it takes a while for the coffee to brew, and you do not want to wait for coffee! If done ahead, you can take the basket of grounds out and empty and clean it. Any utensils that you are through using should be washed and put away before serving time. Cleanup can take a while and anything that can be cleaned ahead of time should be.

Plan how and where the turkeys will be carved and who will do the carving. Timing on this issue is difficult. Try to plan so that the platters of turkey meat are ready shortly before serving. As we are all keenly aware these days, food left out too long can cause illness, and that is the last thing you want to have happen.

Soon after the serving begins, cleanup becomes the big issue. Try to have a separate crew of people just for cleanup. The people who have been preparing need to be able to go home and put their feet up soon after the meal has been served. Church kitchens can get shortchanged when it comes to good "cleanups." Try to impress upon the cleanup crew that it is important to do a good job and leave the kitchen clean. It may be easier to get a committee together for the next function if they don't have to go in and clean for two days before they can prepare a meal.

These tips are not meant to overwhelm anyone. It is a good idea after all is done, to talk over and write down what went well and what should be changed. Making these fund-raisers fun—and they can be!—is important, and the more pitfalls you avoid, the more fun you will have.

Church suppers should be not only tasty but ample. People come and come again when they feel that they have received that "little bit extra." In a commercial restaurant, people wouldn't expect to get the same type of meal or service as they do at a church supper. Always remember that part of your "job" is to fill those attending not only with food, but also with friendship and social nourishment, to feed their souls as well as their stomachs.

The following story, entitled "The Turkey Carving," is one that has brought a few chuckles. It also gives a glimpse of not only the hard work, but also the camaraderie that can be experienced by family and church family by sharing in such events as a turkey—or any other kind of—supper. I have enjoyed being involved in such events, and I am so grateful to my family not only for helping to get tasks done, but also for their wonderful and gracious attitude. "The Turkey Carving" was written by our daughter when she was a young adult.

The Turkey Carving

A minister's child learns quickly to accommodate himself to the different facets of the profession. We learn to work at bake sales, rummage sales, and Christmas bazaars. We also learn to master the famed tradition of church suppers—to cook for them, serve food, sell tickets, and do general, all around go-for-this, go-for-that errands.

Every Friday night during the summer, the ladies in the Women's Fellowship in my father's church put on a public supper. Each week, one or two are in charge of planning the menu and coordinating the works, while the other women help out in the orchestration. In short, one or two are the chiefs and the rest are the Indians. The supper on August 24 was my mother's turn to run the show, and, of course, the whole family was to be pressed into service.

My mother's supper was to be a turkey dinner, the same menu she had served for the past several years. By going over previous years' records and working through various mathematical contortions, she came up with the final figures it would take to feed 100 people, and the cost.

As the days counted down to the big event, the shopping was done and the duty roster grew. The day before the supper, we really launched into action. There were 12 mega-sized loaves of bread to be shredded for the dressing, which was to be made the next morning.

On the eve of the feast, a group gathered at the church, and in the midst of much laughter and good-natured kidding, 60 pounds of potatoes were peeled, 10 pounds of onions diced, and a mountain of celery chopped.

Reveille was early the next day. Over at the church, the clan gathered and began preparing the giant steaming pans of dressing and the fresh vegetables for the vegetable medley. I, however, was stationed at home. It was my duty to keep the workings at the house smooth, fix my father's lunch, and ready the homefront for the climactic preparation of the day: the dreaded turkey carving.

I spent most of that morning in a very domestic stance. I kept my eye on the turkey in the oven, and prepared for the arrival of the other five birds, which would descend on us at 4 o'clock. It was traditional for the turkeys to be carved and the gravy made at our house, because there wasn't enough room in the church kitchen, and it was easy to transport things across the lawn.

I washed all the dishes; cleaned out the drainer; set out the measuring cups, flour, cutting boards, and a new roll of paper towels; and made a fresh batch of iced tea. It was going to be awfully hot about 4 P.M.

My mother went out to lunch with some of the ladies, but my father came home for lunch at noon. I heated up some leftover salmon loaf and poured him a glass of milk. While he ate, I filled him in on what I knew of the preparations for the "turkey circus," as I liked to call it. I also reminded him that we had 13 dozen ears of corn arriving in an hour.

After lunch, we had to fix the table for the carving event, covering it with a layer of newspapers and then plastic tablecloths. Dilemma: Where was the extra leaf? We thought for a moment, ruled out a few possibilities, and then we remembered. It was under the couch. As we struggled to put the leaf in the heavy, iron-clawed oak table, my father smiled and shook his head in his customary fashion. "You don't have to be crazy to get along around here, but it helps," he said wryly. (My father has that invaluable gift of being able to laugh in any situation. I hope it is genetic and will someday turn up in me as a latent tendency.)

The afternoon passed pretty well as scheduled. The corn arrived and the crew to husk it. Everything in the kitchen simmered nicely, and the turkey in our oven browned beautifully.

About 3:45 P.M., the rest of the turkey crew arrived. It was Mr. and Mrs. Vale. (The names have been changed to protect all involved.) They came into the house, Mr. Vale with his knives, apron, and other tools of the carver's trade, and Mrs. Vale carrying a turkey and ready to make gravy. Soon after, Mr. and Mrs. Willis and Mr. Wakely arrived, all on the same mission.

It was quite a show! Each man claimed his territory and set up his work area on the table. They stood there, each with his over-65 bay window and his bald head, wielding his knife like a Samurai.

My mother suddenly whizzed in. "All turkeys please line up," she commanded. Whoops of laughter followed and much flak from the peanut gallery. This was a good-natured bunch, the old shoe. The main purpose was to carve turkeys, but the warm fellowship and friendship were the real prize.

The rest of the birds arrived. I surveyed the goods. Everything looked to be in excellent condition, except for one bird that looked somewhat anemic. I put my worst fears out of my head. "If it ain't broke, don't fix it," I figured.

It was 5:15 and the official proceedings at the church were to start in 15 minutes. The crowd was gathering and everything looked promising, no major flaws yet. All but one of the turkeys had been carved and the gravy brought over to the church. In the center of the table was a large plastic bag filled with the bones, skin, and other remains of the birds.

The final bird to be cut up was the anemic one. A couple of the men commented on its wan appearance, but no one wanted to utter the thought that it might not be done. Mr. Willis and Mr. Vale agreed that the deed had to be performed, so after a bit of turkey carver's etiquette, Mr. Willis won the honor of cutting the bird.

Our fears were confirmed. The turkey was still squawking. Someone had not cooked it long enough or had not thawed it well enough, or something. Whatever it was, it didn't matter. On went the oven and in went the turkey in question. Like expectant fathers, the men waited for the turkey to cook, while the ladies set to work cleaning up the gravy mess. Finally the bird was done, the meat cut and sent over to the church, and we could wash our hands of the whole matter.

The rest is pretty much history, or maybe just a blur. Don't ask me how, but somehow they managed to feed well over 100 people. I think it has something to do with the fishes and the loaves, or more like the turkeys and the loaves. There was only a small amount of turkey left over, which was brought to a family in a state of crisis. Frankly, I could not have eaten turkey for anything. I went to Burger King.

That night, my 15-year-old brother and I sat up talking long after my folks had gone to bed. I filled him in on what had gone on, and he gave me a rundown on the antics at the church while he was over there running the dishwasher.

Then we reminisced a bit about past turkey suppers. There was the year the doorknob broke in the midst of all the traffic between the house and the church. Mom had not been too thrilled when they had to take the gravy out over the dining room rug and out the front door.

Then there was the year Mrs. Wakely dropped a pan of turkey grease on the floor. That was a four-alarm mess!

Yes, except for one slightly raw turkey, the day had been a success. Being a minister's child does have an advantage. You are never in want for excitement. ❧

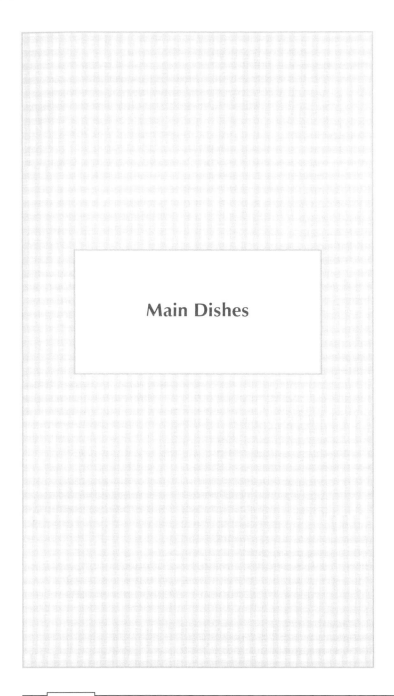

Main Dishes

Turkey Dressing

Serves 6–8

4 CUPS WHITE BREAD, SHREDDED

2 EGGS, BEATEN WITH A FORK

1 CUP DICED CELERY

1 SMALL ONION, CHOPPED FINE

1 TEASPOON POULTRY SEASONING

1 TEASPOON SALT

1/4 TEASPOON PEPPER

1 STICK BUTTER, MELTED

1 CUP (OR MORE) HOT TURKEY STOCK (WATER IN WHICH NECK AND GIBLETS WERE COOKED)

❧ Mix all ingredients except the stock together in a large bowl. Add the stock and mix well. When you think the mixture is moist enough, add some more stock. The dressing mixture needs to be very moist in order not to be too dry when cooked. Prepare more than 1 cup of stock, just to be sure you have enough. Put in a greased pan and bake at 350° until cooked through and slightly crusty on top, about 25–40 minutes. This recipe can be multiplied to the amount needed. *Do not cover.*

Note: Day-old bread from bakery thrift stores works very well in this recipe and it helps save money.

Chicken Pie

Serves 6

1 4–5 POUND WHOLE CHICKEN (OR CHICKEN PARTS)

1 LARGE ONION, CHOPPED

2 CARROTS, PEELED AND CUT INTO CHUNKS

2 CUPS CHICKEN BROTH (BROTH FROM COOKED CHICKEN)

4 TABLESPOONS MARGARINE

4 TABLESPOONS FLOUR

3 CUPS FLOUR

1 CUP SHORTENING

3/8 CUP COLD WATER

1. In a large kettle, cook the chicken along with the onion and carrots in boiling water. Cool. Remove skin and bones. Chicken may be cut up if necessary to fit it in pan.

2. Make a "thinnish" gravy, using the chicken broth. (If possible, cook the chicken the day before you want to make the pie so that the fat will solidify to the top and can be taken off, making a less fatty and less caloric broth.) For the gravy, heat 2 cups chicken broth in a saucepan on the stove or in the microwave. Melt the margarine in the microwave and stir in the 4 tablespoons of flour. Gradually add the broth and either proceed to make the gravy in the microwave or on the stove.

3. For the pie crust, combine the 3 cups of flour with the water and shortening. Divide dough in 1/2. Roll out 1/2 and place in a 10" deep-dish pie plate.*

4. Add the chicken pieces and pour the gravy over the chicken. Roll out the top crust and put in place. Bake at 350° for 45–60 minutes. This will feed at least 6 hungry people. For a large group, just make as many pies as needed for your size group.

*You may omit the bottom crust and put the chicken in the bottom of the pie plate.

Crowded Chicken

Serves 25

16 POUNDS BONELESS, SKINLESS CHICKEN BREASTS (YOU MAY
    INCLUDE A FEW THIGHS IF DESIRED)
7 ENVELOPES ONION SOUP MIX

❧ If chicken pieces are too large for 1 serving, cut in 1/2. Layer chicken in roasting pan(s). Cover each layer with onion soup mix. Cover pan(s) with foil. Bake in a 350° oven. Check for doneness after an hour. Cover again and continue cooking until fork tender.

Chicken Strata

Serves 24

32 SLICES WHITE BREAD
BUTTER
8 CUPS DICED COOKED CHICKEN (3 3-POUND CHICKENS)
2 LARGE ONIONS, CHOPPED (2 CUPS)
2 LARGE GREEN PEPPERS, CHOPPED (2 CUPS)
2 CUPS FINELY CHOPPED CELERY
2 CUPS MAYONNAISE
1 TABLESPOON SALT
1/2 TEASPOON PEPPER
6 EGGS, SLIGHTLY BEATEN
6 CUPS MILK
4 CANS CONDENSED CREAM OF MUSHROOM SOUP
2 CUPS SHREDDED CHEESE

❧ Dry out bread slightly in oven. Butter 8 slices of bread and cut into 1/2" cubes. Set aside. Cut remaining bread into cubes, placing 1/2 in each of 2 9" × 13" × 2" pans. Combine next 7 ingredients; sprinkle over cubes and cover with remaining crumbs. Combine eggs and milk; pour over mixture in pans. Cover and chill 1 hour or overnight. Spoon soup over top and bake at 325° for 50–60 minutes. Sprinkle cheese over top for last few minutes of baking.

Fluffy Chicken Loaf

Serves 12

4 CUPS DICED COOKED CHICKEN

2 CUPS COOKED RICE

2 CUPS SOFT BREADCRUMBS

1/4 CUP PIMIENTO (CUT FINE)

1 4-OUNCE CAN SLICED MUSHROOMS (ADD LIQUID TO BROTH)

2 TEASPOONS SALT

2 1/2 CUPS CHICKEN BROTH

4 EGGS, WELL BEATEN

◈ Combine chicken with rice, crumbs, pimiento, mushrooms, and salt. Combine broth with beaten eggs and mix with chicken, etc. Bake in a 9" × 13" × 2" buttered baking pan. Bake until firm in a moderate 350° oven about 1 hour. Serve with Mushroom Sauce (recipe follows).

Mushroom Sauce:

1 CAN CREAM OF MUSHROOM SOUP

1 CUP CHICKEN BROTH

◈ For the thin sauce, combine condensed mushroom soup and chicken broth. Mix well and heat through thoroughly.

Southern Chicken Salad Casserole

Serves 10–12

4 CUPS DICED COOKED CHICKEN

2 CUPS CONDENSED CREAM OF CHICKEN SOUP

2 CUPS DICED CELERY

4 TABLESPOONS MINCED ONION

2 CUPS SLIVERED ALMONDS

1 CUP MAYONNAISE

3/4 CUP CHICKEN STOCK

1 TEASPOON SALT

1/2 TEASPOON PEPPER

4 TABLESPOONS LEMON JUICE

6 HARD-BOILED EGGS, CHOPPED FINE

1 CUP BUTTERY CRACKER CRUMBS, CRUSHED FINE

◈ Combine the above ingredients, except the cracker crumbs. Put into a 3–4-quart casserole. Cover with crumbs. Bake in 350° oven for 40 minutes. Serve hot. This may be divided for a smaller group or multiplied for a larger group. It can be made the day before the event and baked near serving time. This really works well. It gets the "mess" and the dishes cleaned up the day before! The Atlantic Lime Mold, Cranberry Chutney, and any of the cranberry salads go well with this casserole.

Hawaiian Meatballs

Serves 24

6 POUNDS GROUND BEEF

2³/₄ CUPS CRACKER CRUMBS

1 CUP MINCED ONION

4 EGGS

1 TABLESPOON SALT

1 TEASPOON GINGER

¹/₂ CUP MILK

¹/₂ CUP CORNSTARCH

2 CUPS BROWN SUGAR

2 20-OUNCE CANS PINEAPPLE TIDBITS

1 CUP VINEGAR

¹/₄ CUP SOY SAUCE

1 CUP CHOPPED GREEN PEPPER

❧ Mix together beef, cracker crumbs, onion, eggs, salt, ginger, and milk. Form into meatballs. Brown in oven. Mix together cornstarch and brown sugar. Stir in reserved juice from pineapple tidbits, vinegar, and soy sauce. Stir until smooth and cook over medium heat until thick. Stir and boil 1 minute. Add meatballs, pineapple, and green pepper. Heat through.

Pasta Sauce

Makes 20–25 servings

2 SMALL ONIONS, CHOPPED

2 LARGE CLOVES GARLIC, CHOPPED

4 TABLESPOONS MARGARINE

4 TABLESPOONS OIL

2 POUNDS GROUND BEEF

SALT AND PEPPER TO TASTE

1 LARGE (12-OUNCE) OR 2 SMALL (6-OUNCE) CANS
    TOMATO PASTE

2 LARGE CANS ITALIAN PEAR TOMATOES, CHOPPED

2 28-OUNCE JARS SPAGHETTI SAUCE

1 TABLESPOON BROWN SUGAR

POSSIBLE SPICES—BAY LEAF, BASIL, AND OREGANO—TO TASTE

❧ Fry onions and garlic in margarine and oil. (May be able to cut back a little on margarine and oil.) Add ground beef. When browned, add salt and pepper. Drain excess fat. Add tomato paste, tomatoes, sauce, and water, if necessary. Bring to a boil; then simmer for a couple of hours. Add brown sugar to cut acidity. Add other spices while simmering, such as bay leaf, basil, oregano, etc.

American Chop Suey for 25

3 POUNDS HAMBURGER

2 POUNDS ONIONS, CHOPPED

2 LARGE GREEN PEPPERS, CHOPPED

1 BUNCH CELERY, CHOPPED

2 POUNDS MACARONI

1 #10 CAN TOMATOES (6 POUNDS, 10 OUNCES)

1 15-OUNCE AND 1 6-OUNCE CAN TOMATO PASTE

SALT AND PEPPER TO TASTE

❧ Brown meat, add vegetables, and cook until tender. Cook the macaroni, 20 minutes; drain and add to meat and vegetables. Stir in tomatoes and paste. Add salt and pepper to taste. Heat thoroughly and serve.

Oven-Barbecued Steaks for 25

7½ POUNDS INEXPENSIVE STEAKS (LONDON BROIL OR BLADE STEAK)

¼ CUP SALAD OIL

1 CUP THINLY SLICED ONION

2 CUPS CATSUP

2 CUPS VINEGAR

¼ CUP BROWN SUGAR

3 CUPS WATER

¼ CUP PREPARED MUSTARD

2 TABLESPOONS WORCESTERSHIRE SAUCE

1½ TEASPOONS SALT

¼ TEASPOON PEPPER

❧ Cut steaks in equal portions. Brown on both sides in oil. Put into roasting pans. Fry onion in skillet. Add rest of ingredients to onion. Simmer 5 minutes. Pour over steaks. Cover and roast at 350° for 2–2½ hours.

Scalloped Sweet Potatoes and Apples

Makes 25 1-cup servings

6¼ POUNDS SWEET POTATOES

2½ QUARTS APPLES, PEELED, CORED, AND CUT INTO ½" SLICES

¾ CUP + 3 TABLESPOONS PACKED BROWN SUGAR

5 TABLESPOONS SHORTENING

2¼ TEASPOONS SALT

1 CUP WATER

❧ Scrub potatoes; cover with water and cook until tender. Drain, peel, cut into ½" slices. Equally layer potatoes and apple slices, alternately, in roasting pans. Cook brown sugar, shortening, salt, and water over low heat until sugar is dissolved. Stir constantly. Pour equally over potatoes and apples in each pan. Bake at 350° until apples are tender, approximately 1 hour.

Party Potatoes

A great "do ahead" dish!

Serves 12

8–10 POTATOES

1 CUP SOUR CREAM

8 OUNCES CREAM CHEESE

1 TEASPOON GARLIC SALT

1 TEASPOON ONION SALT

PEPPER TO TASTE

BUTTER

PAPRIKA

❧ Boil potatoes. Drain and mash. Beat sour cream and cream cheese until blended. Add hot potatoes gradually, beating constantly until light and fluffy. Season with garlic and onion salt and pepper. Spoon potatoes into a buttered casserole. Dot with butter and sprinkle with paprika. Brown and bake at 350° for 45 minutes. Much better if refrigerated at least 24 hours before baking. Freezes well. If frozen, bake 1½–2 hours.

Scalloped Noodles

Makes 25 1-cup servings

2¼ QUARTS NOODLES

9¾ CUPS TOMATO PURÉE

2¼ TEASPOONS SALT

½ TEASPOON PEPPER

2 TABLESPOONS SUGAR

3 CUPS GRATED CHEDDAR
   CHEESE

25½ SLICES BACON

Cook noodles according to package instructions. Set aside. Combine tomato purée, salt, pepper, and sugar. Heat to boiling. Arrange alternate layers of noodles, tomato mixture, and cheese in greased roasting pans. Arrange bacon on top of mixture in each pan. Bake at 400° for 20 minutes or until bacon is crisp.

~

Scrambled Eggs

Serves 25

¾ POUND MARGARINE

3 DOZEN EGGS

2¼ CUPS MILK

1 TABLESPOON SALT

PEPPER IF DESIRED

Preheat electric roaster to 400°. Add margarine; as soon as melted, pour in eggs and milk, which have been beaten together. Add salt and pepper. Stir occasionally until eggs are set, about 25–30 minutes. Keep warm at 150°. An Easter breakfast treat!

Baked Grits

Easter breakfast with a Southern flare!

Serves 12

6 CUPS WATER

1½ CUPS GRITS

1½ STICKS MARGARINE

1 POUND CHEDDAR CHEESE, GRATED

3 EGGS

2 TEASPOONS SALT

6–7 DROPS TABASCO SAUCE

PAPRIKA

Bring 6 cups water to a boil and add grits. Cook until well done. Add the margarine and grated cheese to the hot grits. Set aside. Mix 3 eggs, 2 teaspoons salt, and the Tabasco sauce. Add to hot mixture. Pour into an 9" × 13" pan and sprinkle paprika on top. Bake at 250° for 1 hour.

Superb Baked Haddock

Serves 25

12½ POUNDS HADDOCK FILLETS

JUICE FROM 2–3 FRESH LEMONS

1 POUND BUTTER, MELTED

1¼ BOXES OF BUTTERY CRACKERS FINELY CRUSHED

❧ Layer haddock in shallow baking pans. Press together to cover whole pan. Lightly squeeze or pour *fresh* lemon juice over haddock. Combine melted butter with cracker crumbs and cover top of fish. Bake at 350° for 30 minutes or until fish flakes when tested with a fork.

Mashed Potatoes

Serves 25

12½ POUNDS WHITE POTATOES

2–4 CUPS MILK

¼ POUND BUTTER OR MARGARINE

1. Peel and boil the potatoes. The time it takes to cook the potatoes depends on the size of the pans you are using and the age of the potatoes. Do cook them thoroughly so that they mash very well. To ensure that they are well mashed, mash small amounts at a time and then mix together. Mashing well prevents lumpy mashed potatoes.

2. The real secret to *good* mashed potatoes in large quantities is to add sufficient milk and margarine. After the potatoes have been mashed, you are ready to start the whipping process.

3. Heat 2 cups of milk and melt the margarine. Pour into the mashed potatoes, mashing and stirring all the time. (A long-handled masher and a large, heavy whisk are handy tools for this job.) This will probably be about ½ the liquid you will need. It is hard to tell you exactly because potatoes vary in dryness. Using your judgment, add more hot milk and continue until potatoes are the consistency of whipped cream. This may seem too thin—most people think it is the first time—but potatoes are starchy and they will thicken as they wait to be served. One of the problems with cooking for this many people is that the food cannot be served as quickly as it would be at home.

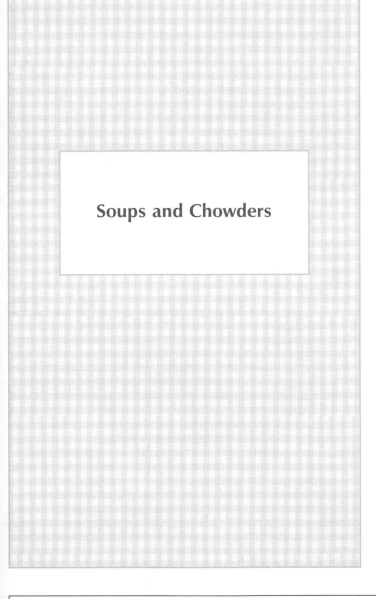

Soups and Chowders

Beef Stew

Serves 25

6¼ POUNDS STEW BEEF
½ CUP SHORTENING
2¼ QUARTS WATER
3 POUNDS POTATOES, DICED
¾ POUND CARROTS, DICED (2¼ CUPS)
3 ONIONS, CUT
1 CUP FLOUR TO THICKEN
½ CUP COLD WATER
2½ TABLESPOONS SALT
1 TEASPOON PEPPER
1 TABLESPOON WORCESTERSHIRE SAUCE

Brown meat in shortening. Cover with 1 quart of water and simmer until tender. Cook potatoes, carrots, and onions in remaining 1¼ quarts water. When tender, combine with meat mixture. Make a paste of flour and ½ cup water. Add to stew, stirring until thick. Season with salt and pepper. Simmer 30 minutes. Before serving, add Worcestershire sauce.

Minestrone Soup

Very hearty—like a stew.

Makes about 21 1-cup servings

4 TABLESPOONS LIGHT OLIVE OIL

1 LARGE ONION, CHOPPED

2 TEASPOONS MINCED GARLIC

1/2 RED PEPPER FINELY CHOPPED

3 LARGE OR 4 SMALL STALKS CELERY, CHOPPED

3 PEELED AND SLICED CARROTS

4 OUNCES SLICED MUSHROOMS

1 CUP FROZEN TENDER PEAS

1 CUP FROZEN CORN

1 LARGE ZUCCHINI, CUT IN 1/2 AND SLICED INTO SMALL CHUNKS

6–8 CUPS CHICKEN, BEEF, OR VEGETABLE BROTH

1 28-OUNCE CAN PEELED ITALIAN TOMATOES, CHOPPED

1 SMALL CAN TOMATO PASTE

1 TEASPOON SUGAR

3/4 TEASPOON ITALIAN SEASONING

SALT AND PEPPER TO TASTE

1 15-OUNCE CAN GARBANZO BEANS (CHICKPEAS), RINSED

1 15-OUNCE CAN DARK RED KIDNEY BEANS, DRAINED
AND RINSED

1/2 10-OUNCE PACKAGE FROZEN, CHOPPED SPINACH,
DEFROSTED AND WELL DRAINED

SPLASH OF RED WINE

2 CUPS DRY PASTA

❧ In a large pot, heat the olive oil and sauté the onion until limp. Add the minced garlic and sauté 1–2 minutes. Add the red pepper, celery, and carrots and sauté until soft. Add the mushrooms; sauté until soft. Add peas, corn, zucchini and cover with broth. Simmer for about 30 minutes. Add tomatoes. Remove 1 cup of broth and stir together with tomato paste; return to pot. Add the remaining ingredients and simmer 1 hour. Adjust seasonings and add a splash of red wine. In a separate pot, cook the pasta al dente—add the pasta to the soup. Sprinkle with Parmesan cheese and serve with garlic toast.

Note: This soup thickens as it sits; therefore, be prepared to add liquid as necessary. To reheat, add liquid—broth or water.

Tomato Bisque

Makes 27 1-cup servings or 12–14 main-dish servings

6 28-OUNCE CANS ITALIAN-STYLE TOMATOES

1 TEASPOON BAKING SODA

1½ TEASPOONS SUGAR

1 TABLESPOON SALT

BLACK PEPPER TO TASTE

6 (OR MORE) 12-OUNCE CANS EVAPORATED MILK

❧ Drain juice from tomatoes into a large pot. Cut hard ends off tomatoes and cut tomatoes into chunks. Add to the juice in pot. Bring to a boil, breaking up tomatoes as you stir occasionally. Purée ¾ of the large tomato pieces in a food processor, leaving small pieces as they are. Return tomato purée to the pot and add baking soda, sugar, salt, and pepper. Add milk and heat but do not boil. Adjust seasonings to taste.

Trixie's Cannellini Bean Soup

This soup is very popular when served in a small café where people gather to chat, play bridge, and just be with each other on a cold wintry afternoon.

Makes 5 quarts, 20 1-cup servings,
or 10 main-dish servings

1 POUND CANNELLINI BEANS

5 CUPS VEGETABLE STOCK (OR 5 VEGETABLE BOUILLON CUBES)

5 CUPS WATER

3–5 POUNDS HAM (OR HAM HOCK) WITH BONE

½ HEAD CELERY, DICED

1 ONION

½ TABLESPOON CHOPPED GARLIC

3 TABLESPOONS FRESH ITALIAN PARSLEY, CHOPPED

½ CUP UNSALTED BUTTER

¼ TEASPOON BLACK PEPPER

1. Pick over, rinse, and soak beans for 1 hour.

2. Combine stock and water in a large pot and bring to a boil.

3. Rinse ham (hock) to remove salt. Remove meat from bone. Remove fat from meat, in large pieces. Add fat and bone to pot. Add drained beans.

4. In another pan, cook vegetables lightly in butter. Add to soup pot. Add pepper.

5. Cut ham into ½" cubes. Remove all fat. Add cubes to pot and cook until vegetables are tender, beans are cooked, and broth is thick. Remove bone and fat. Skim grease off. This is a meal when served with French bread. Freezes well.

Old-Fashioned Fish Chowder

Serves 25

1 POUND SALT PORK, DICED FINE

2½ POUNDS ONIONS, SLICED

12 POUNDS POTATOES, DICED

WATER TO COVER POTATOES

8 POUNDS FISH FILLETS (HADDOCK, COD, CUSK, OR POLLOCK)

4 TEASPOONS SALT

1 TEASPOON PEPPER

3 QUARTS WHOLE MILK

4 LARGE (12-OUNCE) CANS EVAPORATED MILK

❧ Fry salt pork in bottom of heavy kettle until golden brown. Remove pork and let stand. Add onions and cook until yellowed. Add potatoes and enough water so it comes to top of potatoes. Place fish on top of potatoes and sprinkle with seasonings. Cover and bring to a boil; then cook on low heat until potatoes are soft and fish flakes. Pour in both kinds of milk and heat thoroughly but do not boil. Be very careful not to scorch chowder. Add pork scraps. If you do any stirring at all, be gentle as fish should be in large pieces, not flaked apart and certainly not mushed.

Note: If you wish to have a lower-fat chowder, use olive or canola oil instead of pork scraps. You may miss some flavor, but not too much.

Lobster Chowder

Serves 20

8 POUNDS LOBSTER

BUTTER

¼ POUND SALT PORK*

2 QUARTS POTATOES, PEELED AND DICED

6 QUARTS MILK

½ POUND BUTTER

SALT AND PEPPER TO TASTE

❧ Pick lobster meat out of shell or buy fresh or frozen lobster meat and cut in pieces. (Kitchen scissors work well.) Fry lobster pieces, gently, in butter. Dice salt pork and sauté. Add potatoes, diced, and water enough to cover. Cook until potatoes are done. Remove pork. Then add lobster and milk, butter, and seasonings.

*You may substitute olive oil or canola oil instead of salt pork.

Corn Chowder

Serves 25

1/2 CUP CUBED SALT PORK*

1 CUP CHOPPED ONION

2 1/2 TEASPOONS SALT

1 1/4 TEASPOONS BLACK PEPPER

2 1/2 QUARTS CORN (1/2 WHOLE KERNEL CORN AND 1/2 CREAM-STYLE)

2 1/2 QUARTS POTATOES, PEELED AND CUBED

5 CUPS BOILING WATER

1 3/4 CUPS MILK (1/2 REGULAR MILK AND 1/2 EVAPORATED)

Sauté pork, remove from pan, and pour off at least 1/2 of the grease. Add onion and sauté until limp. Add salt and pepper. Add whole kernel corn, potatoes, and water. Cook until potatoes are soft. Add cream-style corn and milk. Heat and serve. A great dish to serve for an all-day snow activity!

*You may substitute olive or canola oil instead of salt pork.

Salads

Cabbage, Apple, and Spinach Salad

Serves 25

10 CUPS SHREDDED CABBAGE

3 CUPS SHREDDED FRESH SPINACH

10 CUPS CHOPPED APPLES, UNPEELED (CORTLANDS WILL NOT DISCOLOR IF YOU MIX APPLES WITH SALAD DRESSING)

1 SCANT TABLESPOON SALT

$^1/_4$ CUP SUGAR

1$^1/_2$ TEASPOONS VINEGAR

$^1/_2$ TEASPOON PEPPER

1$^1/_4$ CUP SALAD DRESSING, MORE IF NEEDED

✣ Mix well in a large bowl or kettle.

Potato Salad

Makes 24 ¾-cup servings

7 POUNDS POTATOES

SALT TO TASTE

4 CUPS DICED CELERY

1½ CUPS CHOPPED PARSLEY

½ CUP FINELY CHOPPED ONION

1 32-OUNCE JAR MAYONNAISE

2 TABLESPOONS SUGAR

2 TABLESPOONS SALT

1 TEASPOON PEPPER

½ CUP CIDER VINEGAR

Eight hours ahead or day before: Cook scrubbed and unpeeled potatoes in boiling salted water. (Using 2 Dutch ovens and medium heat—30 minutes.) Drain. Peel potatoes and when cool enough, slice or cube. Add celery, parsley, and onion. Mix together the mayonnaise, sugar, salt, pepper, and vinegar. Add to potato mixture and mix very well. Put into large pans, cover, and refrigerate overnight. If serving on lettuce, buy 3 heads or the equivalent.

Cauliflower Layered Salad

Serves 10–12

1 HEAD LETTUCE, TORN

1 HEAD CAULIFLOWER FLORETS

1 RED ONION, SLICED

½ POUND BACON, FRIED AND CRUMBLED

1½ CUPS MAYONNAISE

¼ CUP SUGAR

½ CUP PARMESAN CHEESE

In a large bowl, place torn lettuce. Cover with cauliflower florets. Place onion slices on top, then bacon pieces. Spread mayonnaise over all. Sprinkle sugar over mayonnaise. Sprinkle Parmesan over sugar. Seal and refrigerate 24 hours. Toss just before serving.

Atlantic Lime Mold

Serves 10–12 easily

2 3-OUNCE PACKAGES LIME GELATIN

2 CUPS BOILING WATER

2 CUPS CRUSHED PINEAPPLE, DRAINED (SAVE JUICE)

2 CUPS COTTAGE CHEESE, SMALL CURD

MARASCHINO CHERRIES FOR GARNISH

⌀ Dissolve gelatin in water. Add juice from pineapple; chill until slightly thickened. Beat until frothy. Fold in remaining ingredients. Pour into mold. Chill until set. Garnish with cherries.

Cran-Apple Salad

Serves 12

2 1-POUND CANS WHOLE BERRY CRANBERRY SAUCE

2 CUPS BOILING WATER

2 3-OUNCE PACKAGES STRAWBERRY GELATIN

2 TABLESPOONS LEMON JUICE

$1/2$ TEASPOON SALT

1 CUP MAYONNAISE

2 APPLES, PEELED AND CHOPPED

$1/2$ CUP CHOPPED WALNUTS

⌀ Melt cranberry sauce. Mix in boiling water and gelatin. Stir until gelatin is dissolved. Add lemon juice and salt. Chill until mixture thickens slightly. Add mayonnaise; beat until smooth. Add apples and nuts. Pour into 2-quart mold. Chill overnight.

Cranberry-Apple Salad

Cut into 24 squares for serving

4 3-OUNCE PACKAGES ORANGE-FLAVORED GELATIN

3/4 TEASPOON SALT

1 1/2 QUARTS BOILING WATER

3 1-POUND CANS JELLIED WHOLE CRANBERRY SAUCE

1 1/2 1-POUND, 13-OUNCE CANS CRUSHED PINEAPPLE, UNDRAINED

6 LARGE, CRISP APPLES, DICED

Dissolve gelatin and salt in boiling water. Break up cranberry sauce with fork and stir into hot mixture until smooth. Add undrained pineapple with juice. Chill until mixture begins to thicken; then fold in diced apples. Pour into 24 individual molds or a 9" × 13" × 2" pan. Chill until firm.

Macaroni Fruit Salad

Serves 25

Part I:

2 CUPS UNCOOKED MACARONI

1 20-OUNCE CAN PINEAPPLE CHUNKS, DRAINED

1 BOTTLE MARASCHINO CHERRIES

1 CAN MANDARIN ORANGES, DRAINED

6 RED APPLES, UNPEELED AND CUT INTO CHUNKS

Cook macaroni 7 minutes, drain, and rinse. Add drained pineapple, cherries cut in 1/2, oranges, and apples.

Part II:

4 EGGS

2 CUPS SUGAR

1/2 CUP LEMON JUICE

1 8-OUNCE CONTAINER WHIPPED TOPPING

1/2–1 CUP CHOPPED WALNUTS

In saucepan, put beaten eggs, sugar, and lemon juice. Cook slowly until thick, stirring constantly. Add to the macaroni-fruit mixture and chill. Before serving, mix in whipped topping and nuts.

Glorified Waldorf Salad

24 3/4-cup servings

1 1/3 CUPS MAYONNAISE

1/4 CUP MILK

2 TABLESPOONS LEMON JUICE

1 1/2 TEASPOONS NUTMEG

4 LARGE APPLES, DICED

4 LARGE PEARS, DICED

4 CUPS GRAPES, HALVED

2 CUPS DICED CELERY

2 CUPS COARSELY CHOPPED NUTS

3 LARGE HEADS LETTUCE

❧ In a small bowl, mix mayonnaise, milk, lemon juice, and nutmeg about 1 hour before serving. Mix remaining ingredients. Toss with dressing.

Corn Relish for Salad Bar

Makes 20 side-dish servings

2 CANS WHOLE KERNEL CORN

1 TEASPOON MUSTARD SEED

1 TEASPOON DRY MUSTARD

1/2 TEASPOON SALT

1/4 TEASPOON PEPPER

1/2 CUP VINEGAR

2 TABLESPOONS OIL

1/4 CUP BROWN SUGAR

4 CUPS SHREDDED CABBAGE

1 CUP WATER

1/2 CUP CHOPPED ONION

2 CANS PIMIENTO, DRAINED AND CHOPPED

1/4 CUP GREEN PEPPER, MINCED

❧ Drain corn; to liquid add mustard seed, mustard, salt, pepper, vinegar, oil, and sugar. Add cabbage and 1 cup water. Bring to full boil. Combine corn, onion, pimiento, and pepper. Pour hot mixture over; toss. Refrigerate. This type of relish would probably be served buffet style and people would take less than 1/2 cup; therefore, 1 recipe would go a long way.

Cucumber Salad

Serves 6–8

1 3-OUNCE PACKAGE LIME GELATIN

2 CUPS HOT WATER

2 MEDIUM CUCUMBERS, PEELED AND CHOPPED IN FOOD
    PROCESSOR

1 TABLESPOON VINEGAR

1 TABLESPOON SUGAR

1/2 CUP SALAD DRESSING

❧ Dissolve gelatin in 2 cups hot water. Add chopped cucumbers, vinegar, sugar, and salad dressing. Chill overnight.

Mary's Salad

Serves 6

3/4 CUP VINEGAR

1/2 CUP COOKING OIL

1 TEASPOON SALT

1 CUP SUGAR

1 CAN FRENCH-STYLE CUT GREEN BEANS

1 CAN SMALL PEAS

1 CUP DICED CELERY

1 CUP THINLY SLICED ONION, SEPARATED INTO RINGS

1/2 CUP DICED GREEN PEPPER

1 4-OUNCE JAR CHOPPED PIMIENTO

❧ Put vinegar, oil, salt, and sugar in a large mixing bowl and stir until sugar is dissolved. Add remaining ingredients and stir gently. Place in a covered container in refrigerator overnight. Before serving, drain, but reserve liquid for salad dressing. Serve on lettuce.

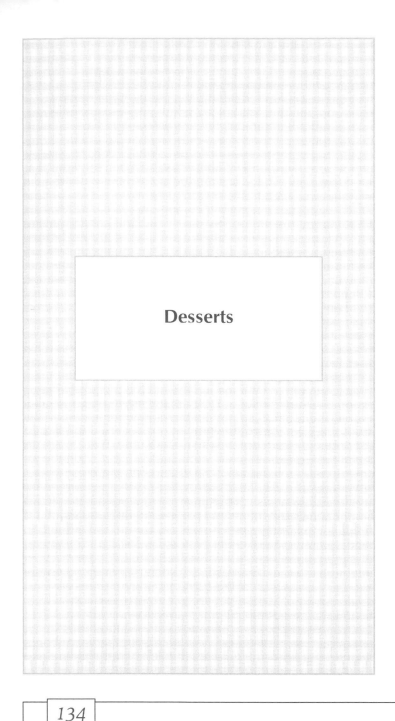

Desserts

Blond Brownies

Makes 24 2" squares

$^2/_3$ CUP BUTTER OR MARGARINE

$2^1/_2$ CUPS BROWN SUGAR

3 EGGS

$2^1/_4$ CUPS FLOUR

2 TEASPOONS BAKING POWDER

1 TEASPOON SALT

$^1/_2$ CUP WALNUTS, CHOPPED (OPTIONAL)

1 TEASPOON VANILLA

❧ Cream together butter or margarine and brown sugar. Add eggs, 1 at a time, beating after each addition. Combine flour, baking powder, and salt and add to butter mixture. Stir in walnuts and vanilla. Bake in a greased 9" × 13" × 2" baking pan. These were often served as the dessert for turkey dinners in the summer.

Note: These brownies may be served with vanilla ice cream on top. For 25 servings of ice cream, you will need approximately $4^1/_2$ half-gallons of ice cream.

Gingerbread

Makes 24 2" squares

1 CUP BOILING WATER
1 CUP SHORTENING
1 CUP BROWN SUGAR
1 CUP LIGHT MOLASSES
2 EGGS, BEATEN
3 CUPS FLOUR
1 TEASPOON SALT
1 TEASPOON BAKING POWDER
1 TEASPOON BAKING SODA
1½ TEASPOONS GINGER
1½ TEASPOONS CINNAMON

❧ Pour water over the shortening; then add sugar, molasses, and eggs. Beat well. Sift the flour, salt, baking powder, baking soda, ginger, and cinnamon together and add to the molasses mixture. Beat until smooth. Bake in a waxed-paper-lined 9" × 13" pan in 350° oven for about 35 minutes. Top with whipped cream or ice cream.

Refrigerator Cheese Dessert

Serves 25

2 CUPS GRAHAM CRACKER CRUMBS
½ CUP CONFECTIONERS' SUGAR, SIFTED
½ CUP BUTTER OR MARGARINE, SOFTENED
6 OUNCES LEMON GELATIN
2 CUPS BOILING WATER
12 OUNCES CREAM CHEESE
2 CUPS SUGAR
2 TABLESPOONS VANILLA
2 CANS EVAPORATED MILK (CHILLED)

❧ For crust, mix crumbs, sugar, and butter thoroughly. Line a 12" × 20" baking pan with crumb mixture, saving ¼ cup crumbs for topping. Dissolve gelatin in boiling water. Chill mixture until it thickens. Beat cream cheese, sugar, and vanilla together. Whip evaporated milk in cold bowl until stiff. Stir whipped evaporated milk and gelatin into cream cheese mixture. Beat until creamy. Pour into pan lined with crumb mixture. Top with remaining crumb mixture. Chill until set.

Grape-Nut Custard

Serves 25

3 CUPS SUGAR	2 TEASPOONS VANILLA
2¼ CUPS GRAPE-NUTS	½ TEASPOON SALT
3 QUARTS MILK	12 EGGS, BEATEN

 Mix together sugar and Grape-Nuts and set aside. Mix last 4 ingredients; then add the sugar and Grape-Nuts. Pour into 12" × 20" baking pan. Bake at 350° for about 45 minutes.

Indian Pudding

Serves 12

3 CUPS CORNFLAKES

½ CUP MOLASSES

2 TABLESPOONS SUGAR

DASH OF SALT

½ TEASPOON GINGER

1 TEASPOON CINNAMON

1 QUART MILK

PIECE OF BUTTER

 Do not crush cornflakes before measuring. Mix all ingredients well. Pour into 9" × 13" pan. Bake 1 hour at 350°. Stir occasionally. Serve with dab of vanilla ice cream.

Indian Pearl Pudding

Serves 20

4 OUNCES LARGE PEARL TAPIOCA

½ CUP CORNMEAL

2 CUPS SCALDED MILK

¼ CUP BUTTER OR MARGARINE

1½ CUPS MOLASSES

1 CUP SUGAR

1 TEASPOON SALT

1½ TEASPOONS CINNAMON

½ TEASPOON GINGER

1 TABLESPOON VANILLA

4 EGGS, BEATEN

1¼ QUARTS MILK

1 CUP COLD MILK

 Soak the 4 ounces of tapioca in water overnight. (Cover generously with water.) Next day, dissolve cornmeal in scalded milk. Remove from stove and add butter, molasses, sugar, salt, cinnamon, ginger, vanilla, eggs, milk, and the drained tapioca. Bake at 300° for 1 hour, and then add 1 cup cold milk and stir. Bake 2 more hours at 200° or until done.

Brownie Pudding

Serves 24–36

2 CUPS FLOUR

1 1/2 CUPS SUGAR

4 TABLESPOONS COCOA

4 TEASPOONS BAKING POWDER

4 TEASPOONS SALT

4 TABLESPOONS BUTTER

1 CUP MILK

1 TEASPOON VANILLA

3/4 CUP CHOPPED NUTS

1 1/2 CUPS BROWN SUGAR

1/2 CUP COCOA

6 1/2 CUPS BOILING WATER

Mix together the flour, sugar, 4 tablespoons cocoa, baking powder, salt, butter, milk, vanilla, and nuts. Spread in bottom of 18" × 13" pan. It will be a thin coating. Mix together the brown sugar, 1/2 cup cocoa, and boiling water. Carefully pour over unbaked brownie mixture. Bake at 350° for 40–45 minutes. Very good!

Dump Cake

Makes 24 2" squares

1 CAN CHERRY PIE FILLING

1 20-OUNCE CAN CRUSHED PINEAPPLE, UNDRAINED

1 PACKAGE YELLOW CAKE MIX, DRY

1 CUP MELTED BUTTER

1 CUP SHREDDED COCONUT

1 CUP CHOPPED NUTS

Preheat oven to 350°. Put ingredients in a 9" × 13" pan in the same order as listed. Do *not* stir. Bake for 1 hour at 350°. May be served with whipped cream.

Maple Walnut Chiffon Cake

Serves 16–18

Step I:
Measure and mix in bowl:
2 CUPS SIFTED FLOUR
1½ CUPS SUGAR
3 TEASPOONS BAKING POWDER
1 TEASPOON SALT

Make a well and add in order:
½ CUP SALAD OIL
7 UNBEATEN EGG YOLKS
¾ CUP COLD WATER
2 TEASPOONS MAPLE FLAVORING

Beat with spoon until smooth.

Step II:
Measure into a large bowl:
1 CUP EGG WHITES (7 OR 8)
½ TEASPOON CREAM OF TARTAR

With electric mixer, beat whites until they form very stiff peaks and are very dry.

Step III:
Pour egg yolk mixture over whites, also:
1 CUP CHOPPED WALNUTS

❧ Gently fold until blended. Pour into large greased tube pan. Bake at 325° for 55 minutes. Turn heat up to 350° for 10 to 15 additional minutes. When done, invert pan until cold. Remove cake by cutting around cake with a large sharp knife.

Timesaver: Beat egg whites before yolks so you don't have to rinse beaters.

Grace's Pumpkin Bread

Serves 20–25

3$\frac{1}{2}$ CUPS FLOUR

1$\frac{1}{2}$ TEASPOONS SALT

2 TEASPOONS BAKING SODA

1 TEASPOON BAKING POWDER

1 TEASPOON NUTMEG

1 TEASPOON CINNAMON

3 CUPS SUGAR

❧ Mix thoroughly and make a well in the middle. Add the following to the well:

1 16-OUNCE CAN PUMPKIN

1 CUP COOKING OIL

$\frac{2}{3}$ CUP WATER

4 EGGS

1 CUP NUTS

❧ Mix together and divide into 4 greased 1-pound coffee tins. Bake at 350° for 1 hour. You may also use various-sized loaf pans.

Browned Butter Icing

1$\frac{1}{2}$ cups

$\frac{1}{3}$ CUP BUTTER

3 CUPS CONFECTIONERS' SUGAR

1$\frac{1}{2}$ TEASPOONS COOKING OIL

3 TABLESPOONS CREAM

2 TEASPOONS VANILLA

1$\frac{1}{2}$ TABLESPOONS HOT WATER

❧ Melt butter then keep over low heat until golden brown. Blend in sugar, cooking oil, cream, and vanilla. Stir in hot water. Stir vigorously until cool enough to spread. (If it becomes too thick to spread, warm slightly over hot water.)

To end this chapter on fund-raising, let me suggest a fun and festive fund-raiser/rite of summer: The Strawberry Festival. Especially for those of us who live in the cold country, the warm days of summer and the taste of freshly picked strawberries are especially wonderful. Following is a recipe for Biscuit Shortcakes.

Biscuit Shortcakes

Makes 18 biscuits

2 CUPS SIFTED FLOUR

3 TEASPOONS BAKING POWDER

2 TABLESPOONS SUGAR

1 TEASPOON SALT

6 TABLESPOONS BUTTER OR MARGARINE

1 EGG

ABOUT $2/3$–$3/4$ CUP MILK

❧ Sift together dry ingredients. Using a pastry blender or 2 knives, cut in butter or margarine. Beat egg slightly, combine with milk, and add to dry ingredients. Mix lightly with a fork. Toss dough onto a lightly floured board. Knead gently for about $1/2$ a minute. Roll or pat dough to $1/2$" thick. Cut with floured biscuit cutter. Bake on an ungreased or parchment paper–lined cookie sheet in a 450° oven for 12–15 minutes. Serve while hot, if possible.

Serving the shortcakes: Split the hot shortcakes. Spoon a generous amount of crushed, sugared strawberries over the bottom shortcake. Add the top and spoon more strawberries over. Top with whipped cream and serve in a soup bowl! Worth having struggled through the long winter for!!

Note: One package (16 ounces) frozen strawberries or 1 quart of fresh berries is enough for about 16 biscuits. Crush the fresh berries and add $1/2$–1 cup of sugar. To 1 cup whipping cream, add 1 tablespoon sugar and 1 teaspoon vanilla.

Chapter Three

The Church Entertains and Caters

From time to time the opportunity comes for a church to cater a special event, or to entertain for some special occasion. Sometimes these are also fund-raising opportunities, but in any case they provide a means for helping to bring people together and to build community among the participants.

There will be some crossover between this chapter and the chapter on fund-raising, and it is suggested that you consult "Fund-Raising" for tips on the planning process. This chapter centers on more intimate events than the usual public fund-raising activities. Examples are: a wedding reception, a rehearsal dinner, a luncheon for a community group, a special after-worship reception, a dinner for new church members or a class of confirmands, and gatherings following a funeral or memorial service.

White table paper may be fine for an informal occasion, while other events may call for white cloth tablecloths. Centerpieces are always in order, possibly in keeping with the season as well as the event. Arranging the napkins, utensils, and chinaware carefully reinforces that, even if the activity is simple, it nonetheless is important. Always keep in mind that "you feast first with your eyes."

If your ladies fellowship meets at the church for a meal or refreshments, set an attractive table. If possible, use a cloth tablecloth. The addition of flowers, arrangements of fruit, or a plant along with candles adds an even finer touch. The flowers can be ordered from the florist, but just as appropriate are garden flowers, pine or spruce, a few springs of bittersweet or holly in season. Create your own centerpiece.

People need those special times when an attractive table is set and a mood of friendship and fellowship permeates the room. Why not let the regular social functions at the church provide such opportunities? The speaker, program, or devotion should naturally be the most important nourishment of the day, but there is nourishment as well in tastefully done entertaining within the church.

Catering a Wedding Reception

Note: The "family" will be referred to in the following section. However, if the bride or bridal couple is making the arrangements, substitute in your mind wherever "family" appears.

Occasionally the church is asked to cater a wedding reception. Churches can provide a wonderful reception for people at a very reasonable cost to the family while realizing an acceptable profit for the treasury. Weddings are such fun, too!

One or two people from the church should meet with the family who is requesting the catering service as soon as possible. Determine first if what is being asked for is within your capabilities. When you have settled on the menu (and don't forget to determine exactly who will be providing the wedding cake), figure out what the cost will be. As with church fund-raising suppers, do not rely on memory. Plan everything out on paper. Determine what all of your needs will be, including any items that may need to be rented.

Once this chore has been completed, you can give the family a price per plate. Decide with the family on a date by which they will give you a close approximate count on how many will be attending the reception. This figure will be the minimum number for which the family will be responsible. Always be ready to serve a few more people if necessary. Don't be rigid. Be as accommodating as possible. Give the kind of warm family-type service that cannot possibly be gotten from a strictly commercial arrangement.

Further discuss with the family the colors the bride has chosen, so that those colors may be carried out in your napkins, flowers, candles, et cetera.

Churches are in a fine position to cater small rehearsal dinners or perhaps birthday or anniversary occasions. Always remember that it is a joy and a privilege to be a part of a special celebration for someone in your church or community.

Supporting Those in Need

Through the generations people have joined hands in times of sadness. Even more so today the church should be ready to help bereaved families and friends. It is a time in which the church family can often make a major contribution to the lives of others.

The church is an appropriate place for people to gather following a service. In earlier years, it may have been the home, but space at home is increasingly an issue as people move into condominiums or smaller homes or apartments. The church has plenty of space for people, coats (in winter), cars, et cetera. As family and friends gather from near and far, the family is relieved of the work and responsibility of hosting a gathering. Gatherings are appropriate and important so people can visit together with the unspoken message that life goes on.

The church needs to be ready with very little notice. It is a good idea, if possible, to have a small standing committee that is responsible for the preparation and delivery of a gathering. A "field office" should be kept well stocked at the church with the basic supplies, such as white napkins, assorted sizes of white paper lace doilies, candles, and easy-care white cloth tablecloths. Having these basic supplies on hand cuts down on the running around when time is short.

A procedure that works well is to have the clergyperson let the family know that there is a small group at the church willing to put a gathering together. Someone from the committee can then call or visit to make the final arrangements. It is difficult to know how many people to expect, but when you know about how many relatives are expected, you can make an educated guess. It usually comes out pretty close when you know your community well.

Although similar service should be provided to each family, each situation is different and you need to tailor your services to fit the family's needs. Tell each family what the service includes. If they have special requests that are within your capabilities, try to accommodate them.

Set a dignified serving table with a white tablecloth and an understated arrangement. The family can provide the centerpiece, but often a single rose with greenery or baby's breath is sufficient. White candles burning look lovely and serene. The committee can provide the candles and the rose. At the end of the gathering, the rose can be given to the nearest relative to take home. I have always been gratified at how lovingly and enthusiastically the rose has been received.

Assorted sweets along with fruit and cheese are the usual fare. If the family needs more than that, small finger rolls can be provided as well. Usually the simple fare is sufficient. Ample amounts of coffee and tea should be available. Also punch or cider, in season, should be served.

When you have a thumbnail idea of how many may attend, figure out the amount of baked goods, fruit, and cheese that will be needed. You want to be sure that there is a nice variety of sweets, and not too many of any one item. Plan to offer three to four pieces of dessert, fruit, and cheese per person, and do the math from there. A hint: Usually when you ask people to bake for these occasions, they bring you a "batch" of squares or cookies. That is a rather nebulous amount! Be specific—suggest two dozen (or three, as you think necessary). This will help assure variety and avoid mountains of food in the kitchen. It also allows the person doing the baking to keep something for their family or to freeze for another time.

It is always good to ask for assistance from people who may know the bereaved as a neighbor or a special friend. These people may be willing to bake as well as serve. If using a silver service, these are the people to ask to pour coffee and tea or dip punch. They will consider it an honor to help in this way.

In my experience, a fee has not been set for this service. However, donations from the family are gratefully accepted so that the assistance may continue and the expenses are met. People are so grateful for this help that they are usually very generous in making a donation. There may be circumstances where you do not wish to accept a donation.

It is important to remember that every situation is different. Remember, as well, the whole purpose of this gathering is to give the family an opportunity to have a few minutes with those who care about them. In catering the gathering, a church provides a most important service in a loving and supportive way. ❧

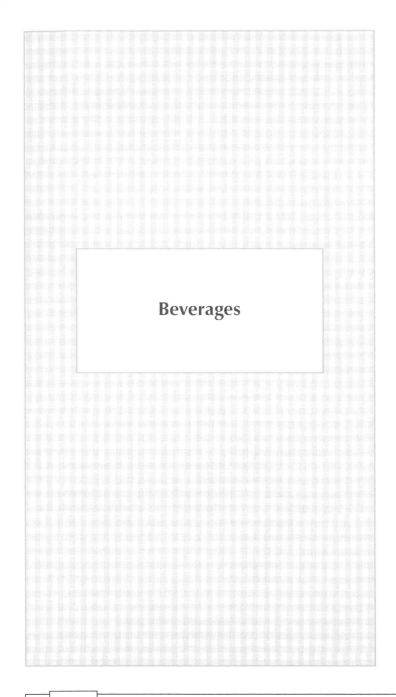

Beverages

Lemon-Strawberry Punch

32 punch-cup servings

1 16-OUNCE PACKAGE FROZEN STRAWBERRIES, THAWED

3 6-OUNCE CANS FROZEN LEMONADE, PARTIALLY THAWED

1/2 CUP SUGAR (OPTIONAL)

2 QUARTS ICE WATER

1 QUART GINGER ALE, CHILLED

Purée strawberries in blender. Add lemonade concentrate and sugar. Blend to mix. Let stand at least 30 minutes. At serving time pour over ice in punch bowl and add water and ginger ale. Strawberry-lemonade base may be made the day ahead or the morning of the event.

Zesty Fruit Punch

Serves 20

2 32-ounce bottles ginger ale, chilled

6 cups pineapple-orange juice, chilled or 3 cups
    pineapple juice and 3 cups orange juice

1 6-ounce can frozen lemonade concentrate, thawed

1 large fresh orange, thinly sliced

1 fresh lime, thinly sliced

Combine ingredients in a large punch bowl with ice ring. May also be served chilled from 2 large pitchers.

Easy Refreshing Punch

About 16 servings

1 64-ounce bottle cranberry juice or cranberry-
    raspberry juice cocktail

1 32-ounce bottle fruit-flavored seltzer

1 or more ice molds depending on weather and length
    of gathering.

Have all ingredients well chilled. Mix in punch bowl and serve. Have plenty MIK (More in Kitchen).

Mulled Cider Punch

Makes 25 1/2-cup servings

2 quarts cider

1/4 cup brown sugar, packed

1 1/2 teaspoons whole cloves

1 1/2 quarts cranberry juice

4 3" cinnamon sticks

1 lemon, thinly sliced

Additional thinly sliced lemon for punch-cup garnish

Combine all ingredients in large kettle. Heat to boiling, reduce heat, and simmer 15–20 minutes. Remove cinnamon, cloves, and lemon. Float fresh lemon slice in each cup.

Sherbet Punch

Makes 25 punch-cup servings

1 quart pineapple juice

1 can frozen orange juice with enough water to make
    1 quart

1/4 cup lemon juice

1 quart ginger ale

1 quart pineapple sherbet

1 quart orange sherbet

Mix all together.

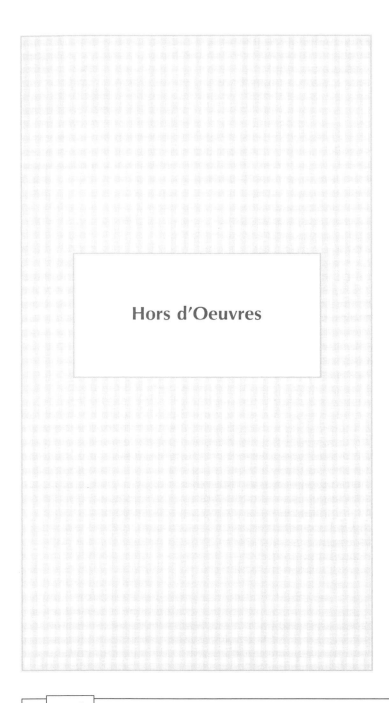

Hors d'Oeuvres

Crab Hors d'Oeuvres

Makes 48 bites

1 5-OUNCE JAR SHARP PROCESSED CHEESE SPREAD

1/2 TEASPOON SEASONED SALT

1/4 TEASPOON GARLIC POWDER

1 STICK BUTTER OR MARGARINE

1 TABLESPOON MAYONNAISE

1 6-OUNCE CAN CRABMEAT

1 PACKAGE OF 6 ENGLISH MUFFINS

◣ Mix first 5 ingredients. Fold in crabmeat. Split the English muffins and place on a cookie sheet. Spread the mixture on each of the 12 halves. Broil until cheese is melted and they are bubbly and hot. Remove from oven and cut each muffin into 8 wedges.

Note: These may be made ahead of time and frozen. Simply take out of wrapper, put on cookie sheet, and broil. Do not thaw first.

Veggie Pizza

About 150 1" squares (if using a 10" × 15" baking sheet)

2 TUBES OF CRESCENT ROLLS

Topping:

2 8-OUNCE PACKAGES CREAM CHEESE, SOFTENED

1 TEASPOON DRIED DILL WEED

1/4 TEASPOON GARLIC SALT

3/4 CUP MAYONNAISE

1/4 CUP MILK

Veggies:

Chop veggies by hand. A food processor makes them too mushy.

1/4 CUP CHOPPED ONION

1 CUP FINELY CHOPPED CAULIFLOWER

1 CUP FINELY CHOPPED GREEN PEPPER

1 CUP FINELY CHOPPED BROCCOLI

1 CUP FINELY CHOPPED GRATED CARROTS

1 CUP CHOPPED BLACK OLIVES

On 1 large or 2 small cookie sheets (with a lip and not dark), flatten crescent rolls and pinch together to eliminate perforations. Bake for 8–10 minutes at 375° until golden. Let cool.

Topping: Blend together cream cheese, dill weed, garlic salt, mayonnaise, and milk. Spread topping on crust. Sprinkle chopped veggies on top, patting the veggies gently into the cheese mixture. Refrigerate overnight. Cut into small squares and serve chilled.

Party Cheese Ball

Makes 2¼ pounds

2 8-OUNCE PACKAGES CREAM CHEESE

1/4 POUND BLUE CHEESE

1/2 POUND EXTRA SHARP CHEDDAR CHEESE, GRATED

1 TABLESPOON WORCESTERSHIRE SAUCE

1/2 TEASPOON SALT

1/2 TEASPOON GARLIC POWDER

1/2 TEASPOON ONION POWDER

1 CUP CHOPPED WALNUTS

Mix together cheeses until well blended. Add remaining ingredients, reserving 1/2 cup walnuts. Chill; shape into 2 small balls or 1 large one. Roll in reserved 1/2 cup walnuts. Chill thoroughly. Serve with crackers and/or fresh fruit.

Taco Dip

This is a traditional Super Bowl dip at our house.

Serves 10

12 OUNCES CREAM CHEESE, SOFTENED

1/2 CUP DAIRY SOUR CREAM

2 TEASPOONS CHILI POWDER

1 1/2 TEASPOONS GROUND CUMIN

1/8 TEASPOON GROUND RED PEPPER

1/2 CUP SALSA (MILD OR WILD, SUIT YOUR TASTE)

SHREDDED LETTUCE OR LETTUCE LEAVES

1 CUP (4 OUNCES) SHREDDED CHEDDAR CHEESE

1 CUP (4 OUNCES) SHREDDED MONTEREY JACK CHEESE

1/2 CUP DICED PLUM TOMATOES

1/3 CUP SLICED GREEN ONIONS

1 SMALL CAN SLICED BLACK OLIVES, DRAINED

1/4 CUP PIMIENTO-STUFFED GREEN OLIVES

TORTILLA CHIPS AND BLUE CORN CHIPS

ક Combine cream cheese, sour cream, chili powder, cumin, and red pepper in large bowl; mix until well blended. Stir in salsa. Cover a 10" quiche dish or platter with lettuce and spread dip mixture over. Garnish with cheeses, tomatoes, green onions, and olives. Serve with chips. A colorful presentation!

Dill Dip

Makes 2 1/2 cups

2 TEASPOONS ONION FLAKES

1 TEASPOON DRIED DILL WEED

2 TEASPOONS GARLIC SALT

2 TEASPOONS PARSLEY FLAKES

1 1/2 CUPS SOUR CREAM

1 CUP SALAD DRESSING OR MAYONNAISE

ક Blend all ingredients together well. Serve as dip for raw vegetables.

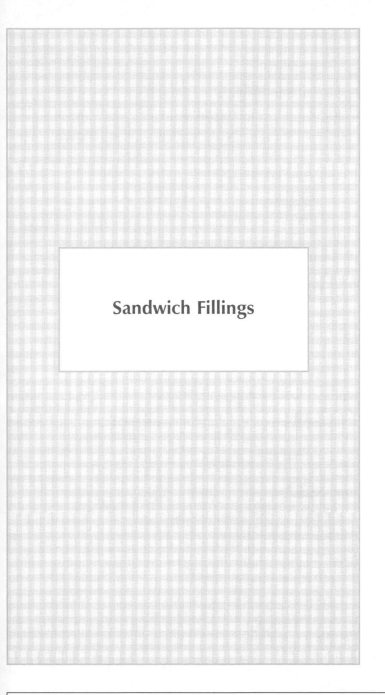

Sandwich Fillings

Zion's Hill Delights

Makes 3 whole sandwiches or 12 canapés

1 CUP DICED COOKED CHICKEN (ABOUT 1 WHOLE BREAST)
$^1/_2$ CUP FINELY CHOPPED DATES (NOT PRECUT)
$^1/_4$ CUP CHOPPED HAZELNUTS (FILBERTS)
$^1/_4$ CUP CRUMBLED CRISP BACON (ABOUT 4 STRIPS)
$^1/_2$ CUP MAYONNAISE
SALT TO TASTE
10 THIN SLICES WHITE BREAD, BUTTERED

1. Chicken should be diced in $^1/_4$" cubes. If hazelnuts have their skins, place in a 350° oven for 10–15 minutes, until skins split. When cool, rub skins off.

2. Combine all ingredients, except bread, adding salt if necessary. Spread on buttered bread slices; trim crusts. Cut into quarters for canapés, in halves for teatime, or top with another slice of bread, trim crusts, and cut in $^1/_2$ for lunch. May be doubled.

Sandwich Fillings for 25

Chicken or Turkey Salad

5 CUPS CHICKEN OR TURKEY CHOPPED FINE

$1^1/2$ CUPS CELERY, CHOPPED FINE

1 CUP SWEET PICKLE, CHOPPED FINE

$1^1/2$ CUPS MAYONNAISE

$1^1/2$ TABLESPOONS LEMON JUICE

2 TEASPOONS SALT

❧ Combine all ingredients and mix thoroughly.

Corned Beef Sandwiches

3 POUNDS CANNED CORNED BEEF, CHOPPED OR GROUND IN FOOD PROCESSOR

1 DOZEN HARD-BOILED EGGS, GRATED

1 CUP MINCED ONION

2 CUPS MAYONNAISE

$1/2$ TEASPOON DRY MUSTARD OR 1 TABLESPOON REGULAR MUSTARD

❧ Combine meat, eggs, and onion. Add mayonnaise and mustard.

Egg Salad Sandwiches

4 DOZEN HARD-BOILED EGGS

2 4-OUNCE JARS PIMIENTOS, CHOPPED OR 1 10-OUNCE JAR SALAD OLIVES

1 CUP SWEET RELISH

2 CUPS MAYONNAISE OR $1^1/2$ CUPS PLUS 2 TABLESPOONS PREPARED MUSTARD

❧ Combine all ingredients.

Ham Salad

3 POUNDS CHOPPED COOKED HAM

1 DOZEN HARD-BOILED EGGS, CHOPPED OR GRATED

$1^1/2$ CUPS CHOPPED CELERY

1 CUP SWEET PICKLE RELISH

2 TABLESPOONS PREPARED MUSTARD

2 CUPS MAYONNAISE

❧ Combine all ingredients; mix well.

Tuna Salad

4 13-OUNCE CANS TUNA, DRAINED

2 CUPS CHOPPED CELERY

1 CUP RELISH OR CHOPPED SWEET PICKLES

2 TABLESPOONS LEMON JUICE

$1^1/2$ CUPS MAYONNAISE

❧ Mix together well.

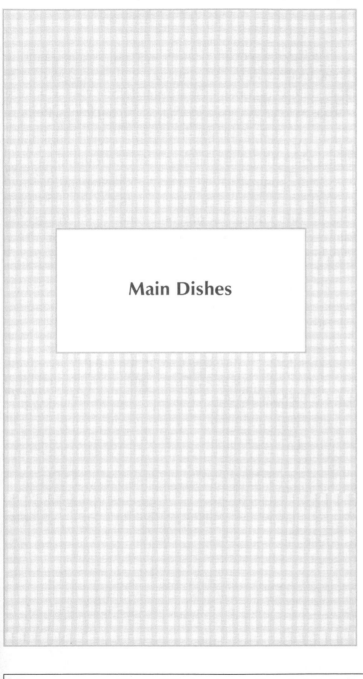

Main Dishes

Secrets of the Sea

Serves 6

3 SLICED HARD-COOKED EGGS

1 CAN EACH WHITE TUNA, SHRIMP, CRABMEAT, AND LOBSTER
   (OTHER FISH MAY BE SUBSTITUTED FOR LOBSTER AS LONG
   AS QUANTITY REMAINS THE SAME)

1 CUP BREAD CUBES

1 4-OUNCE CAN MUSHROOMS, DRAINED

2 CUPS MEDIUM WHITE SAUCE

1/2 CUP BUTTER OR MARGARINE, MELTED

1/4 POUND CHEDDAR CHEESE, GRATED

BREADCRUMBS

In a buttered casserole, place ingredients in order given with dabs of white sauce on each layer. Top with cheese and breadcrumbs that have been sautéed in butter. Bake at 350° for 45 minutes. Mix ahead to combine flavors.

Seafood au Gratin

Serves 4–6

1/2 POUND SCALLOPS

1/2 POUND SKINLESS FISH FILLETS, SUCH AS HADDOCK, COD,
    OR CUSK

1/2 POUND CRABMEAT OR SHELLED SHRIMP

1/2 CUP WATER

1/4 CUP BUTTER OR MARGARINE

2 TEASPOONS FINELY CHOPPED ONION

5 TABLESPOONS FLOUR

1/2 TEASPOON SALT

1/8 TEASPOON PEPPER

1 1/2 CUPS HALF-AND-HALF OR MILK PLUS 1/2 CUP RESERVED
    SEAFOOD LIQUID

1 CUP SHREDDED CHEDDAR CHEESE

1 TABLESPOON SHERRY, OPTIONAL

1/4 CUP FINE BUTTER CRACKER CRUMBS

1 TABLESPOON BUTTER OR MARGARINE, MELTED

1. In a large saucepan, simmer scallops, fish, and crab or shrimp together in 1/2 cup water just until sheen goes off fish. Drain, reserving cooking liquid. Let seafood cool. Cut large scallops in 1/2 across grain and flake fish into chunks. Remove bits of shell from crabmeat. Set aside.

2. In same saucepan, melt 1/4 cup butter. Add onion; cook and stir in flour, salt, and pepper. Add half-and-half and seafood liquid; cook and stir until mixture is thick and smooth. Add cheese, stirring until melted. Stir in scallops, fish, crabmeat, and, if desired, sherry. Turn mixture into a buttered 1 1/2-quart casserole.

3. Combine cracker crumbs with melted butter. Sprinkle evenly over top of casserole. Bake in a 350° oven for 20–25 minutes or until hot and bubbly.

Note: This rather festive dish may be made a day ahead and baked near serving time. Easily multiplied. Served at a catered birthday party.

Seafood Casserole

Serves 12 generously

4 1/2 CUPS LOBSTER MEAT, CUT UP, WITH TAMALE, OR 1 CAN
    SHRIMP, 1/4 POUND SCALLOPS, 3/4 POUND COOKED
    HADDOCK, 1/2 POUND SEA LEGS CRAB, AND 1 6-OUNCE
    CAN CRABMEAT OR 6–8 OUNCES FRESH CRAB

1 1/2 CUPS SOFT BREADCRUMBS

3 CUPS MILK (USING PART EVAPORATED MILK IS GOOD)

3 EGGS, WELL BEATEN

6 TABLESPOONS BUTTER, MELTED

3 TABLESPOONS LEMON JUICE

A FEW DROPS ONION JUICE

1 1/2 TEASPOONS SALT

PEPPER TO TASTE

BUTTERED CRUMBS FOR TOPPING (THESE IN ADDITION TO
    ABOVE CRUMBS)

🥄 Mix all ingredients except buttered crumbs in a large bowl in order given, stirring well after each addition. Pour into a large casserole and cover with buttered crumbs. Bake at 350° for 30 minutes. Good if made ahead and flavors allowed to blend.

Shrimp and Artichoke Casserole

Serves 8

2 15-OUNCE CANS, OR 2 10-OUNCE PACKAGES FROZEN
    ARTICHOKE HEARTS

1 1/2 POUNDS COOKED SHRIMP

1 POUND FRESH MUSHROOMS, SLICED

3/4 CUP UNSALTED BUTTER

1/2 CUP FLOUR

2 CUPS HEAVY CREAM

1 CUP MILK

SALT AND PEPPER TO TASTE

1 TABLESPOON WORCESTERSHIRE SAUCE

1/2 CUP SHERRY

GRATED PARMESAN CHEESE

PAPRIKA

🥄 Butter a 10" casserole. Drain artichoke hearts (if using frozen artichokes, cook and drain before layering in bottom of casserole) and layer in bottom of casserole. Cover with shrimp. Sauté mushrooms in 1/4 cup butter and add to casserole. Melt remaining 1/2 cup butter. Add flour 1 tablespoon at a time. Slowly add cream and milk. Season with salt and pepper, Worcestershire sauce, and sherry. Pour over ingredients in casserole. Grate Parmesan cheese on top and sprinkle with paprika. Bake 20–25 minutes in 350° oven.

Company Eggs

One real advantage of this recipe is that the casserole is assembled the day before it is needed, so all the mess is cleaned up! This makes a wonderful Easter breakfast. Our family uses it for Christmas morning. The only work is to heat the oven!

Serves 10

8 SLICES OF BREAD, CUBED

$2/3$ STICK OF SHARP CHEDDAR CHEESE, SHREDDED
(1 10-OUNCE BLOCK IS FINE)

8 EGGS

4 CUPS MILK

$1/2$ TEASPOON DRY MUSTARD

1 TEASPOON SALT

PEPPER

1. Butter a 9" × 9" pan. Layer cubed bread in bottom. Cover with cheese. Combine the remaining ingredients. Pour egg mixture over cheese. Cover and refrigerate overnight.

2. In the morning, heat oven to 325° and bake about 1 hour. You may crumble cooked bacon or vegetables over top of egg/cheese mixture. If using vegetables, allow more baking time. The vegetables seem to be watery and require more baking time. Making $1/2$ recipes easily serves 12–15. Fresh fruit served in punch cups is a very nice accompaniment to the eggs.

Brunch Strata

Serves 8 generously

8 SLICES AIRY FRESH BREAD, CUBED

1 POUND BULK SAUSAGE, COOKED, CHOPPED, AND DRAINED

2 CUPS GRATED CHEDDAR CHEESE

4 EGGS

$2^{1}/2$ CUPS MILK

$3/4$ TEASPOON DRY MUSTARD

1 CAN CREAM OF MUSHROOM OR CELERY SOUP

$1/2$ CUP MILK

1. Place bread cubes on bottom of greased 9" × 13" pan or large round casserole. Top with sausage and sprinkle with cheese. Mix eggs, milk, and mustard and pour over cheese. Cover and refrigerate overnight.

2. Next day heat oven to 300°. Mix soup and $1/2$ cup milk. Spread over top of casserole and bake for $1^{1}/2$ hours or until firm, bubbly, and golden on top. Serve with muffins and salad.

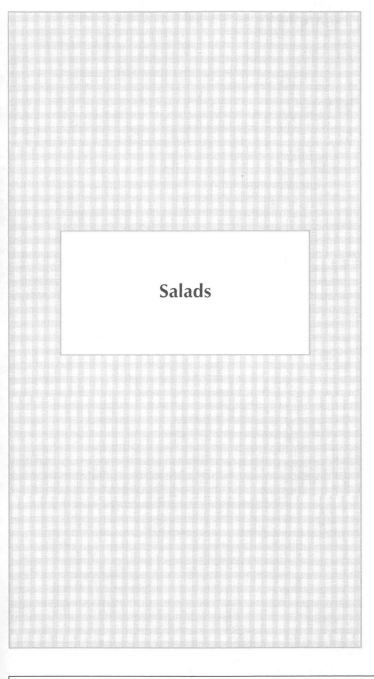

Salads

Chutney Turkey Salad

Serves 8–10

1 CUP MAYONNAISE

1/4–1/2 CUP MANGO CHUTNEY, CHOPPED

1 TEASPOON CURRY POWDER

2 TEASPOONS GRATED LIME ZEST

1/4 CUP FRESH LIME JUICE

1/2 TEASPOON SALT

4 CUPS DICED COOKED TURKEY BREAST

2 8-OUNCE CANS PINEAPPLE CHUNKS

1/2 CUP THINLY SLICED GREEN ONIONS

1/2 CUP SLIVERED ALMONDS, TOASTED

LETTUCE

❧ Mix well first 6 ingredients. Combine the next 3 ingredients. Pour first mixture over and top with almonds. Serve on lettuce leaves.

Strawberry Cream Squares

Serves 20–24

4 3-OUNCE PACKAGES STRAWBERRY GELATIN
4 CUPS BOILING WATER
4 10-OUNCE PACKAGES FROZEN STRAWBERRIES, THAWED
4 LARGE, FINELY DICED BANANAS
2 CUPS SOUR CREAM

❧ Dissolve the strawberry gelatin in boiling water. Add the remainder of ingredients except the sour cream. Pour 1/2 mixture into 9" × 13" dish. Chill firmly. Spread sour cream over and top with remaining mixture. Chill until firm. While first 1/2 of gelatin mixture is chilling, keep the remainder of the mixture at room temperature so that it does not firm up.

Asheville Salad

Serves 8

1 CUP CONDENSED TOMATO SOUP
3 3-OUNCE PACKAGES CREAM CHEESE
2 TABLESPOONS GELATIN
1/2 CUP COLD WATER
1 CUP MAYONNAISE
1 1/2 CUPS CHOPPED CELERY
GREEN PEPPER, ONION, AND SLICED GREEN OLIVES TO TASTE

❧ Bring soup to a boil. Add cheese and stir until smooth. Add gelatin softened in cold water. When partly cool, add mayonnaise and finely chopped veggies. Refrigerate in an oiled mold. Cut in squares.

Pineapple Lime Salad

Serves 8

16 LARGE MARSHMALLOWS
1 CUP MILK
1 SMALL PACKAGE LIME GELATIN
2 3-OUNCE PACKAGES CREAM CHEESE
1 20-OUNCE CAN UNDRAINED CRUSHED PINEAPPLE
1 CUP WHIPPED CREAM OR WHIPPED TOPPING
2/3 CUP MAYONNAISE

❧ Melt marshmallows in 1 cup milk in top of double boiler. Pour mixture over 1 package lime gelatin. Stir until gelatin is dissolved. Stir in 2 packages cream cheese. Add undrained pineapple. Let cool. Blend in 1 cup whipped cream or topping and mayonnaise. Refrigerate.

Wesley's Favorite Salad

Serves 8 generously

1 3.4-ounce package lemon-flavor instant pudding
1 20-ounce can crushed pineapple in its own juice
1/3 of a 10.5-ounce package mini marshmallows
1 cup sweetened coconut flakes
1 15-ounce can mandarin oranges, drained
1 8-ounce container lite whipped topping, defrosted

✑ Empty pudding mix into medium/large bowl. Add the pineapple with its juice and stir until all the pudding mix is absorbed. Add remaining ingredients and stir well to combine. Refrigerate 4 hours minimum—6 hours or overnight is best.

Note: Bananas or cherries cut up and/or nuts could be added.

Curried Chicken Salad with Raisins and Honey

Serves 6

2 large bone-in, skin-on chicken breasts
1 tablespoon vegetable oil or olive oil
Salt

✑ Preheat oven to 400°. Put chicken breasts in a foil-lined pan, brush with olive oil, and sprinkle with salt. Add onions and garlic, if you wish. Roast until a meat thermometer registers 160°. This will take 35–40 minutes. Cool chicken, remove from bone, and cut into bite-size pieces.

Salad:
2 medium celery ribs, diced (quite small)
2 medium scallions, white and green parts minced
2 tablespoons minced fresh cilantro or parsley leaves
3/4–1 cup mayonnaise
1–2 tablespoons fresh lemon juice
6 tablespoons golden raisins
2 teaspoons curry powder
1 tablespoon honey
Salt and freshly ground black pepper

✑ Mix all together in a large bowl. Serve chicken on lettuce leaves.

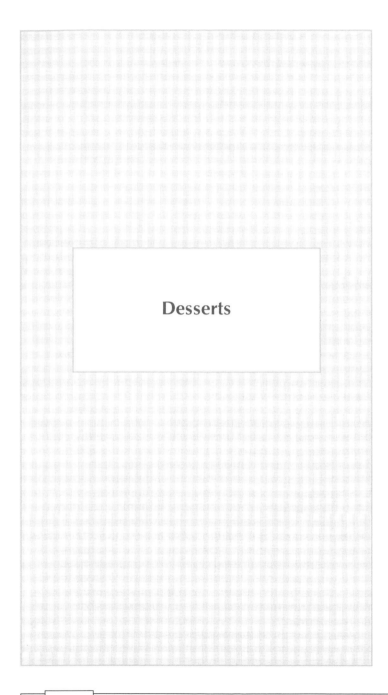

Desserts

Hummingbird Cake

Serves at least 16

3 CUPS FLOUR

2 CUPS SUGAR

1 TEASPOON BAKING SODA

1 TEASPOON CINNAMON

$\frac{1}{2}$ TEASPOON SALT

1$\frac{1}{2}$ CUPS VEGETABLE OIL

3 EGGS, SLIGHTLY BEATEN

1 TABLESPOON MELTED BUTTER

1 8-OUNCE CAN CRUSHED PINEAPPLE, UNDRAINED

2 LARGE BANANAS, MASHED AND BLENDED TO LIQUID

1 CUP CHOPPED NUTS

✺ Mix together dry ingredients. Set aside. In a large bowl, mix together oil, eggs, and butter until well blended. Add flour mixture, pineapple and juice, and bananas; blend until smooth. Stir in nuts. Pour into greased and floured Bundt pan. Bake at 350°, 60–70 minutes or until toothpick inserted in center comes out clean. Let cool in pan 1 hour before removing. Ice or glaze as desired.

Strawberry Shortcut Cake

Serves about 20

2 CUPS FROZEN STRAWBERRIES IN SYRUP, THAWED

1 3-OUNCE PACKAGE STRAWBERRY-FLAVORED GELATIN

1 CUP MINIATURE MARSHMALLOWS

1 PACKAGE PLAIN YELLOW CAKE MIX

WHIPPED CREAM OR ICE CREAM

◆ Combine strawberries with gelatin. Set aside. Put marshmallows in bottom of a generously greased 9" × 13" pan. Prepare cake mix as directed on package. Pour this mixture over marshmallows. Spoon strawberry mixture over batter. Bake at 375° for 40–50 minutes or until toothpick comes out clean. Top with whipped cream or ice cream when served.

Raspberry Nut Cake

Serves 10–12

2 CUPS FLOUR

1/2 TEASPOON SALT

1 1/2 TEASPOONS BAKING POWDER

1/2 TEASPOON BAKING SODA

1 TEASPOON CINNAMON

1/2 CUP SHORTENING

1 1/4 CUPS SUGAR

3 EGGS, ADDED 1 AT A TIME

3/4 CUP SOUR MILK

1 TEASPOON VANILLA

1/2 CUP CHOPPED NUTS

1 CUP FRESH RASPBERRIES

◆ Sift together flour, salt, baking powder, soda, and cinnamon. Blend together the shortening, sugar, eggs, sour milk, and vanilla. Add sifted ingredients. Add nuts. Fold in raspberries. Bake at 350° for 45 minutes.

Raspberry Frosting:

1/3 CUP MARGARINE

3 CUPS CONFECTIONERS' SUGAR

2 TABLESPOONS HOT CREAM

1/2 TEASPOON SALT

2 TABLESPOONS MASHED RASPBERRIES

1 TEASPOON VANILLA

◆ Mix all together and frost cake.

Peach Cake

Serves 20

1 LARGE CAN PEACHES
1 PACKAGE YELLOW CAKE MIX
1½ STICKS BUTTER OR MARGARINE
½ CUP CHOPPED NUTS
1 CUP WHIPPED CREAM OR WHIPPED TOPPING

❧ Empty canned peaches into a 9" × 2" × 13" baking pan and cut into bite-size pieces. Sprinkle dry cake mix evenly over peaches. Slice and arrange butter or margarine slices over cake mix. Top with nuts. Bake at 350° for 30 minutes. Cool and top with whipped cream or whipped topping and sprinkle with nuts.

Apple Cake

Serves 10–12

4 EGGS
2 CUPS SUGAR
1 CUP OIL
2 CUPS FLOUR
4 TEASPOONS BAKING POWDER
½ TEASPOON SALT
2 TEASPOONS VANILLA
5–6 APPLES, PEELED AND CUT INTO SMALL PIECES
1 CUP CHOPPED NUTS

❧ Mix first 7 ingredients and fold in apples and nuts. Mix topping and sprinkle on cake before baking. Bake at 350° for 50 minutes.

Topping:
2 TABLESPOONS SUGAR
2 TABLESPOONS CINNAMON

Cranberry Cake

Serves 10–12

2 CUPS FLOUR

1 TEASPOON BAKING POWDER

1 TEASPOON BAKING SODA

1/2 TEASPOON SALT

1 STICK BUTTER OR MARGARINE

1 CUP SUGAR

2 EGGS

1/2 PINT SOUR CREAM

1 TEASPOON ALMOND FLAVORING

1 CUP NUTS

1 8-OUNCE CAN WHOLE CRANBERRY SAUCE

ꙮ Sift together flour, baking powder, baking soda, and salt. Cream butter, sugar, and eggs. Add sour cream to creamed mixture. Add flour mixture, almond flavoring, and nuts. Beat until smooth. Reserve 1/4 cup cranberry sauce. In a greased tube pan add 1/2 of remaining cranberry sauce, cover with 1/2 of the batter, other 1/2 of sauce, rest of batter, and on top put the reserved 1/4 cup sauce. Bake at 350° for 45 minutes. Add glaze.

Glaze:

1/2 CUP CONFECTIONERS' SUGAR

1–2 TABLESPOONS WATER

1/4 TEASPOON ALMOND FLAVORING

ꙮ Mix all the ingredients to a spreading consistency and use to glaze the cake.

Company Cake

Serves 8–12

1/2 CUP BUTTER

1/2 CUP SUGAR

4 EGGS, SEPARATED

4 TABLESPOONS MILK

3/4 CUP FLOUR

1 TEASPOON BAKING POWDER

1 TEASPOON VANILLA

1 CUP SUGAR

ꙮ Cream together butter and 1/2 cup sugar. Add egg yolks, milk, flour, baking powder, and vanilla. Beat well and put into 2 greased pans. Beat egg whites with 1 cup sugar. Put on top of layers. Bake for 20 minutes at 350°. Cool 10 minutes. Remove from pans. Put layers together with ice cream and/or fruit.

Cemetery Cake

This recipe was copied from the "Maine Old Cemetery Association" newsletter, Fall 1971 issue. The members raved about the cake as an easy one to carry on their excursions into cemeteries. Therefore, the name Cemetery Cake. When made for weddings it is called Chocolate Wedding Cake!

Serves 12–14

3 CUPS FLOUR

2 CUPS SUGAR

6 TABLESPOONS COCOA

2 TEASPOONS BAKING SODA

1 TEASPOON SALT

2 TEASPOONS VANILLA

$2/3$ CUP OIL

2 TEASPOONS VINEGAR

2 CUPS COLD WATER

❧ Beat all ingredients together until smooth. (There are no eggs.) Bake at 350° for 35 minutes in a 9" × 13" pan or 2 9" pans.

Date Cake

Serves 10–12

1 CUP HOT WATER

1 TEASPOON BAKING SODA

1 PACKAGE DATES

$1/4$ CUP SHORTENING

1 CUP SUGAR

1 EGG, BEATEN

2 CUPS FLOUR

1 CUP NUTS

❧ Pour hot water and soda on dates. Cool. Cream shortening and sugar. Add egg, date mixture, flour, and nuts. Bake at 350° for 25–30 minutes.

Second Generation Chocolate Cake

Serves 12–15

4 SQUARES BAKING CHOCOLATE
1 2/3 CUPS ALL-PURPOSE FLOUR
2 TEASPOONS BAKING POWDER
1/2 TEASPOON SALT
2 TEASPOONS BAKING SODA
2/3 CUP SHORTENING
2 CUPS SUGAR
2 EGGS
2 TEASPOONS VANILLA
2 CUPS BOILING WATER

&. Make 1 day ahead, for 2 layer-cake pans or 1 large pan. Melt baking chocolate and set aside. Sift together flour, baking powder, salt, and soda. Cream shortening and sugar. Add eggs. Add chocolate and vanilla. Add water and dry ingredients. Bake at 325° for 30 45 minutes, depending on pan size. Frost with your favorite frosting.

Chocolate Sheet Cake

Makes 30 large squares

1 STICK MARGARINE
1/2 CUP COOKING OIL
4 TABLESPOONS COCOA
1 CUP WATER
2 CUPS SIFTED FLOUR
2 CUPS SUGAR
1/2 CUP BUTTERMILK
2 EGGS
1 TEASPOON BAKING SODA
1 TEASPOON VANILLA

&. Put margarine, oil, cocoa, and water in saucepan and bring to a boil. Sift together flour and sugar. Pour chocolate sauce over dry ingredients and mix well. Add buttermilk, eggs, soda, and vanilla. Pour into greased jelly roll pan. Bake 20 minutes at 400°. While sheet cake is hot, frost with the following frosting.

Frosting:

1 STICK MARGARINE
4 TABLESPOONS COCOA
1/3 CUP BUTTERMILK
1 POUND CONFECTIONERS' SUGAR
1/2 TEASPOON SALT
1 TEASPOON VANILLA
1 CUP CHOPPED NUTS

&. Bring margarine, cocoa, and buttermilk to boiling point; remove from heat and add rest of ingredients. Frost. When cool, cut into squares. Remove from pan.

Lemon Bars

Makes 20 squares

1/2 CUP BUTTER, MELTED
1/4 CUP POWDERED SUGAR
1 CUP FLOUR
2 EGGS, WELL BEATEN
2 TABLESPOONS LEMON JUICE
GRATED RIND OF 1 LEMON
2 TABLESPOONS FLOUR
1 CUP GRANULATED SUGAR

❧ Combine butter, sugar, and 1 cup flour in an 8" × 8" pan. Press flat and bake for 10 minutes at 350°. Mix and pour remaining ingredients on top of first mixture and bake 350° for 20 minutes.

Pumpkin Bars

Makes 35 2" squares using a jelly roll pan

2 1/2 CUPS FLOUR
2 TEASPOONS BAKING POWDER
1 TEASPOON BAKING SODA
2 TEASPOONS CINNAMON
1 TEASPOON PUMPKIN PIE SPICE
1 CUP SUGAR
1 CUP OIL
4 EGGS
2 CUPS PUMPKIN
1 CUP NUTS

❧ Put all ingredients in bowl and mix. Put in a large greased jelly roll pan or 2 cake pans. Bake at 350° for 15–20 minutes. Frost when cool. Frosting recipe follows.

Frosting:

1 3-OUNCE PACKAGE CREAM CHEESE
3/4 STICK MARGARINE
1 TEASPOON VANILLA
2 CUPS CONFECTIONERS' SUGAR (APPROXIMATELY)
1 TEASPOON MILK

❧ Mix all together and beat until fluffy.

Mint Chocolate Squares

Serves 16

2 EGGS, BEATEN
1 CUP SUGAR
1/2 TEASPOON VANILLA
1/2 CUP BUTTER, MELTED
2 SQUARES UNSWEETENED CHOCOLATE, MELTED
1/2 CUP FLOUR

❧ Combine all but flour and beat well. Blend in flour. Pour into a greased and floured 8" × 8" baking pan. Bake at 350° for 25 minutes. Spread following frosting on cooled squares.

Frosting:

2 TABLESPOONS BUTTER
1 1/2 CUPS SIFTED CONFECTIONERS' SUGAR
FEW DROPS GREEN FOOD COLORING
2 TABLESPOONS CREAM
1/2 TEASPOON PEPPERMINT EXTRACT

Chocolate Topping:

1 TABLESPOON BUTTER, MELTED
1 SQUARE UNSWEETENED CHOCOLATE, MELTED

❧ Mix together and pour over green frosting.

Strawberry Dessert

This is a lovely dessert. You will note that the recipe requires 2 egg whites. It is recommended that when making this dessert, you use only pasteurized liquid egg whites or dried egg whites.

Serves 18–20

1 CUP FLOUR
1/4 CUP BROWN SUGAR
1/2 CUP CHOPPED WALNUTS
1/2 CUP MARGARINE
2 PASTEURIZED EGG WHITES
2/3 CUP SUGAR
1 10-OUNCE PACKAGE FROZEN STRAWBERRIES, THAWED
2 TABLESPOONS LEMON JUICE
1 CUP CREAM

❧ Mix flour, brown sugar, walnuts, and margarine. Bake in a shallow pan at 350° for 20 minutes, stirring occasionally. Sprinkle 2/3 of crumbs in a 9" × 13" pan. Combine egg whites, sugar, strawberries, and lemon juice. Beat on high speed for 10 minutes. Whip cream and fold into strawberry mixture. Spoon over crumbs in pan and sprinkle rest of crumbs on top of mixture. Freeze several hours. May be made ahead and kept frozen until needed if properly wrapped. Very rich.

Dump Bars

Makes 24–28 bars

2 STICKS BUTTER OR MARGARINE

1 POUND BROWN SUGAR

4 EGGS

1 TEASPOON VANILLA

1/2 TEASPOON SALT

2 CUPS + 1 TABLESPOON FLOUR

1 TEASPOON BAKING POWDER

1 CUP COCONUT

NUTS, DATES, OR CHOCOLATE BITS (OPTIONAL)

🍮 Melt margarine and sugar together. Add eggs, vanilla, and salt. Mix well. Add flour, baking powder, and coconut. Pour into greased 9" × 13" pan. May add nuts, dates, or chocolate bits on top. Bake at 325° for 35–40 minutes.

Penuche Bars

Makes 24–28 bars

1/2 CUP BUTTER

1/2 CUP BROWN SUGAR

1 CUP FLOUR

1/2 TEASPOON SALT

1 CUP BROWN SUGAR

2 EGGS, BEATEN

2 TABLESPOONS FLOUR

1/2 TEASPOON BAKING POWDER

1/4 TEASPOON SALT

1 1/2 CUPS COCONUT

1 CUP COARSE NUT MEATS

1 TEASPOON VANILLA

🍮 Cream butter and 1/2 cup brown sugar. Add 1 cup flour and 1/2 teaspoon salt. Spread this mixture in a 9" × 13" pan and brown in a 350° oven. Mix remaining ingredients and spread over first layer and bake for 20–25 minutes.

Dot's Bars

Makes about 35 squares

2/3 CUP OIL

3/4 CUP COCOA

1/4 CUP OIL (YES, THIS IS CORRECT)

2 EGGS, UNBEATEN

2 CUPS SUGAR

2 1/2 CUPS FLOUR

1 TEASPOON BAKING POWDER

1 1/2 CUPS COLD WATER

1 TEASPOON VANILLA

1 CUP CHOCOLATE CHIPS

1 CUP CHOPPED WALNUTS

❧ Mix all ingredients in order given. Pour into a jelly roll pan. Put 1 cup chocolate chips and 1 cup chopped walnuts on top. Bake 20 minutes or a little longer at 350°. Freezes very well. Cut into small squares.

Hello Dolly Bars

Makes 20–24 squares

1 STICK MARGARINE

1 CUP GRAHAM CRACKER CRUMBS

1 CUP CHOCOLATE CHIPS

1 CUP BUTTERSCOTCH CHIPS

1 CUP SHREDDED COCONUT

1 CUP CHOPPED NUTS

1 CAN SWEETENED CONDENSED MILK

❧ Use a 9" × 13" pan. Melt margarine and cool slightly. Pour into baking pan. Cover with graham cracker crumbs. Sprinkle each of the following over crumbs, layer upon layer: chocolate chips, butterscotch chips, coconut, and chopped nuts. Pour condensed milk evenly over all. Do *not* stir. Bake in a 350° oven for 25 minutes. Cool. Cut into squares.

Split Levels

Makes 24 bars

1 CUP (6-OUNCE PACKAGE) SEMISWEET CHOCOLATE PIECES

1 3-OUNCE PACKAGE CREAM CHEESE

1/3 CUP EVAPORATED MILK OR LIGHT CREAM

1/2 CUP CHOPPED WALNUTS

2 TABLESPOONS SESAME SEEDS

1/2 TEASPOON ALMOND EXTRACT

1 1/2 CUPS FLOUR

1/2 TEASPOON BAKING POWDER

1/4 TEASPOON SALT

3/4 CUP SUGAR

1/2 CUP BUTTER OR MARGARINE, SOFTENED

1 EGG

1/4 TEASPOON ALMOND EXTRACT

❧ In saucepan, combine chocolate pieces, cream cheese, and milk. Melt over low heat, stirring constantly. Remove from heat. Stir in walnuts, sesame seeds, and almond extract. Blend well. Set aside. In large bowl, combine remaining ingredients. Blend at low speed just until particles are fine. Press 1/2 of mixture into a greased 11" × 7" pan. Spread with chocolate mixture. Sprinkle with remaining crumbs. Bake at 375° for 20–25 minutes. Cool. Can also use a 9" square pan. Easily doubled.

Chip and Nut Bars

Makes 35 squares

1 CUP SOFT MARGARINE

1 3/4 CUPS FIRMLY PACKED BROWN SUGAR

2 EGGS

2 TEASPOONS BAKING POWDER

1/2 TEASPOON BAKING SODA

1 TEASPOON VANILLA

2 CUPS FLOUR

1 TABLESPOON INSTANT COFFEE GRANULES

1 CUP CHOPPED NUTS

1 6-OUNCE PACKAGE CHOCOLATE CHIPS (DIVIDED)

❧ Put all ingredients except nuts and chips in large bowl. Mix at lowest speed of mixer until blended. Stir in 1/2 of the nuts and chips. Grease a jelly roll pan and spread dough evenly in pan. Sprinkle top with remaining nuts and chips. Bake at 350° 20–25 minutes. Cool and cut into squares.

Fruitcake Bars

Makes 20–24 squares

1 CUP WALNUTS
1/2 CUP PITTED PRUNES
1/2 CUP DRIED APRICOTS
1/3 CUP ORANGE JUICE
1 1/2 CUPS FLOUR
1/2 TEASPOON BAKING POWDER
1/2 TEASPOON SALT
1/2 TEASPOON CINNAMON
1/2 CUP BUTTER
1/2 CUP SUGAR
1/4 CUP BROWN SUGAR
2 EGGS
1 CUP DICED CANDIED FRUIT

Fruit Glaze:

1 CUP CONFECTIONERS' SUGAR
1 TABLESPOON HOT WATER
1 1/2 TEASPOONS BUTTER, MELTED
1/4 CUP FINELY DICED CANDIED FRUIT

❧ Chop walnuts; set aside. Cut prunes and apricots into small pieces and combine with orange juice. Sift together flour, baking powder, salt, and cinnamon; set aside. Cream together butter, sugar, and brown sugar. Beat 2 eggs. Stir in fruit mixture and flour mixture. Stir in walnuts and candied fruit. Spread in a greased 9" × 13" pan and bake at 375°. Cool and spread with Fruit Glaze.

Chocolate Bars

Makes 35 bars

1 CUP MARGARINE
2 CUPS BROWN SUGAR
2 EGGS
2 TEASPOONS VANILLA
2 1/2 CUPS FLOUR
1 TEASPOON BAKING SODA
1 TEASPOON SALT (OPTIONAL)
3 CUPS ROLLED OATS

❧ Cream margarine and sugar until fluffy; add eggs and vanilla. Sift flour, soda, and salt. Add rolled oats, then dry ingredients, to creamed mixture. Mix and set aside.

Filling:

1 12-OUNCE PACKAGE CHOCOLATE CHIPS
1 14-OUNCE CAN SWEETENED CONDENSED MILK
2 TABLESPOONS MARGARINE
1/2 TEASPOON SALT
1 CUP NUTS (OPTIONAL)
2 TEASPOONS VANILLA

❧ In top of double boiler, mix chocolate chips, condensed milk, margarine, and salt. Cook over hot water to melt. When smooth, add nuts and vanilla. Spread 2/3 of oatmeal mixture into a jelly roll pan. Cover evenly with chocolate filling mixture. Dot with remaining oatmeal mixture. Bake at 350° for 25–30 minutes.

Raisin Bars

Makes 20–24 bars

1 CUP SEEDLESS RAISINS

1 CUP BOILING WATER

1 CUP SUGAR

1/2 CUP COOKING OIL

1 EGG

1 3/4 CUPS FLOUR

1/2 TEASPOON SALT

1 TEASPOON BAKING SODA

1 TEASPOON CINNAMON

1/2 TEASPOON ALLSPICE

🍃 Bring first 2 ingredients to a boil and cool. Mix everything together and pour into greased 10" × 12" or 9" × 13" pan. Bake at 375° for 30–35 minutes. Cut into bars and ice while warm.

Icing:

2 CUPS CONFECTIONERS' SUGAR

2 TABLESPOONS SOFT BUTTER

2 TABLESPOONS LEMON JUICE

1 TEASPOON VANILLA OR ALMOND EXTRACT

🍃 Mix together sugar, butter, and vanilla or almond extract. Add the lemon juice a little at a time, beating well as juice is added. Make thin enough to spread.

Brownies

Very good!

Makes 16

2/3 CUP UNSIFTED FLOUR

1/2 TEASPOON BAKING POWDER

1/4 TEASPOON SALT

1/3 CUP BUTTER OR MARGARINE

2 SQUARES UNSWEETENED CHOCOLATE

2 EGGS

1 CUP SUGAR

1 TEASPOON VANILLA

1 CUP CHOPPED NUTS

🍃 Mix flour with baking powder and salt. Melt butter and chocolate over hot water. Beat eggs well; gradually add sugar, beating well. Beat in chocolate and vanilla. Mix in flour; stir in nuts. Spread in greased 8" square pan. Bake at 350° for 25 minutes. Cool before cutting.

Cocoa Brownies

Makes 20–24 brownies

1$\frac{1}{2}$ CUPS FLOUR
1$\frac{1}{2}$ CUPS SUGAR
$\frac{1}{2}$ TEASPOON SALT
$\frac{1}{2}$ CUP COCOA
1 CUP SHORTENING
4 EGGS
2 TEASPOONS VANILLA
1 CUP WALNUTS

☙ Sift dry ingredients into a large bowl. Add shortening, eggs, and vanilla and beat on medium speed 3 minutes. Fold in nuts. Pour into greased 9" × 13" pan. Bake at 350° for 25 minutes or until done. Cool in pan for 5–6 minutes on cake racks. Cut into squares and finish cooling out of pan.

Caramel Cuts

Makes 16–18 bars

$\frac{1}{4}$ CUP MARGARINE
1 CUP LIGHT BROWN SUGAR
1 UNBEATEN EGG
$\frac{1}{2}$ TEASPOON VANILLA
$\frac{3}{4}$ CUP FLOUR
1 TEASPOON BAKING POWDER
$\frac{1}{2}$ CUP CHOPPED NUTS

☙ Melt margarine in saucepan. Add light brown sugar and blend well. While mixture is warm, add egg and vanilla. Sift and add flour, baking powder, and nuts. Bake at 325° for 20 minutes in greased and floured 9" square pan. Quick and easy!

Variations:
Add raisins or chocolate chips.

Marshmallow Fudge Bars

Makes 24 bars

1/2 CUP SHORTENING

3/4 CUP SUGAR

3/4 CUP SIFTED FLOUR

1/4 TEASPOON BAKING POWDER

1/4 TEASPOON SALT

2 TABLESPOONS COCOA

2 EGGS, WELL BEATEN

1 TEASPOON VANILLA

1/2 CUP CHOPPED NUTS

MARSHMALLOWS, CUT IN 1/2, AS NEEDED

&. Cream shortening and sugar until fluffy. Into this, sift other dry ingredients. Blend in the eggs. Add vanilla and chopped nuts and spread in greased 12" × 8" pan. Bake at 350° for 25–30 minutes. Cover baked bars with halved marshmallows and return to oven about 3 minutes. When cool, frost with Fudge Frosting.

Fudge Frosting:

1 SQUARE CHOCOLATE

1/2 CUP BROWN SUGAR

1/4 CUP WATER

1 TABLESPOON BUTTER

1 TEASPOON VANILLA

CONFECTIONERS' SUGAR

&. Boil together 3 minutes. Remove from heat; add vanilla. Cool slightly and add enough confectioners' sugar to make a spreading consistency.

Chocolate Chip Cookie Bars

Makes 20–24 bars

2 8-OUNCE PACKAGES CREAM CHEESE

1 EGG

3/4 CUP SUGAR

2 PACKAGES OF ROLLED CHOCOLATE CHIP COOKIE DOUGH
(FOUND IN THE REFRIGERATED SECTION OF SUPERMARKET)

&. Mix cream cheese, egg, and sugar together. Spread a roll of cookie dough in 9" × 13" pan. Spread cream cheese mixture over it. Spread the other roll on top. Bake at 350° for 30–35 minutes.

Peanut Oat Bars

Makes 4 dozen bars

^{2}/$_3$ CUP BUTTER OR MARGARINE

^{1}/$_4$ CUP PEANUT BUTTER

1 CUP PACKED BROWN SUGAR

^{1}/$_4$ CUP LIGHT CORN SYRUP

^{1}/$_4$ TEASPOON VANILLA EXTRACT

4 CUPS QUICK-COOKING OATS

Topping:

1 CUP MILK CHOCOLATE CHIPS

^{1}/$_2$ CUP BUTTERSCOTCH CHIPS

^{1}/$_3$ CUP PEANUT BUTTER

1. In a mixing bowl, combine butter, peanut butter, brown sugar, corn syrup, and vanilla; gradually add the oats.

2. Press into greased 9" × 13" × 2" pan. Bake at 400° for 12–14 minutes or until edges are golden brown. Cool on a wire rack for 5 minutes.

3. For topping, melt chips and peanut butter in a microwave or saucepan. Stir until blended; spread over warm bars. Cool completely; refrigerate for 2–3 hours before cutting.

Note: This recipe contains no flour.

Cherry Dream Squares

Makes 20–24 squares

1 PACKAGE WHITE CAKE MIX

^{1}/$_2$ CUP BUTTER OR MARGARINE, SOFTENED

1^1/$_4$ CUPS ROLLED OATS

1 EGG

1 21-OUNCE CAN CHERRY PIE FILLING

^{1}/$_2$ CUP CHOPPED NUTS (OPTIONAL)

^{1}/$_4$ CUP FIRMLY PACKED BROWN SUGAR

1. In a large bowl, combine cake mix, 6 tablespoons butter, and 1 cup rolled oats. Mix until crumbly. Reserve 1 cup crumbs for topping.

2. To remaining crumbs, add 1 egg. Mix until well blended. Press into 9" × 13" pan. Pour cherry pie filling and spread over crust.

3. To reserved crumbs in bowl, add remaining ^{1}/$_4$ cup rolled oats, 2 tablespoons butter, nuts, and brown sugar. Beat until well mixed. Sprinkle over cherry mixture. Bake at 350° until done. Cool completely. May be served as dessert with whipped cream; you may wish to cut the squares a little larger.

Variation:

You may substitute a carrot cake mix and a raisin pie filling.

Stained-Glass Fruitcakes

Makes 80

2 CUPS WALNUT HALVES

2 CUPS PECAN HALVES

1$\frac{1}{2}$ CUPS CANDIED PINEAPPLE, CUT UP

1$\frac{1}{2}$ CUPS LIGHT RAISINS

1$\frac{1}{3}$ CUPS PITTED WHOLE DATES

$\frac{3}{4}$ CUP WHOLE RED CANDIED CHERRIES

$\frac{3}{4}$ CUP WHOLE GREEN CANDIED CHERRIES

1 14-OUNCE CAN SWEETENED CONDENSED MILK

❧ In large bowl, combine walnuts, pecans, candied pineapple, raisins, dates, and cherries. Stir in condensed milk. Mix thoroughly. Pack firmly into buttered 1$\frac{3}{4}$" muffin pans. Bake in 275° oven for 25 minutes. Cool.

Cream Cheese Tarts

Makes 24

2 CUPS CRUSHED GRAHAM CRACKERS

1$\frac{1}{4}$ CUPS SUGAR

1 STICK MARGARINE, MELTED

1 POUND CREAM CHEESE

2 TEASPOONS VANILLA

2 EGGS, BEATEN

1 CAN CHERRY PIE FILLING

❧ Mix together graham crackers, $\frac{1}{4}$ cup sugar, and margarine. Place a small amount in paper baking cups in 24 muffin tins. Whip the cream cheese, vanilla, 1 cup sugar, and eggs until smooth. Fill each cup and bake at 375° for 15 minutes. Cool. Top each with cherry pie filling.

Apple Squares I

Makes 20–24 squares

3 CUPS CHOPPED, PEELED APPLES

2 CUPS SUGAR

2 TEASPOONS CINNAMON

1 TEASPOON NUTMEG

3 CUPS FLOUR

1 TEASPOON SALT

2 TEASPOONS BAKING SODA

2 EGGS, BEATEN

1 CUP OIL

2 TEASPOONS VANILLA

❧ Toss apples, sugar, and spices in large bowl. Add flour, salt, and soda sifted together. Beat eggs, oil, and vanilla. Add to dry mixture. Blend well with spoon. Bake in a 9" × 13" × 2" pan for 40 minutes at 350°. Nice and moist.

Apple Squares II

Makes 16–18 bars

1 EGG

3/4 CUP SUGAR

1/4 CUP UNDILUTED EVAPORATED MILK

1 TEASPOON VANILLA

3/4 CUP SIFTED FLOUR

1 TEASPOON BAKING POWDER

1/4 TEASPOON SALT

1 TEASPOON CINNAMON

1 CUP PEELED AND CHOPPED APPLES

1/2 CUP CHOPPED NUTS

1 TABLESPOON SUGAR

1/2 TEASPOON CINNAMON

❧ Beat egg; add sugar, milk, and vanilla. Mix flour with baking powder, salt, and cinnamon. Add dry ingredients to creamed mixture. Add apples and nuts. Spread batter in a buttered 9" × 9" pan. Mix 1 tablespoon sugar and 1/2 teaspoon cinnamon and sprinkle over batter. Bake 25–30 minutes at 350°. Cool and cut into squares or bars.

Sour Cream Rhubarb Squares

Makes 20–24 squares

1 CUP BROWN SUGAR, PACKED

1/2 CUP BUTTER OR MARGARINE

1 EGG

1 CUP SOUR CREAM

2 CUPS FLOUR

1 TEASPOON BAKING SODA

2 CUPS FINELY CUT RHUBARB

❧ Mix first 4 ingredients together well. Add rest of ingredients and blend well. Pour batter into a greased 9" × 13" × 2" pan.

Topping:

1/2 CUP SUGAR

1/2 CUP CHOPPED NUTS

1 TABLESPOON MARGARINE, MELTED

1 TEASPOON CINNAMON

❧ Mix well; mixture will be crumbly. Spread 1/2 of topping on batter. Bake at 350° for 45–50 minutes. Remove from oven and sprinkle with the rest of the topping.

Raspberry Oatmeal Squares

Makes 20–24 squares

1 1/2 CUPS OATMEAL

1 3/4 CUPS FLOUR

1/2 TEASPOON BAKING SODA

1/2 TEASPOON SALT

1 CUP WALNUT PIECES

1 CUP BROWN SUGAR

1 TEASPOON CINNAMON

1 CUP BUTTER, MELTED

RASPBERRY JAM

❧ Mix all ingredients, except jam, well, in order given. Put 1/2 the mixture on bottom of greased 9" × 13" × 2" pan. Spread with raspberry jam. Crumble the remaining oatmeal mixture over top of jam. Bake at 325° for 30 minutes or until done. Very good!

Strawberry Squares

Makes 15–18 squares

2¼ CUPS GRAHAM CRACKER CRUMBS (RESERVE ¼ CUP
    FOR TOPPING)
½ CUP BUTTER OR MARGARINE
1 10-OUNCE BOX FROZEN STRAWBERRIES
1 3-OUNCE PACKAGE STRAWBERRY GELATIN
½ CUP LEMON JUICE
½ CUP SUGAR
1 CUP WHIPPED CREAM, DIVIDED
2 TEASPOONS SUGAR OR TO TASTE
¼ TEASPOON VANILLA

❧ Combine cracker crumbs with butter. Press into a 9" × 13" pan and bake 10 minutes in 325° oven. Thaw frozen strawberries on stove in saucepan and bring to boil. Add gelatin, lemon juice, and sugar. Stir until all dissolved. Let cool. When cool, add ½ cup whipped cream. Spread on base and put in refrigerator to cool. Top with ½ cup whipped cream flavored with sugar and vanilla. Spread ¼ cup crumbs on top. Best kept in refrigerator.

Cherry Squares

Makes 30–35 squares

1 CUP SHORTENING
2 CUPS SUGAR
4 EGGS, BEATEN
1 TEASPOON VANILLA
3 CUPS FLOUR
½ TEASPOON SALT
1 CAN CHERRY PIE FILLING

❧ Blend shortening and sugar. Add eggs and vanilla, flour and salt. Mix well; batter will be cookie consistency. Spread ¾ batter on ungreased jelly roll pan. Spread cherry pie filling over batter. Put remaining batter "here and there" over top. Bake at 350° for 35 minutes, no longer. Good with apple, lemon, pineapple, or blueberry pie filling.

Spritz Cookies

Makes about 125 cookies

1 POUND BUTTER

1 1/3 CUPS SUGAR

2 EGGS

1 TEASPOON VANILLA

5 CUPS SIFTED FLOUR

1 TEASPOON CREAM OF TARTAR

1/2 TEASPOON BAKING SODA

❧ Cream butter and sugar. Add eggs and beat well. Add the vanilla. Add the flour, which has been mixed and sifted with the cream of tartar and soda. (If you do not have cream of tartar and soda, use 2 teaspoons baking powder.) Press the dough through a cookie press for S-shape, B-shape, or O-shape. Bake at 400° for about 10 minutes or until they are light yellow.

Cathedral Cookies

Makes at least 2 dozen cookies

2 TABLESPOONS MARGARINE

1 12-OUNCE PACKAGE CHOCOLATE CHIPS

1 EGG, BEATEN

1/2 TEASPOON SALT

3 CUPS COLORED MINIATURE MARSHMALLOWS

1/2 CUP NUTS

COCONUT

❧ Melt margarine in double boiler with chocolate chips. Cool slightly. Add egg, salt, marshmallows, and nuts. Sprinkle bread board with coconut. Make chocolate mixture into rolls and roll in coconut. Place in refrigerator, wrapped in waxed paper. Slice into cookies.

Thin Crisp Molasses Cookies

Makes 4 dozen cookies

$3/4$ CUP SHORTENING

1 CUP SUGAR

1 EGG

$1/4$ CUP MOLASSES

2 CUPS SIFTED FLOUR

2 TEASPOONS BAKING SODA

$1/4$ TEASPOON SALT

1 TEASPOON CINNAMON

$3/4$ TEASPOON GROUND CLOVES

$3/4$ TEASPOON GINGER

✌ Mix shortening, sugar, egg, and molasses together thoroughly. Sift together and stir in remaining ingredients. Mix thoroughly. Place by teaspoonfuls on a greased cookie sheet, about 2" apart. (You may use parchment paper instead of greasing the cookie sheet.) Flatten with the bottom of a glass dipped in cold water. Sprinkle with granulated sugar. Bake in moderate oven, 375°, about 8 or 9 minutes.

Jenifer House Molasses Cookies

Makes 6 dozen

2 CUPS MARGARINE

$3/4$ CUP MOLASSES

$1/4$ CUP WATER

$1/2$ TABLESPOON SALT

3 CUPS BROWN SUGAR

3 LARGE EGGS

$6^1/2$ CUPS UNSIFTED FLOUR

1 TABLESPOON BAKING SODA

1 TABLESPOON CINNAMON

2 TEASPOONS CLOVES

$2^1/2$ TEASPOONS GINGER

✌ Cream margarine, molasses, water, salt, and brown sugar together. Beat in eggs. Add dry ingredients and mix well. (You'll have to mix it in by hand after the first 2 cups of flour.) Refrigerate for 24 hours. Roll into balls 2" in diameter. Roll in granulated sugar. Bake for 15–18 minutes at 350°.

Raspberry Swirl Coconut Cookies

Yields 5 dozen cookies

1/2 CUP SHORTENING

1/2 CUP BUTTER

1 CUP PACKED BROWN SUGAR

3/4 CUP WHITE SUGAR

2 EGGS

1 TEASPOON ALMOND EXTRACT

3 1/4 CUPS FLOUR

1 TEASPOON BAKING SODA

1/2 TEASPOON SALT

2 CUPS FLAKED COCONUT

1/2 CUP WATER

RASPBERRY JAM

❧ Cream together shortening, butter, brown sugar, white sugar, eggs, and almond extract. Combine the flour, soda, and salt. Add to the creamed mixture alternately with the water, ending with dry mixture. Beat well. Stir in coconut. Drop mixture by level tablespoonfuls 2" apart on ungreased baking sheet. Make a small cavity in each cookie with back of spoon. Place 1/4 teaspoon raspberry jam on each cookie. Top with 1/2 teaspoon cookie dough. Bake at 400° for 10–12 minutes.

Cornmeal Cookies

Makes 3 dozen

3/4 CUP BUTTER OR MARGARINE

3/4 CUP SUGAR

1 EGG

1 1/2 CUPS FLOUR

1/2 CUP CORNMEAL

1 TEASPOON BAKING POWDER

1/4 TEASPOON SALT

1 TEASPOON VANILLA

1/2 CUP RAISINS (OPTIONAL)

❧ Mix butter and sugar in bowl. Add egg and beat well; add rest of ingredients and mix well. Drop dough from teaspoon onto a greased baking sheet. Bake at 350° about 15 minutes.

Variation:

If you want chocolate cookies, mix 1/4 cup cocoa into dry ingredients. Add 1/4 cup milk.

Beacon Hill Cookies

Makes 2½–3 dozen

1 CUP CHOCOLATE CHIPS
2 EGG WHITES
⅛ TEASPOON SALT
½ CUP SUGAR
½ TEASPOON VANILLA
½ TEASPOON VINEGAR
¼ CUP CHOPPED NUTS
½ CUP PACKED COCONUT (OPTIONAL)

❧ Melt chocolate over hot water. Beat egg whites and salt until foamy; add sugar gradually, beating well after each addition. Continue beating until mixture will stand in stiff peaks. Add vanilla and vinegar and beat well. Fold in chocolate, nuts, and coconut, if desired. Drop from a teaspoon onto a greased cookie sheet. Bake in a moderate, 350°, oven for 10 minutes. You may omit coconut and use pecans for nuts.

Ginger Crisps

Very old recipe but very good!

Makes 3 dozen cookies

⅔ CUP OIL
1 CUP WHITE SUGAR
1 EGG
¼ CUP MOLASSES
1 TEASPOON VANILLA
½ TEASPOON SALT
2 CUPS SIFTED FLOUR
1 TEASPOON GINGER
1 TEASPOON CINNAMON
¼ TEASPOON GROUND CLOVES
2 LEVEL TEASPOONS BAKING SODA

❧ Mix oil and sugar. Add egg and beat well. Stir in molasses. Add vanilla and salt. Sift dry ingredients and add to mixture. Dough will seem dry but that is okay. Using a spoon, form into small balls and press lightly on greased cookie sheet. Dip tops into sugar if desired. Bake at 350° for 12 minutes.

Pineapple Cookies

Makes 3 dozen

1/2 CUP MARGARINE

1 CUP BROWN SUGAR

1 EGG

3/4 CUP CRUSHED PINEAPPLE

2 CUPS FLOUR

1/4 TEASPOON SALT

1/4 TEASPOON BAKING SODA

1 TEASPOON BAKING POWDER

1 TEASPOON VANILLA

WALNUTS (OPTIONAL)

Cream together margarine, brown sugar, and egg. Spoon pineapple from the can in order to get a little juice. Sift flour, salt, soda, and baking powder. Mix with above. Add vanilla. Mix in a few chopped walnuts if desired. Drop on cookie sheet and bake in 400° oven for 12–15 minutes.

Cocoa Mint Meringue Drops

Makes about 30 meringue drops

2 EGG WHITES AT ROOM TEMPERATURE

1 TABLESPOON COCOA

2/3 CUP SUGAR

1/8 TEASPOON MINT FLAVORING

Before you start to mix cookies, turn oven to 375°. Cover cookie sheet with aluminum foil. Beat egg whites until they hold up in peaks. Mix cocoa and sugar together and gradually add to egg whites. Add mint flavoring. Beat until mixture is very stiff. Drop mixture by teaspoon onto covered cookie sheet. Put pan in oven; close door and turn oven off. Leave pan of cookies in oven overnight. Drops can be baked at 200° for 2 hours if this is more convenient.

Fruit Chews

Makes 20–24 bars

1 POUND LIGHT BROWN SUGAR
1/4 POUND (1 STICK) BUTTER OR MARGARINE
3 EGGS
2 CUPS SIFTED FLOUR
2 TEASPOONS BAKING POWDER
1 TEASPOON BAKING SODA
1 TEASPOON VANILLA
1 CUP FINELY CHOPPED APRICOTS

❧ Cream sugar and margarine thoroughly. Add eggs 1 at a time. Add flour, baking powder, soda, extract, and fruit. Bake in a well-greased 9" × 13" pan at 325° for 50 minutes. Cool and cut into squares.

Variation:
Use dark brown sugar and replace apricots with dates.

Apple Chunk Cake

Serves 15–18

4 MEDIUM-SIZED APPLES
1/2 CUP RAISINS
1/2 CUP CARAMEL CHIPS OR CHOCOLATE CHIPS
    (CARAMEL CHIPS ARE BEST)
1/4–1/2 CUP CHOPPED BLACK WALNUTS
2 1/2 CUPS UNSIFTED FLOUR
1 1/2 CUPS SUGAR (1/2 WHITE AND 1/2 BROWN)
1 TEASPOON BAKING POWDER
1 TEASPOON CINNAMON
1 CUP WATER
1 STICK BUTTER OR MARGARINE
1 TEASPOON VANILLA
1 TEASPOON BAKING SODA
2 EGGS

❧ Peel and dice apples into a large bowl. Add raisins. Add caramel chips, black walnuts, flour, sugar, baking powder, and cinnamon. Mix this all together. Mix until flour has completely covered all ingredients. (Mix with a wooden spoon.) Heat 1 cup water to boiling. Add butter, vanilla, and soda to water immediately when water is taken off stove. Add liquid mixture to dry ingredients and stir until well mixed. Add unbeaten eggs; mix until well blended with spoon. Pour into a large, well-greased and floured pan. (A round tube pan is fine.) Bake at 350° for 1 hour or until a toothpick comes out clean. Remove from oven and let cool in pan overnight. Remove carefully. This makes a large cake—it's a very old Virginia recipe. Cake may be glazed.

Easy Angel Cake Dessert

Serves 12–15

❧ Bake an angel food cake in a 10" angel food cake pan. Cool and remove.

1½–2 CUPS WHIPPING CREAM
½ CUP SUGAR
¼–⅓ CUP COCOA
½ TEASPOON VANILLA*

❧ Whip cream until stiff and add sugar, cocoa, and vanilla. Slice angel food cake into serving-size pieces and top with whipped cream. May be garnished with a cherry, sprinkles, or whatever appeals to you. You may use Amaretto, Crème de Menthe, or any other flavored liqueur.

*Flavored liqueur may be used instead of vanilla, ½ teaspoon or to taste.

Molded Ambrosia

A make-ahead dessert!

Serves 9

1 CUP GRAHAM CRACKER CRUMBS
¼ CUP MARGARINE, MELTED
1 9-OUNCE CAN CRUSHED PINEAPPLE
1 3-OUNCE PACKAGE ORANGE GELATIN
1 CUP BOILING WATER
⅓ CUP SUGAR
1 CUP SOUR CREAM
¼ TEASPOON VANILLA
1 CUP MANDARIN ORANGE SECTIONS, DICED
½ CUP COCONUT

❧ Combine crumbs and margarine. Reserve ⅓ cup for topping. Press crumbs into 8" × 8" pan. Drain pineapple, reserving liquid. Dissolve gelatin in hot water with sugar. Stir in pineapple liquid. Chill until partially set; then add sour cream and vanilla; whip until fluffy. Fold in pineapple, oranges, and coconut. Pour over crumbs in pan. Top with crumbs; chill until firm. Cut in squares; trim with maraschino cherries.

Note: Tripling this recipe would feed 25 people.

Banana Bread

Serves 8

1 3/4 CUPS SIFTED FLOUR

1 TEASPOON BAKING SODA

1 TEASPOON CREAM OF TARTAR

1/2 TEASPOON SALT

1/3 CUP SHORTENING

2/3 CUP SUGAR

2 EGGS, WELL BEATEN

1 CUP MASHED BANANA

❧ Mix and sift flour, soda, cream of tartar, and salt. Cream shortening and beat in sugar; add eggs, mixing well. Mash ripe bananas, as soon as peeled, with a fork (3–4 bananas yield 1 cup). Add flour alternately with bananas, mixing well after each addition. Pour into greased loaf pan and bake in a 350° oven for 1 hour or until done.

Pumpkin Bread

Makes 2 good-sized loaves

1/3 CUP FLOUR

2 LEVEL TEASPOONS BAKING SODA

1 1/2 TEASPOONS SALT

1 TEASPOON CINNAMON

1 TEASPOON NUTMEG

3 CUPS SUGAR

4 EGGS

2 CUPS PUMPKIN OR 1 CAN PUMPKIN PIE FILLING

1 CUP COOKING OIL

2/3 CUP COLD WATER

❧ Sift dry ingredients. Beat eggs until thick and light in color. Add pumpkin, oil, and water. Add dry ingredients and beat well. Bake at 350° for 1 hour.

Lemon Loaf Bread

1 loaf

1/2 CUP MARGARINE

1 CUP SUGAR

2 MEDIUM EGGS

1 1/2 CUPS FLOUR

1 TEASPOON BAKING POWDER

1/2 TEASPOON SALT

1/2 CUP MILK

1 LEMON

CRUSHED NUTS (OPTIONAL)

1/4 CUP SUGAR

Cream margarine. Add sugar. Blend together and add eggs. Beat thoroughly. Add sifted dry ingredients alternately with milk. Add grated lemon rind and some crushed nuts, if desired. Pour into well-greased loaf pan and bake at 350° for 55 minutes. (Time depends on size of loaf pan.) Mix the juice of 1 lemon with 1/4 cup sugar and pour over top. Return to oven for 5 minutes more.

Chapter Four

Food Sales

Food Sales have been an early and constant part of the landscape of church fund-raising. They are a great source of income, with very little overhead.* The food sale may be a part of a larger church fair, or it may stand alone. Communities that have a summer tourist population can usually do very well with a food sale on a Saturday morning. Baked beans, breads, cakes, and pies are usually very popular. Of course, it is a given, if you have lots of pies, everyone wants cakes and vice versa. Have you experienced that?

If you are serious about your contribution to the food sale earning money for your church, try to plan what you will bake, and how much money your baking will bring. Check out the price list that is being used and plan what you will need to make to earn what you want your contribution to be. If you are unable to bake for the sale, monetary donations are always appreciated.

There are many changes in the way our society lives today, and that lends itself to a different "twist" to consider for your sale. I submit for your consideration a frozen food sale, which may be a part of a regular food sale or just a frozen food sale. Many families are now one or two people. Sometimes these people live in retirement communities. Little cooking is done, but there are times when pulling out of the freezer a small amount of lasagna, muffins, soup, or whatever would be helpful and a nice change. People living in their own homes may have more freezer space, and a frozen homemade bread or casserole would be a treat. In addition to frozen foods, small quantities of "good keepers" such as jellies, chutneys, pickles, and candies, for example, may just hit the spot for some of your customers. These people may not make these items anymore, but love that homemade taste.

An advantage of a frozen food sale from the cook's point of view is that you make and freeze your contributions ahead of time, at your convenience.

When offering frozen items at your sale, be sure to have the sale near your church freezer, or use coolers. The frozen foods should be sold frozen.

With few exceptions, food sale items should be made from scratch. ❣

*Overhead would result from the purchase of disposable containers for baked beans or some type of food that cannot be put into a paper bag. Also, you may need plastic wrap or foil. Still, this is quite modest overhead.

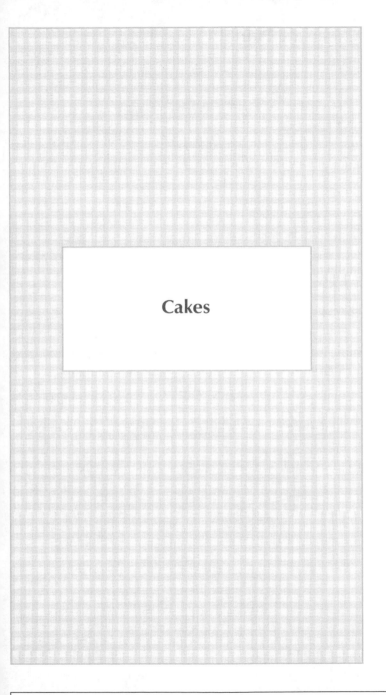

Cakes

Cold Oven Pound Cake I

Serves 12–15

2 CUPS ALL-PURPOSE FLOUR

1½ CUPS WHITE SUGAR

2 TEASPOONS BAKING POWDER

1 TEASPOON SALT

½ CUP MARGARINE

½ CUP VEGETABLE SHORTENING

4 EGGS

½ CUP SWEET MILK

2 TEASPOONS VANILLA

In a large bowl, combine all above ingredients. Beat for 20 minutes with electric mixer. Put in ungreased 10" tube pan. Place in a cold oven and turn oven to 350°. Bake 1 hour. Do *not* open door while baking.

Cold Oven Pound Cake II

Serves 20–25 if slices are slightly less than 1/2" thick

1/2 CUP VEGETABLE SHORTENING

2 STICKS MARGARINE

3 CUPS SUGAR

5 EGGS

1 TEASPOON VANILLA

1 TEASPOON ALMOND EXTRACT

1 TEASPOON LEMON EXTRACT

3 CUPS FLOUR

1/2 TEASPOON BAKING POWDER

1/2 TEASPOON SALT

1 CUP SWEET MILK

❧ With electric mixer, cream vegetable shortening, margarine, and sugar. Add eggs, 1 at a time, mixing well after each addition. Blend in vanilla and almond and lemon extracts. Sift together flour, baking powder, and salt. Add alternately with milk to the mixture. Pour into well-greased 10" tube cake pan and place in a cold oven. Turn oven to 325° and bake 1 1/2 hours. Do *not* open oven door during baking time. May be frosted or not as you desire. This cake can be cut very thin. Wonderful with fresh fruit or sherbet.

Chocolate Pound Cake

Serves at least 15–18

1/2 POUND BUTTER (2 STICKS)

3 CUPS SUGAR

1/2 CUP VEGETABLE SHORTENING

6 EGGS

3 CUPS FLOUR

4 TABLESPOONS COCOA

1/2 TEASPOON BAKING POWDER

1 CUP MILK

1 TABLESPOON VANILLA EXTRACT

❧ Cream butter, sugar, and vegetable shortening. Add eggs and blend well. Add sifted dry ingredients alternately with milk. Add vanilla. Pour into greased 10" tube pan and bake in a preheated 350° oven for 1 hour and 40 minutes.

Sponge Cake I

Serves 10–12

6 EGGS, SEPARATED
1 1/2 CUPS SUGAR
1 1/2 CUPS SIFTED FLOUR
1/2 TEASPOON SALT
1 TEASPOON LEMON EXTRACT
6 TABLESPOONS COLD WATER
1 1/2 TEASPOONS BAKING POWDER

✌ Beat egg yolks until lemon colored; add sugar and beat again. Add flour, salt, lemon extract, and cold water. Beat egg whites with baking powder until stiff. Fold into mixture. Bake in ungreased tube pan. Bake at 350° for 50–60 minutes.

Sponge Cake II

Serves 18–20

6 EGG YOLKS
1/2 CUP COLD WATER
1 1/2 CUPS SUGAR
1/2 TEASPOON VANILLA
1/2 TEASPOON ORANGE OR LEMON EXTRACT
1 1/2 CUPS SIFTED CAKE FLOUR
1/4 TEASPOON SALT
6 EGG WHITES
3/4 TEASPOON CREAM OF TARTAR

✌ Beat egg yolks until thick and lemon colored; add water; continue beating until very thick. Gradually beat in sugar, then vanilla and orange or lemon extract. Sift flour with salt and fold into egg yolk mixture a little at a time. Beat egg whites with cream of tartar until stiff peaks form. Fold into first mixture, turning bowl gradually. Bake in ungreased 10" tube pan in slow oven, 325°, for about 1 hour. Invert pan to cool. May be frosted, but good served plain with fruit or ice cream.

Lemon Sponge Cake

Serves 18–20

1½ CUPS CAKE FLOUR	½ CUP WHITE SUGAR
1 CUP WHITE SUGAR	½ CUP EGG YOLKS (6)
½ TEASPOON BAKING POWDER	¼ CUP COLD WATER
¾ CUP EGG WHITES (6 MEDIUM)	1 TEASPOON VANILLA
1 TEASPOON CREAM OF TARTAR	EXTRACT
½ TEASPOON SALT	1 TEASPOON LEMON EXTRACT

☙ Sift flour, 1 cup sugar, and baking powder. Set aside. Beat egg whites, cream of tartar, and salt until soft peaks form. Do not underbeat (15 minutes). Combine egg yolks, water, vanilla extract, and lemon extract. Add to dry ingredients all at once. Beat for 1 minute on high speed. Fold batter, ¼ at a time, into beaten egg whites using a wire whip or spatula. Blend thoroughly after each addition. Pour into an ungreased 10" tube pan. Bake at 350° for 40–50 minutes. Invert immediately when cake is removed from oven and let cool in pan. Cut cake into 3 layers and fill with Lemon Filling.

Lemon Filling:

1 CUP SUGAR

¼ CUP CORNSTARCH

⅛ TEASPOON SALT

1½ CUPS COLD WATER

2 EGG YOLKS, SLIGHTLY BEATEN

2–3 TEASPOONS GRATED LEMON RIND

¼ CUP FRESH LEMON JUICE

2 TABLESPOONS BUTTER

☙ Combine sugar, cornstarch, and salt in saucepan. Add cold water a little at a time and cook over medium heat, stirring constantly until thick and clear. Blend in egg yolks to which a little of the hot mixture has been added. Cook for 2 minutes, stirring constantly. Remove from heat; stir in grated lemon rind, lemon juice, and butter. Cool before putting on cake layers. Frost with Fluffy Marshmallow Frosting.

Fluffy Marshmallow Frosting:

1 CUP WHITE SUGAR

⅓ CUP COLD WATER

¼ TEASPOON CREAM OF TARTAR

8 MARSHMALLOWS (QUARTERED)

1 TEASPOON VANILLA

⅓ CUP PASTEURIZED EGG WHITES, BEATEN UNTIL STIFF

☙ Combine sugar, cold water, and cream of tartar in saucepan and bring to boil. Continue to boil until 6"–8" strands appear or mixture reaches 242° on candy thermometer. Beat in marshmallows and vanilla. Add syrup to beaten egg whites. Will cover entire sides and top of cake.

Hot Milk Sponge Cake

Serves 14–16

2 EGGS

1 CUP SUGAR

2 TEASPOONS VANILLA

1 CUP FLOUR

1 TEASPOON BAKING POWDER

1/4 TEASPOON SALT

1/2 CUP HOT MILK

2 TABLESPOONS BUTTER

❧ Beat eggs until very thick. Add sugar, gradually, and vanilla, beating well. Sift together flour, baking powder, and salt. Gradually sift this mixture over the egg mixture and fold in. Heat together 1/2 cup milk and 2 tablespoons butter. Add all at once to the flour/egg mixture and fold in. Pour into a greased 8" × 8" pan and bake at 350° for 20–25 minutes.

Chocolate Cake

Makes 24 2" squares

1/2 CUP SHORTENING

2 CUPS SUGAR

2 CUPS FLOUR

1/2 TEASPOON BAKING POWDER

1 TEASPOON BAKING SODA

1/2 TEASPOON SALT

3/4 CUP WATER

3/4 CUP SOUR MILK

2 EGGS

1 TEASPOON VANILLA

4 OUNCES UNSWEETENED CHOCOLATE, MELTED

❧ Cream shortening with sugar and add flour, baking powder, soda, and salt. Add remaining ingredients. Mix all together; beat 3 minutes. Bake in a 9" × 13" baking pan or in layer pans. Very moist.

Blueberry Cake

Tried and true over 200 times—always good!

Makes 20–24 servings if using a 9" × 13" pan

1/2 CUP BUTTER

1 1/2 CUPS SUGAR

2 EGGS

3 CUPS FLOUR

1 TEASPOON CREAM OF TARTAR

1/2 TEASPOON BAKING SODA

1 CUP MILK

1 PINT FRESH BLUEBERRIES

&- Cream butter, sugar, and eggs. Add sifted dry ingredients alternately with milk. Dust berries with flour. Add berries and fold in. Bake in well-greased pan at 375° for 50 minutes. May be made in 2 small pans for bake sale at church. May also be made in a tube pan or 9" × 13" pan.

Rum Cake

Serves 18–20

1 PACKAGE YELLOW CAKE MIX

4 EGGS

1 CUP WATER

1 TABLESPOON VANILLA

1 STICK BUTTER OR MARGARINE, MELTED

1 PACKAGE INSTANT VANILLA PUDDING MIX

1/2 CUP CHOPPED NUTS

1 CUP SUGAR

1/2 CUP WATER

1 BOTTLE RUM EXTRACT

1–2 TABLESPOONS RUM

&- Mix together cake mix, eggs, water, vanilla, and butter. Add vanilla pudding mix and nuts. Bake 55–60 minutes in well-greased tube pan at 350°. Boil sugar and water until dissolved. Let cool and then add rum extract and rum. Pour over cake while still in pan. Let cool and wrap in foil until ready to use. Better after mellowing a short time.

Lemon (Summer Squash) Pound Cake

This keeps well if it lasts that long!

Serves 18–20

1 CUP MARGARINE

1 1/2 CUPS SUGAR

2 TEASPOONS LEMON PEEL

4 EGGS

1/2 CUP SOUR CREAM

3 CUPS FLOUR

1 TEASPOON BAKING POWDER

1/4 TEASPOON SALT

1 1/2 CUPS SHREDDED AND DRAINED SUMMER SQUASH

❧ Cream together the margarine, sugar, and lemon peel. Add eggs and sour cream. Stir in the flour, baking powder, and salt. Last add the summer squash. Pour into a 10" tube pan and bake at 350° for 50–60 minutes. Cool 15–20 minutes in pan and turn out onto serving plate. Drizzle with the following icing:

1 CUP CONFECTIONERS' SUGAR

2 TABLESPOONS LEMON JUICE

Note: Add a few drops more lemon juice if needed to make barely pourable from a spoon.

Date Nut Cake

Serves 18–20

4 EGGS, SEPARATED

1 CUP SUGAR

1/2 POUND BUTTER, MELTED

1 TEASPOON VANILLA

1 CUP FLOUR

2 TEASPOONS BAKING POWDER

1 QUART SHELLED PECANS, CHOPPED

1 POUND DATES, CHOPPED

❧ Beat egg yolks very well. Add sugar, melted butter, and vanilla, mixing well. Add flour, baking powder, dates, and nuts. Mix all together. Beat egg whites until stiff. Fold into batter. Bake in a 9" tube pan at 300° for 2 hours. This cake is very rich. Small pieces are quite sufficient.

Milk Chocolate Cake

Very good seller.

Serves 18–20

2¼ CUPS SUGAR

3 TABLESPOONS WATER

2 SQUARES UNSWEETENED CHOCOLATE, MELTED

¾ CUP SOFT BUTTER

1 TEASPOON VANILLA

4 EGGS, SEPARATED

2¼ CUPS SIFTED CAKE FLOUR

1 TEASPOON CREAM OF TARTAR

½ TEASPOON BAKING SODA

½ TEASPOON SALT

1 CUP MILK

❧ Stir ¼ cup sugar and the water into melted chocolate. Set aside. Cream butter and remaining 2 cups sugar. Add vanilla, and then egg yolks, 1 at a time, beating well after each addition. Add chocolate mixture and blend. Add sifted flour, cream of tartar, soda, and salt, alternating with 1 cup milk. Beat until smooth. Fold in stiffly beaten egg whites. Bake at 350° in a well-greased and floured 10" tube pan. When cool, dust with confectioners' sugar.

Torta di Mandorla (Almond Cake)

Serves 14–16

2 CUPS UNPEELED ALMONDS

1⅓ CUPS SUGAR

8 EGG WHITES

SALT

GRATED RIND OF 1 LEMON

6 TABLESPOONS FLOUR

❧ Put almonds and sugar in blender or food processor and grind to a fine consistency. Beat egg whites with a pinch of salt to form stiff peaks. Fold ground almonds and grated lemon peel into the egg whites gently but thoroughly. Add flour by shaking it through a strainer, mixing gently. Thickly smear an 8" or 9" springform pan with butter. Pour the batter into the pan, shaking it to level it off. Bake at 350° for 1 hour. Test with a toothpick to be sure cake is dry. When slightly cooled, remove from springform pan. Serve completely cold.

Cookies, Bars, and Squares

Prastgards Kaker
(Swedish Parsonage Cookies)

Makes about 2 dozen

1/2 CUP BUTTER OR MARGARINE

1 CUP SUGAR

2 EGGS

2 1/2 CUPS SIFTED FLOUR

1 TEASPOON BAKING POWDER

1/2 TEASPOON SALT

1 TEASPOON ALMOND FLAVORING

EGG YOLK

SUGAR

CHOPPED WALNUTS

☙ Cream butter and sugar, add unbeaten eggs, and beat well. Sift flour, baking powder, and salt. Add almond flavoring to creamed mixture, then sifted dry ingredients. Place on long, greased cookie sheet in 2 long flat strips. Brush with egg yolk; sprinkle top with white sugar and chopped walnuts. Bake at 375° for 15–20 minutes. Cut into diagonal strips while hot.

Faghtigman (pronounced fut-ee-mahn)

Makes 2–3 dozen

6 EGG YOLKS
6 TEASPOONS SUGAR
6 TABLESPOONS CREAM
1 1/2 CUPS FLOUR
1/8 TEASPOON SALT
1 TEASPOON GROUND CARDAMOM
OIL OR SHORTENING FOR FRYING

  Beat egg yolks and sugar. Add cream, flour, salt, and ground cardamom. Heat salad oil or shortening to frying temperature (350°). Roll dough very thin and cut with pastry cutter into diamond shapes with a slit. Fry in oil just until browned. Cool on paper toweling. Sprinkle with powdered sugar, if desired.

Sandbakkels

Makes 3–4 dozen

1 CUP SHORTENING, PART MARGARINE
1 CUP SUGAR
1 EGG
1 TEASPOON ALMOND EXTRACT
2 1/2 CUPS FLOUR

  Mix ingredients together. Press into sandbakkel tins. Bake at 350° until lightly browned. Let cool slightly, then gently remove cookies from tins.

Sugar Cookies with Almond Glaze

Makes 3½ dozen

1 CUP BUTTER OR MARGARINE, SOFTENED
¾ CUP SUGAR
1 TEASPOON ALMOND EXTRACT
2 CUPS FLOUR
½ TEASPOON BAKING POWDER
¼ TEASPOON SALT

Combine butter, sugar, and almond extract in large mixer bowl. Beat at medium speed until creamy, scraping sides and beaters often. Reduce speed to low and add all remaining ingredients. Beat until well mixed. Roll dough into 1" balls and place on parchment paper on cookie sheet. Butter and sugar the bottom of a glass. Bake at 400° for 7–9 minutes. Cool 1 minute before removing from sheets. Glaze as follows:

Glaze:

1½ CUPS CONFECTIONERS' SUGAR
1 TEASPOON ALMOND EXTRACT
4–5 TEASPOONS WATER
SLICED ALMONDS

Sift ingredients together in a small bowl. Mix with wire whisk. Spread on cookies when cool, and sprinkle sliced almonds on top.

Crispee Bars Deluxe

Makes 20–24 bars

½ CUP PEANUT BUTTER
½ CUP LIGHT BROWN SUGAR
½ CUP LIGHT CORN SYRUP
4 CUPS CRISPED RICE CEREAL
6 TABLESPOONS BROWN SUGAR
3 TABLESPOONS CREAM OR MILK
3 TABLESPOONS BUTTER OR MARGARINE
1 CUP CONFECTIONERS' SUGAR
1 CUP CHOCOLATE CHIPS

1. Heat until blended peanut butter, light brown sugar, and light corn syrup. *Do not boil.* Mix this with the crisped rice cereal and pack into a greased 9" × 13" pan.

2. Mix together in saucepan 6 tablespoons brown sugar, cream or milk, and butter. Bring to a boil and boil 1 minute. Add 1 cup or a little more confectioners' sugar and spread over top of cereal mixture in pan. Melt 1 cup chocolate chips, thinned with a little butter, and spread over top. Let cool before slicing.

Chocolate Almond Bark

Makes 35–50 pieces

3/4 CUP MARGARINE, SOFTENED

1/3 CUP SUGAR

1/3 CUP BROWN SUGAR

2 TABLESPOONS COFFEE LIQUEUR

1 1/2 CUPS FLOUR

1 6-OUNCE PACKAGE CHOCOLATE CHIPS

1/2 CUP SLIVERED ALMONDS

❧ Preheat oven to 375°. In large bowl of electric mixer, cream margarine and sugars, beating until light and fluffy. Blend in liqueur. Gradually add flour; mix all until blended. Stir in chocolate chips. Spread mixture into an ungreased jelly roll pan. Sprinkle evenly with almonds, pressing them lightly into the dough. Bake until well browned, 18–20 minutes. Cool completely. Break into pieces. Delicious! Makes many pieces of various sizes.

Crunchy Surprise Bars

Makes 20–24 bars

1 CUP SUGAR

1 CUP BUTTER OR MARGARINE, SOFTENED

1/4 CUP MOLASSES

1 EGG YOLK

1 TEASPOON VANILLA

2 CUPS FLOUR

1 12-OUNCE PACKAGE SEMISWEET CHOCOLATE CHIPS

1 CUP RAISINS

1 CUP PEANUTS

1/3 CUP PEANUT BUTTER

❧ Mix sugar, butter, molasses, egg yolk, and vanilla with spoon. Stir in flour and 1 cup chocolate chips. Press dough into ungreased 9" × 13" pan. Bake until golden brown, 25–30 minutes at 350°. Mix remaining chocolate chips, raisins, peanuts, and peanut butter in a 2-quart saucepan. Heat over medium-low heat, stirring constantly until chocolate chips are melted. Spread over crust in pan. Refrigerate at least 2 hours. Cut into bars.

Note: Top will not crack if put on when mixture is warm.

Toffee Bars

Makes 20–24 bars

1/2 CUP BUTTER
1/2 CUP SUGAR
1 CUP FIRMLY PACKED BROWN SUGAR
2 CUPS FLOUR
1 CUP BUTTERMILK
1 TEASPOON BAKING SODA
1 EGG
1 TEASPOON VANILLA

Topping:
6 TOFFEE CANDY BARS, CRUSHED
1/4 CUP CHOPPED NUTS
1/2 CUP RESERVED DRY INGREDIENTS

৯ Cream butter thoroughly. Add sugars gradually, beating well after each addition. Blend in flour and mix well. Reserve 1/2 cup of this mixture for later use. To remainder of mixture, add buttermilk, soda, egg, and vanilla. Beat until completely blended. Pour batter into greased 9" × 13" pan and sprinkle topping* evenly over surface. Bake at 350° 35–40 minutes.

*To prepare topping, crush candy bars and mix with chopped nuts and reserved 1/2 cup dry mixture. To make it easier to crush toffee bars, put them in the freezer until ready to crush.

Congo Bars

Makes 30–35 squares

1 POUND DARK BROWN SUGAR
2/3 CUP BUTTER OR MARGARINE
3 EGGS
2 3/4 CUPS FLOUR
2 1/2 TEASPOONS BAKING POWDER
1/2 TEASPOON SALT
1 TEASPOON VANILLA
1 6-OUNCE PACKAGE CHOCOLATE CHIPS
1 CUP NUTS

৯ Cream brown sugar and butter well. Add eggs, beating well. Sift together the flour, baking powder, and salt. Add dry ingredients and vanilla to egg mixture. Beat well. Add chocolate chips and nuts. Spread into greased jelly roll pan and bake at 350° for 20–25 minutes.

Tea Time Tassies

Makes 2 dozen

1 3-OUNCE PACKAGE CREAM CHEESE

1/2 CUP MARGARINE

1 TEASPOON VANILLA

1/2 TEASPOON SALT

1 CUP SIFTED FLOUR

1 EGG

3/4 CUP BROWN SUGAR

1 TABLESPOON SOFT MARGARINE

2/3 CUP COARSELY BROKEN PECANS

1. For the pastry, soften the cream cheese and 1/2 cup margarine to room temperature. Blend. Stir in flour; chill slightly, about 1 hour. Shape into 2 dozen 1" balls. Place in tiny ungreased muffin cups. Press dough on bottom and up sides of cups.

2. For the filling, beat together egg, sugar, 1 tablespoon margarine, vanilla, and salt just until smooth. Divide 1/2 the pecans among pastry-lined cups. Add egg mixture and top with remaining pecans. Bake at 350° for 25 minutes.

Lemon Bars I

Makes 36 1 1/2" squares

1 1/2 CUPS GRAHAM CRACKER CRUMBS

1/2 CUP BUTTER, MELTED

1/3 CUP BROWN SUGAR (PACKED)

3/4 CUP SIFTED FLOUR

1/2 TEASPOON BAKING POWDER

1/4 TEASPOON SALT

1 1/3 CUPS (15-OUNCE CAN) SWEETENED CONDENSED MILK

1/2 CUP LEMON JUICE

1 TEASPOON GRATED LEMON RIND

Mix graham cracker crumbs, butter, brown sugar, flour, baking powder, and salt. Spread 2/3 mixture in 8" × 12" pan or 9" square pan, patting down well on sides and bottom of pan. Blend condensed milk, lemon juice, and lemon rind well. Spread this filling on bars. Sprinkle remaining crumbs over lemon filling and bake at 350° for 20 minutes.

Lemon Bars II

Makes 48 1½" squares

½ CUP CONFECTIONERS' SUGAR

2 CUPS FLOUR

1 CUP BUTTER, SOFTENED

4 EGGS

2 CUPS SUGAR

DASH SALT

⅓ CUP FRESH LEMON JUICE

¼ CUP FLOUR

½ TEASPOON BAKING POWDER

❧ Sift confectioners' sugar and flour. Cut in butter until mixture clings together. Press into a 9" × 13" pan. Bake at 350° for 20 minutes until light brown. Beat eggs, sugar, salt, and lemon juice. Sift ¼ cup flour and baking powder. Add to egg mixture. Pour on baked crust. Bake at 350° for 25 minutes. Sprinkle with confectioners' sugar.

Gingerbread Cupcakes

Makes about 12 cupcakes

½ CUP SHORTENING

⅔ CUP MOLASSES

½ CUP SUGAR

2 EGGS, BEATEN

2 CUPS FLOUR

1 TEASPOON BAKING POWDER

1 TEASPOON BAKING SODA

½ TEASPOON SALT

1 TEASPOON GINGER

1 TEASPOON CINNAMON

1 CUP SOUR MILK

❧ Heat first 3 ingredients to the boiling point. Cool. Add beaten eggs. Blend in dry ingredients alternately with sour milk. Line muffin tin with cupcake cups and spoon in batter. Bake at 350° for 15 minutes.

Pies

Classic Blueberry Pie

Serves 6

PASTRY FOR 2-CRUST PIE

1 CUP SUGAR

2 TABLESPOONS FLOUR

4 CUPS BLUEBERRIES

DASH SALT

1/4 TEASPOON NUTMEG

1/4 TEASPOON CINNAMON

1 TABLESPOON BUTTER

Line pie plate with pastry. Mix sugar and flour; spread about 1/4 of it on lower crust. Fill with blueberries. Sprinkle the rest of sugar mix over berries. Add salt and sprinkle with nutmeg and cinnamon. Dot with butter. Place top crust on pie, flute edges, and cut slits. Bake at 425° for 40 minutes.

Custard Pie

Makes 6 servings

PASTRY FOR 1-CRUST PIE

4 EGGS, SLIGHTLY BEATEN

1/2 CUP SUGAR

1/2 TEASPOON SALT

3 CUPS MILK

1/2 TEASPOON VANILLA

NUTMEG

❧ Line a 9" pie plate with pastry. Flute edge of pie crust. Combine eggs, sugar, and salt. Add milk and vanilla. Pour into unbaked pie shell. Sprinkle nutmeg over filling. Bake at 450° for 10 minutes. Reduce heat to 350° and continue baking 30 minutes longer.

Coconut Pie

Makes 6 servings

2 CUPS MILK

3/4 CUP SUGAR

1/2 CUP BISCUIT MIX

4 EGGS

1/4 CUP BUTTER OR MARGARINE

1 1/2 TEASPOONS VANILLA

1 CUP FLAKED COCONUT

❧ Combine milk, sugar, biscuit mix, eggs, butter, and vanilla in electric mixer. Blend on low speed for 3 minutes. Pour into greased 9" pie pan. Let stand about 5 minutes; then sprinkle with coconut. Bake at 350° for 40 minutes. Serve warm or cold.

Lemon Meringue Pie

Serves 6

½ CUP COLD WATER

7 TABLESPOONS CORNSTARCH

1½ CUPS HOT WATER

1¼ CUPS WHITE SUGAR

3 EGG YOLKS, SLIGHTLY BEATEN

JUICE AND GRATED RIND
    OF 1 LEMON

1 TABLESPOON BUTTER

1 BAKED PIE SHELL

3 EGG WHITES

6 TABLESPOONS SUGAR

1. Combine cold water and cornstarch to thin paste.

2. Combine hot water and 1¼ cups sugar in top of double boiler over direct heat and bring to boil. Stirring constantly, add cornstarch paste and cook until mixture begins to thicken. Over hot water in double boiler cook until thick and smooth (about 15 minutes).

3. Stir a small amount of mixture into beaten egg yolks and return to double boiler for a couple minutes more. Add lemon juice, rind, and butter. Blend well. Cool, stirring occasionally. Pour into pie shell.

Note: To get more juice from a fresh lemon, wash the lemon and put in microwave for 40–45 seconds. When you cut into it, the juice will flow freely. Be careful, sometimes the lemon will get quite hot even in that short time.

Meringue:
Beat egg whites until stiff. Add 6 tablespoons sugar gradually, beating constantly. Swirl onto the lemon filling. Bake in a slow 325° oven until firm and lightly browned.

Angel Lemon Pie

Serves 6–8

Meringue for Shell:

4 EGG WHITES

¼ TEASPOON CREAM OF TARTAR

1 CUP SIFTED POWDERED SUGAR

Beat egg whites with cream of tartar until stiff. Gradually add sugar until stiff peaks form. Butter pie plate and line with meringue. Bake 1 hour at 275°.

Filling:

4 EGG YOLKS, SLIGHTLY BEATEN

½ CUP SUGAR

3 TABLESPOONS FRESH LEMON JUICE

3 TABLESPOONS FINELY GRATED LEMON RIND

⅛ TEASPOON SALT

1 CUP HEAVY CREAM, WHIPPED

Blend all ingredients, except cream, in double boiler until thick. Fold in cream. Pour into shell. Serve chilled.

French Silk Pie

Serves 6

PASTRY FOR SINGLE-CRUST PIE

1 CUP SUGAR

3/4 CUP BUTTER (NOT MARGARINE)

3 SQUARES (3 OUNCES) UNSWEETENED CHOCOLATE, MELTED
AND COOLED

1 1/2 TEASPOONS VANILLA

3 PASTEURIZED EGGS*

1. Prepare and roll out pastry. Line a 9" pie plate. Trim pastry to 1/2" beyond edge of pie plate. Flute edge; prick bottom and sides of pastry with tines of a fork. Bake at 450° for 10–12 minutes. Cool on wire rack.

2. In a small mixer bowl, cream sugar and butter for about 4 minutes or until light. Blend in cooled chocolate and vanilla. Add eggs, 1 at a time, beating on medium speed for 2 minutes after each addition, scraping sides of bowl constantly. Turn into baked pastry shell. Chill overnight. Cover and chill to store.

*The eggs in this pie are not cooked, so it is imperative that pasteurized eggs be used. Pasteurized eggs are readily available in the supermarket.

Gram's Pine Grove Chess Pie

Serves 4–5

PASTRY FOR 8" 1-CRUST PIE, UNCOOKED

1 CUP BROWN SUGAR, PACKED

1/2 CUP GRANULATED SUGAR

1 TABLESPOON FLOUR

2 EGGS

2 TABLESPOONS MILK

1 TEASPOON VANILLA

1/2 CUP MELTED BUTTER

1 CUP WALNUTS

Mix together brown sugar, granulated sugar, and flour. Beat in eggs, milk, vanilla, and butter. Fold in walnuts. Pour into pastry-lined pie shell. Bake at 375° for 40–50 minutes.

Rhubarb Custard Pie

Serves 6–7

2 EGG YOLKS
1 CUP SUGAR
2 TABLESPOONS FLOUR
1/4 TEASPOON SALT
2 TABLESPOONS BUTTER OR MARGARINE
2 CUPS DICED RHUBARB
UNBAKED 9" PIE SHELL
2 EGG WHITES
4 TABLESPOONS SUGAR

1. Mix together egg yolks, sugar, flour, and salt until well blended. Add butter or margarine. Pour mixture over diced rhubarb in a bowl and mix well. Pour into pie shell and bake at 350° for 25 minutes.

2. Beat egg whites until stiff and gradually add 4 tablespoons sugar.

3. Continue beating until meringue is stiff and sugar is well beaten in.

4. Remove pie from oven and cover with meringue. Bake at 400° for 10 minutes or until golden brown.

Pecan Pie I

Very rich.

Serves 6–8

1 CUP WHITE CORN SYRUP
1 CUP DARK BROWN SUGAR
1/3 TEASPOON SALT
1/3 CUP BUTTER OR MARGARINE, MELTED
1 TEASPOON VANILLA
3 WHOLE EGGS, SLIGHTLY BEATEN
1 HEAPING CUP PECANS
9" PIE SHELL, UNBAKED

Combine syrup, sugar, salt, butter, vanilla, and mix well. Add slightly beaten eggs. Add pecans. Pour into a 9" unbaked pie shell. Bake in a preheated 350° oven for approximately 45 minutes.

Pecan Pie II

"Eat to the strum of banjoes!"

Makes 6–8 servings

1–1½ CUPS CHOPPED PECANS
9" PIE SHELL, UNBAKED
3 WHOLE EGGS
2 TABLESPOONS BUTTER, MELTED
2 TABLESPOONS FLOUR
½ TEASPOON VANILLA
½ TEASPOON SALT
½ CUP SUGAR
1 CUP DARK CORN SYRUP

❧ Sprinkle the chopped nuts over the pie shell. Beat eggs; blend in melted butter, flour, vanilla, salt, sugar, and syrup. Pour over the nuts and bake at 425° for 10 minutes. Then reduce heat to 325° and bake 40 minutes more.

Lemon Sponge Pie

Serves 6

2 CUPS SUGAR
4 TABLESPOONS BUTTER OR MARGARINE
4 TABLESPOONS FLOUR
4 EGG YOLKS
2 CUPS MILK
JUICE FROM 2 LEMONS
GRATE RIND OF 2 LEMONS
4 EGG WHITES, BEATEN STIFF
9" PIE CRUST, UNBAKED

❧ Cream sugar and butter together. Add the flour, stirring until mixed. Add the yolks. Beat this mixture until smooth and add the milk, lemon juice, and rind. Fold in the stiffly beaten egg whites and pour mixture into pie crust. Bake in a hot oven for 10 minutes and then lower heat to 325°. Bake until firm to the touch and nicely browned. Serve when cool.

Jamestown Rich Squash or Pumpkin Pie

Serves 6

1 CUP SQUASH OR PUMPKIN
1 CUP HEAVY CREAM OR EVAPORATED MILK
1 CUP SUGAR
3 EGGS, SLIGHTLY BEATEN
1 TEASPOON CINNAMON
1 TEASPOON NUTMEG
3/4 TEASPOON GINGER
3/4 TEASPOON SALT
1/4 TEASPOON MACE
4 TABLESPOONS BRANDY
UNBAKED 9" PIE CRUST

❧ Mix all ingredients except pie crust together well in large bowl. Pour mixture into unbaked 9" pie crust. Bake at 425° for 15 minutes and at 325° for 45 minutes.

Pumpkin Sponge Pie

Serves 6–8

10" PIE CRUST, UNBAKED
2 EGG WHITES, BEATEN
3/4 CUP SUGAR
2 EGG YOLKS
2 CUPS PUMPKIN
2 TABLESPOONS MOLASSES
2 HEAPING TABLESPOONS FLOUR
1 TEASPOON SALT
2 CUPS MILK
CINNAMON FOR TOP

❧ Line a 10" pie pan with pastry. Beat egg whites until stiff; add a small amount of sugar to them. (Use a small amount of the 3/4 cup.) Beat egg yolks; add rest of sugar and remaining ingredients. Fold in egg whites and pour into the prepared pie shell. Sprinkle cinnamon on top. Bake at 425° for 15 minutes and then at 325° for 45 minutes longer.

West Pond Apple Pie

The peacefulness surrounding this lovely little pond tucked down in a valley deep in the woods, makes sharing food very special. This pie, hot from the oven and lovingly prepared for our arrival, is a flavor delight. Beyond the flavor, it makes one feel warm all over to be in such a setting with good friends and with our adorable toy poodles, Daisy and Sven, playing at our feet. Nourishment of body and soul!

Serves 6–8

3/4 CUP SUGAR (IF APPLES ARE VERY TART, MAY NEED MORE SUGAR)

1 1/2 TABLESPOONS CREAM OF TARTAR

1/2 TEASPOON CINNAMON

1/4 TEASPOON NUTMEG

3–4 POUNDS OF MACINTOSH APPLES

PASTRY FOR 2-CRUST PIE

8–9 DABS BUTTER

SEVERAL DROPS MILK

A PINCH OF SUGAR

1. Preheat oven to 425°. Place a foil-covered pan below baking level to catch possible drips. Line 9" or 10" pie pan with bottom crust.

2. Combine sugar, cream of tartar, cinnamon, and nutmeg. Mix thoroughly!

3. Peel apples and slice quite thinly into a bowl. Between every 2 or 3 sliced apples, sprinkle a little of the dry mixture over the slices. (Reserve 2 tablespoons of dry mixture for later use.) Mix all the slices to ensure that they are covered with dry mixture. Carefully place slices on bottom crust and slightly round in center. Sprinkle the reserved dry mixture over the slices. Put the 8–9 dabs of butter randomly over the slices.

4. Put on top crust, pinching the top and bottom crust together to seal in the juices during baking. Gently spread milk, a drop at a time, over the top crust. Sprinkle a pinch or two of sugar over the top crust. Using a sharp knife or a fork, cut slits in top crust. Bake at 425° for 10 minutes; reduce heat to 350° for additional 40 minutes. Crust should be golden brown. Remove from oven and cool.

Delicious!

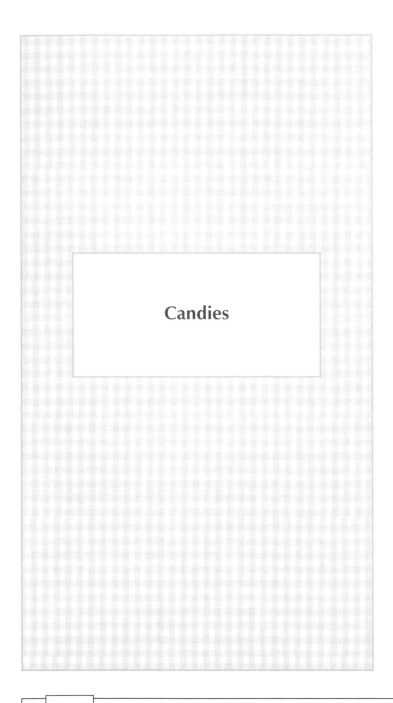

Candies

Aunt Lou's Fudge

Makes 77 1" squares

3 CUPS WHITE SUGAR

4 TABLESPOONS COCOA

1 CUP EVAPORATED MILK

1 CUP PEANUT BUTTER

1 CUP MARSHMALLOW FLUFF

1 CUP CHOPPED NUTS

3/4 STICK MARGARINE

1 TEASPOON VANILLA

⤸ Mix white sugar, cocoa, and milk and boil for 7 minutes. Remove from heat. Add remaining ingredients and mix. Pour into buttered 7" × 11" pan.

Peanut Butter Fudge

Makes 64 1" squares

2 CUPS SUGAR

1 CUP EVAPORATED MILK, UNDILUTED

1/4 CUP MARGARINE

1 12-OUNCE JAR NUTTY PEANUT BUTTER

1 CUP MINIATURE MARSHMALLOWS

1 TEASPOON VANILLA

Boil sugar, milk, and margarine in an iron or very heavy pan, stirring constantly. Add peanut butter, marshmallows, and vanilla. Pour into a buttered 8" square pan.

Soda Cracker Fudge

Makes 64 1" squares

2 CUPS WHITE SUGAR

2/3 CUP MILK

4 TABLESPOONS PEANUT BUTTER

1 7 1/2-OUNCE JAR MARSHMALLOW FLUFF

1/2 TEASPOON GINGER

3/4 CUP SALTINE CRACKERS, CRUSHED FINE

1 CUP WALNUTS

Mix sugar and milk and boil for 5 minutes (or softball stage). Add remaining ingredients. Grease an 8" × 8" pan and pour in mixture.

Chocolate Fudge

Makes 5 pounds

1/2 POUND MARGARINE

1 LARGE (12-OUNCE) CAN EVAPORATED MILK

5 CUPS SUGAR

1 SMALL AND 1 LARGE PACKAGE CHOCOLATE CHIPS

1 LARGE JAR MARSHMALLOW FLUFF

2 TEASPOONS VANILLA

1 CUP WALNUTS

Mix together in saucepan margarine, milk, and sugar. Bring to boil and boil for 10 minutes. Remove from stove and blend in the chocolate chips, Marshmallow Fluff, vanilla, and walnuts. Pour mixture into a buttered 9" × 13" pan. Fudge will be creamy. For easier handling, let set to dry out a little.

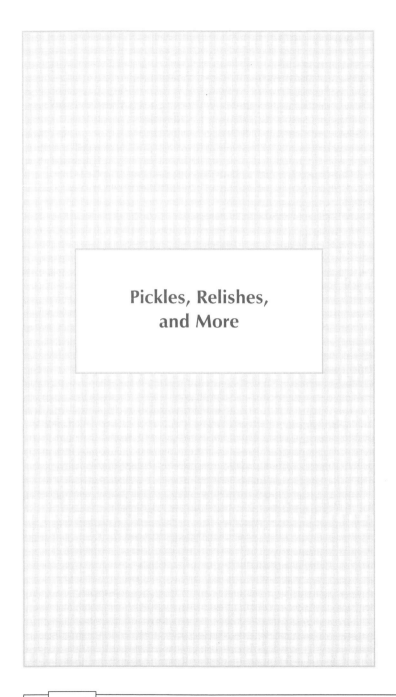

Pickles, Relishes, and More

Brandied Cranberries

Makes about 3 cups

4 CUPS FRESH CRANBERRIES

2 CUPS SUGAR

1/3 CUP BRANDY

🖎 Place cranberries in a 13" × 9" × 2" baking pan. Sprinkle evenly with sugar. Cover with foil; bake in 300° oven for 1 hour. Stir carefully. Stir in brandy. Store in screw-top 1/2-pint jars. Great for Christmas gifts or food sales.

Zucchini Relish

About 12 pints

12 CUPS ZUCCHINI, SLICED
4 CUPS SLICED ONIONS
5 TABLESPOONS SALT
6 CUPS SUGAR
1 TABLESPOON DRY MUSTARD
3/4 TEASPOON NUTMEG
3/4 TABLESPOON CORNSTARCH
3/4 TABLESPOON TURMERIC
1 1/2 TEASPOONS CELERY SEEDS
1/2 TEASPOON BLACK PEPPER
2 1/2 CUPS VINEGAR
1 RED BELL PEPPER, CHOPPED
1 GREEN PEPPER, CHOPPED

Put zucchini and onions through food chopper. Mix with 5 tablespoons salt. Let stand overnight. Rinse well with cold water. Drain well in colander. In large kettle mix sugar and all spices and vinegar. Let boil until it starts to thicken. Add all vegetables. Cook slowly 30 minutes. Can in hot sterilized jars at once.

Chili Sauce

Makes about 4 pints

12 RIPE TOMATOES, CUT IN SMALL PIECES (SCALD OFF SKINS FIRST)
3 SWEET RED PEPPERS, CUT UP
3 ONIONS, CUT UP
1 CUP VINEGAR (3/4 VINEGAR, 1/4 WATER)
1 SCANT CUP SUGAR

In a bag (cheesecloth) tie:
1 TEASPOON CINNAMON
1 TABLESPOON CELERY SEED
1 TABLESPOON ALLSPICE (GROUND)

Bring to boil, simmer, cook down, stir, and stir flavoring out of bag. Clean and sterilize 1/2-pint jars before filling. Seal.

Note: Recipe may be doubled; do *not* double spices. Instead, use 1 3/4 teaspoons cinnamon, 5 teaspoons celery seed, and 5 teaspoons allspice.

Sweet Ripe Cucumber Pickles

About 6–8 pints

5 POUNDS CUCUMBERS, PEELED AND CUBED
5 POUNDS SUGAR
VINEGAR TO COVER

Tie in cheesecloth:
2 TEASPOONS CINNAMON
1/4 TEASPOON CLOVES
1/4 TEASPOON GINGER

❧ Bring all ingredients except cucumbers to a boil. Pour over cucumbers. Cook slowly until cucumbers look quite transparent. Pour into hot jars and seal. Makes about 6 pints.

Refrigerated Pickles

About 12 pints

25 CUCUMBERS (NOT TOO LARGE)
3 MEDIUM-SIZED ONIONS
1/2 CUP PICKLING SALT
4 CUPS CIDER VINEGAR
5 CUPS SUGAR
1 TEASPOON TURMERIC
1 1/2 TEASPOONS CELERY SEED
1 1/2 TEASPOONS MUSTARD SEED

❧ Wash and wipe cucumbers. Peel onions. Slice unpared cucumbers and onions as for table use, making thin slices. Set aside. Mix all other ingredients; bring to boil and then cool down. Pour over cucumbers and onions. Place in glass jars, and just store in refrigerator, using as wanted. Delicious and so easy!

Dilled Beans or Carrots

About 4 pints

FRESH BEANS OR CARROTS (SLICE AS MANY AS NEEDED
    TO FILL JARS)
1 CLOVE GARLIC PER PINT
1 TABLESPOON DILL SEED PER PINT
2 1/2 CUPS WATER
2 1/2 CUPS WHITE VINEGAR
1/4 CUP PICKLING SALT

Pack raw vegetables into hot jars (leaving 1" head space). Add garlic and dill seed. Combine water, vinegar, and salt. Boil. Pour boiling liquid over vegetables in jars. Seal. Process 10 minutes in boiling water bath.

Miniature Meat and Cheese Loaves

These are an example of selling frozen foods in small quantities for small families.

8 loaves

2 POUNDS GROUND CHUCK
2 3/4 CUPS FRESH BREADCRUMBS
3/1 CUP CHOPPED ONIONS
1/2 CUP CHOPPED GREEN PEPPER
2 TABLESPOONS CHOPPED FRESH PARSLEY
1 TEASPOON SALT
1/4 TEASPOON PEPPER
1/4 TEASPOON BASIL LEAVES
1/4 CUP MILK
1 CAN CONDENSED VEGETABLE SOUP
1/2 CUP CUBED SWISS CHEESE
1 16-OUNCE JAR SPAGHETTI SAUCE

Mix together lightly all ingredients except cheese and spaghetti sauce. Shape into 8 small meatloaves and place on a jelly roll pan. Press cheese cubes into each loaf, covering with meat mixture. Bake at 400° for 35 minutes. Cool and refrigerate or freeze. To serve, heat in spaghetti sauce until well blended.

Note: These little meat loaves could be baked in small foil pans and frozen for the food sale. A note of instruction could accompany them for reheating with sauce. When reheated, they may not even need the sauce because they have a can of soup in the mixture as well as a little milk.

Hot Pepper Jelly

Fills 4–5 small jelly glasses

$1^1/_2$ CHOPPED RED SWEET PEPPERS
2 LONG RED HOT PEPPERS, CHOPPED
$1^1/_2$ CUPS CIDER VINEGAR
$5^1/_2$ CUPS SUGAR
1 6-OUNCE BOTTLE FRUIT PECTIN

❧ Combine peppers in bowl. Place $^1/_2$ in blender or food processor, with $^1/_2$ cup vinegar. Cover; whirl until smooth. Pour into large kettle; repeat with remaining peppers, $^1/_2$ cup vinegar. Rinse blender with remaining vinegar and add vinegar to kettle. Bring to boil; stir in sugar; until boil cannot be stirred down, stir constantly. Boil 1 minute. Remove from heat; stir. Add pectin and stir well; cool 5 minutes. Ladle into hot jars. Seal with wax and cover. Cool completely before moving. Store in cool place.

Hot Tea Mix

Makes 2 cups mix

1 9-OUNCE JAR ($1^1/_4$ CUPS) ORANGE-FLAVORED BREAKFAST
    DRINK POWDER
$^3/_4$ CUP ICED TEA MIX WITH LEMON AND SUGAR
1 TEASPOON GROUND CINNAMON
$^1/_2$ TEASPOON GROUND ALLSPICE
$^1/_4$ TEASPOON GROUND CLOVES

❧ Combine all ingredients; mix well. Store in airtight containers. Directions: For 1 serving, mix 2 tablespoons of Hot Tea Mix and 1 cup boiling water in a cup or mug.

Chicken Coating Mix

Makes about 3½ cups

2 TABLESPOONS PARSLEY FLAKES

1 TABLESPOON GROUND OREGANO

1 TABLESPOON GROUND MARJORAM

1 TABLESPOON GROUND THYME

2 TEASPOONS GROUND ROSEMARY

1 TEASPOON GARLIC SALT

1 TEASPOON ONION SALT

1 TABLESPOON CELERY SALT

1 TABLESPOON GROUND GINGER

1 TEASPOON PEPPER

1 TEASPOON GROUND SAGE

1 TABLESPOON PAPRIKA

1 14–16-OUNCE PACKAGE CORNFLAKES, CRUSHED FINE

❧ Combine all ingredients in a bowl until evenly distributed. Put into a small airtight container. Store in a cool, dry place. Use within 6 months.

Cranberry Relish

1 POUND RAW CRANBERRIES

4 GOOD-SIZED APPLES, CORED BUT NOT PEELED

¾ CUP SUGAR

❧ Put cranberries and apples through grinder. Add sugar to 1 cup pulp. Do not cook. Mix well with remaining pulp and put into jars. This is good with meats, chicken, and turkey.

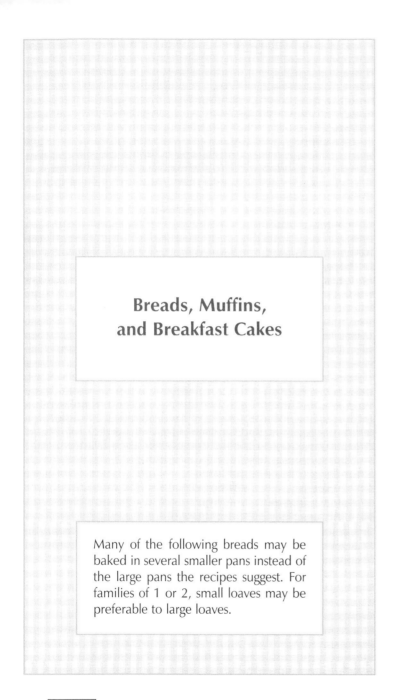

Breads, Muffins, and Breakfast Cakes

Many of the following breads may be baked in several smaller pans instead of the large pans the recipes suggest. For families of 1 or 2, small loaves may be preferable to large loaves.

Swedish Coffee Bread

Makes 1 large coffee ring or 2 smaller rings

2 CUPS MILK, SCALDED

1/2 CUP SHORTENING

3/4 CUP SUGAR

2 EGGS

6–7 CRUSHED CARDAMOM SEEDS

3/4 TEASPOON SALT

6–7 CUPS FLOUR

1 PACKAGE DRY YEAST (DISSOLVED IN LUKEWARM WATER WITH LITTLE SUGAR)

MELTED BUTTER, SUGAR, AND CINNAMON

❧ Mix all together. Knead by hand on floured board or with bread kneader. Let rise until double. Roll dough about 1/2" thick and spread with melted butter. Sprinkle with sugar and cinnamon. Roll up like a jelly roll, cut, and form into a coffee ring or rolls. Let rise until double. Bake at 350° for 30 minutes for coffee ring and 15 minutes for rolls.

Molasses Shredded Wheat Bread

Makes 4 loaves

3 CUPS BOILING WATER

4 LARGE SHREDDED WHEAT BISCUITS

2 TEASPOONS SALT

2/3 CUP SUGAR

2/3 CUP MOLASSES

6 TABLESPOONS SHORTENING

1 CUP COLD WATER

2 YEAST CAKES

1 CUP LUKEWARM WATER

10–12 CUPS FLOUR

1. Pour boiling water over shredded wheat biscuits and add salt, sugar, molasses, and shortening. Cool mixture of first 5 ingredients with cold water after shortening is melted.

2. Add yeast cakes dissolved in 1 cup lukewarm water. Stir in flour, kneading in last 2 or 3 cups until dough is no longer sticky. Let rise until double in bulk.

3. Divide into 4 equal parts. Place in 4 greased bread pans. Let rise until double. Bake at 375° for 20–30 minutes. Lower heat to 350° and finish baking.

Oatmeal Bread

Makes 2 loaves

1 PACKAGE DRY YEAST

1/4 CUP LUKEWARM WATER

1 CUP QUICK OATS

1/4 CUP SHORTENING

1/4 CUP BROWN SUGAR

1 TABLESPOON SALT

1 CUP BOILING WATER

1 CUP COLD MILK

5 1/2 CUPS WHITE FLOUR

Sprinkle yeast over lukewarm water in small bowl. Set in warm place. Combine oats, shortening, sugar, and salt in large bowl. Add boiling water and stir until shortening melts. Add milk. Let cool to lukewarm. Add yeast mixture, then flour. Knead at least 5 minutes on floured board. Place in greased bowl; cover with damp cloth and let rise for 2 hours. Place on floured board; cut into 2 parts. Shape into 2 loaves and place in greased 8 1/2" × 4 1/2" loaf pans. Let rise 1 hour. Bake at 350° for about 40 minutes.

Wheat Bread

Makes 1 loaf

1 PACKAGE DRY YEAST

1 CUP WARM WATER

1 CUP WHOLE WHEAT FLOUR

1³/₄ CUPS WHITE FLOUR

1 TEASPOON SALT

4 TABLESPOONS DARK BROWN SUGAR

2 TABLESPOONS BUTTER

❧ Stir yeast into warm water. In food processor, put flours, salt, and brown sugar. Cut butter into pieces and add to flour mixture. Run processor to chop butter. Run processor while adding water and yeast a little at a time. If too moist, add a little extra white flour. Process 45 seconds to knead. Place in floured plastic bag until double in bulk. Punch down and let rest 5 minutes. Shape and place in greased pan. Let rise until double. Bake about 30 minutes at 375°.

Date Bran Bread

Makes 2 loaves

7–8 CUPS FLOUR

1 TABLESPOON SALT

3 PACKAGES DRY YEAST

3 CUPS BRAN CEREAL

1¹/₂ CUPS MILK

³/₄ CUP WATER

6 TABLESPOONS HONEY

¹/₂ CUP MARGARINE

3 EGGS

1 CUP CHOPPED DATES

¹/₂ CUP CHOPPED NUTS

❧ Combine 1¹/₂ cups flour, salt, yeast, and cereal. Heat milk, water, honey, and margarine until very warm. Add to dry ingredients and beat 2 minutes. Add eggs and ¹/₂ cup flour; beat at high speed 2 minutes. Stir in flour to make stiff dough. Knead until smooth. Place in a greased bowl; let rise until double in size, about 1 hour. Punch down; knead in dates and nuts. Form 2 loaves. Place in 9" × 5" loaf pans and let rise until doubled. Bake at 375° for about 40 minutes.

Variett's Oatmeal Bread

Makes 3 loaves

2–3 PACKAGES DRY YEAST (USUALLY USE 3)
1 CUP WARM WATER
PINCH SUGAR
1 CUP RAW OATMEAL
1/2 CUP SUGAR
1 TEASPOON SALT
2 CUPS BOILING WATER
2 ROUNDED TABLESPOONS SHORTENING
1/2 CUP MOLASSES
2 EGGS
7–8 CUPS FLOUR

✏ Sprinkle yeast over 1 cup warm water and dab of sugar. Mix next 5 ingredients together and add to yeast mixture. Add molasses, eggs, and flour. Let rise in a warm place 1½–2 hours. Punch down and knead. Divide into 3 parts and put in pans that have been greased with margarine. Cover and let rise 1½ hours. Bake at 350° for 45 minutes.

Rag-Brod (Swedish Rye Bread)

Makes 6–8 loaves

6 CUPS WARM WATER
2 PACKAGES DRY YEAST
2 TEASPOONS SUGAR
4 CUPS RYE FLOUR
1 CUP DARK MOLASSES
6 TABLESPOONS SHORTENING, MELTED
2 SCANT TABLESPOONS SALT
16 CUPS WHITE FLOUR (APPROXIMATELY)

1. In 1 cup warm water dissolve yeast with 2 teaspoons sugar.

2. Sift rye flour into large mixing bowl. Make a well in the flour and add the molasses, melted shortening, salt, 5 cups lukewarm water, and 4 cups of white flour to make a very soft dough. Beat until dough becomes very smooth. Add yeast mixture to dough. Mix well.

3. Add remaining 12 cups white flour until dough is stiff. On floured board to prevent sticking, knead for at least 10 minutes. Put back into mixing bowl; spread top of dough with small amount of soft shortening. Let rise 1–1½ hours or until double in size.

4. Punch down; turn out onto board and mold into loaves. Place in greased bread pans. Let rise 1½ hours. Bake at 350° for 20–30 minutes. Remove from pans and place on racks. Brush tops with melted shortening.

Puckerbrush Black Bread

Makes 1 large loaf or 4 mini loaves

1 1/2 CUPS MEDIUM RYE OR GRAHAM FLOUR
2 CUPS WHITE FLOUR
1/2 TEASPOON SALT
1/2 CUP LIGHT BROWN SUGAR
2 TEASPOONS BAKING SODA
1/2 CUP MOLASSES
2 CUPS SOUR MILK OR BUTTERMILK

Mix all dry ingredients, except soda. Add molasses. At last minute add baking soda to milk, and add to other ingredients. Mix well. Pour into well-greased 5" × 9" loaf pan or 4 3" × 5" loaf pans. Bake at 350° for 1 hour (5" × 9") or 30 minutes (3" × 5").

Note: There are no eggs and no shortening in this recipe. This bread is wonderful hot from the oven with soups and chili. It is also great toasted.

Banana Bread I

Makes 1 loaf

1 TEASPOON BAKING SODA
1 TEASPOON WARM WATER
3 MASHED BANANAS
1 3/4 CUPS FLOUR
1/2 TEASPOON CINNAMON
1/2 TEASPOON NUTMEG
1/2 CUP BUTTER (OR VEGETABLE SHORTENING)
1 CUP SUGAR
2 EGGS

Dissolve 1 teaspoon baking soda in 1 teaspoon warm water and add to mashed bananas. Sift dry ingredients together and set aside. Cream butter and sugar. Add eggs, mashed bananas, and dry ingredients. Mix well. Bake at 350° for 45 minutes in an 11" × 7 1/4" × 1 1/2" pan or any other suitable pan. Makes a nice, moist loaf. Makes 22 1/2" slices. These slices will be wide, so you may wish to cut them in 1/2.

Note: Small slices make tasty tea sandwiches spread with cream cheese.

Banana Bread II

Makes 1 loaf

2 CUPS SIFTED FLOUR

1 TEASPOON BAKING SODA

1 TEASPOON SALT

1/2 CUP SHORTENING

1 CUP SUGAR

2 EGGS

1 CUP MASHED RIPE BANANAS (2 TO 3 BANANAS)

1 TABLESPOON VINEGAR PLUS MILK TO MAKE 1/2 CUP LIQUID

🐛 Sift together flour, soda, and salt. Cream shortening, blend in sugar, add eggs 1 at a time, and beat mixture until fluffy. Add flour mixture alternately with bananas and liquid, beating well after each addition. Pour in greased 9 1/2" × 5 1/2" × 2 3/4" loaf pan. Bake at 350° for 60–70 minutes or until done. Cool several hours or overnight before slicing. Makes 1 loaf. May be divided into small loaves if desired.

Date-Nut Bread

Makes 1 large loaf

1 1/2 CUPS BOILING WATER

1 CUP DATES, CUT UP

2 3/4 CUPS FLOUR

1 TEASPOON BAKING SODA

1 TEASPOON SALT

1 TABLESPOON BUTTER

1 1/2 CUPS SUGAR

1 EGG

1/2 CUP CHOPPED NUTS

2 TEASPOONS VANILLA

1. Pour boiling water over dates and let stand until cool. Sift flour, soda, and salt. Set aside.

2. Cream butter and sugar as much as possible and add egg. Mix well. Pour cooled juice from dates into the mixture and add dry ingredients.

3. Add dates, nuts, and vanilla. Bake in 1 large loaf pan at 325–350° for 1 1/4 hours. May be divided into smaller pans. Adjust baking time.

Zucchini Bread

Makes 2 loaves

3 EGGS
1 CUP VEGETABLE OIL
2 CUPS GRATED ZUCCHINI
1½ CUPS SUGAR
1 TEASPOON SALT
3 CUPS FLOUR

1 TEASPOON BAKING SODA
1 TEASPOON BAKING POWDER
1 TEASPOON CINNAMON
1 TEASPOON VANILLA
1 CUP BROKEN NUT MEATS
    (WALNUTS OR PECANS)

৯ Mix together and beat eggs, vegetable oil, zucchini, and sugar. Sift dry ingredients and add to egg mixture, beating well. Add vanilla and stir in nuts. Bake at 350° for about 1 hour.

Blueberry Molasses Bread

2 CUPS FLOUR
1 CUP WHOLE WHEAT FLOUR
½ CUP SUGAR
1 TEASPOON SALT

½ CUP MOLASSES
1 TEASPOON BAKING SODA
1½ CUPS MILK
1½ CUPS BLUEBERRIES

৯ Combine flours, sugar, and salt in large bowl. Add molasses. Dissolve soda in milk; add to flour mixture. Stir in berries. Pour into greased 9" × 5" loaf pan and bake about 1½ hours at 325°.

Lemon Bread

Makes 1 loaf

1½ CUPS FLOUR
½ TEASPOON SALT
1 TEASPOON BAKING POWDER
¼ CUP SHORTENING
1 CUP WHITE SUGAR
2 EGGS
½ CUP MILK
½ CUP FINELY CHOPPED WALNUTS
JUICE AND RIND OF 1 LEMON
¼ CUP SUGAR

৯ Sift flour, salt, and baking powder. Cream shortening and sugar; add eggs and grated rind. Blend together. Add milk alternately with sifted dry ingredients. Add walnuts, which have been coated with flour. Bake in 350° oven in a greased 9" × 5" loaf pan for 45–50 minutes. When bread comes out of oven, mix juice of 1 lemon and ¼ cup sugar together in small bowl. Brush top and sides of warm bread with this mixture. To help with absorption of this mixture into bread, poke the tines of a fork into the top of the bread in several places. Bread is quite sweet. Cut in ½" slices; makes 18 slices. Could be cut even a little thinner if you wish.

Apricot Bread

Makes 1 loaf

1/2 CUP DRIED APRICOTS

1 LARGE ORANGE

1/2 CUP RAISINS

2 TABLESPOONS MARGARINE

1 CUP SUGAR

1 TEASPOON VANILLA

1 EGG

1/2 CUP CHOPPED NUTS

2 CUPS SIFTED FLOUR

2 TEASPOONS BAKING POWDER

1/2 TEASPOON BAKING SODA

1/2 TEASPOON SALT

1. Soak apricots in water to cover for 1 1/2 hours.

2. Squeeze orange and add enough boiling water to juice to make 1 cup of liquid.

3. Put drained apricots, orange peel, and raisins through food chopper twice. If using food processor, pulse to chop well.

4. Cream margarine and sugar. Add vanilla and beat in egg. Add fruit mixture and nuts. Mix together flour, baking powder, soda, and salt. Stir in sifted ingredients alternating with orange juice mixture. Pour batter into a well-greased and floured 9" × 5" loaf pan. Bake in a 350° oven for 1 hour or until toothpick thrust in center comes out clean. Cool slightly before removing from pan. Makes 18 1/2" slices. Frost if desired. (Recipe follows.)

Cream Cheese Frosting:

1 3-OUNCE PACKAGE CREAM CHEESE, SOFTENED

2 TABLESPOONS LIGHT CORN SYRUP

2 1/4 CUPS SIFTED CONFECTIONERS' SUGAR

1/2 TEASPOON VANILLA

Mix all ingredients and beat until fluffy. Makes 1 cup.

Grape-Nut Bread

Makes 1 large loaf or 2 small ones

1 CUP GRAPE-NUTS
2 CUPS SOUR MILK
$1/2$ CUP SUGAR
4 HEAPING TEASPOONS BAKING POWDER
1 TEASPOON BAKING SODA
$1/4$ TEASPOON SALT
1 EGG
$3 1/2$ CUPS FLOUR

❧ Soak Grape-Nuts in sour milk for 30 minutes. Add sugar, baking powder, soda, salt, egg, and flour. Mix all ingredients and bake in a greased loaf pan for 1 hour at 350°. The large loaf would make 18–20 slices.

Note: To make 1 cup sour milk, measure 1 cup sweet (regular) milk and add 1 to 2 tablespoons vinegar or lemon juice.

Molasses Muffins

Makes 16

$2 1/4$ CUPS SIFTED FLOUR
$1/2$ TEASPOON SALT
3 TEASPOONS BAKING POWDER
$3/4$ CUP MILK
$1/4$ CUP OIL
$3/4$ CUP MOLASSES
1 EGG, WELL BEATEN
6 TEASPOONS WHEAT GERM, IF DESIRED

❧ Mix and sift together dry ingredients. Add milk, oil, and molasses to beaten egg. Stir liquid and dry ingredients lightly together. Do not beat. Fill greased muffin tins $2/3$ full. Bake 20 minutes at 350°. You may add 6 teaspoons wheat germ to batter if you wish.

Blueberry Muffins I

Makes 8 large muffins

2 CUPS FLOUR

2 TEASPOONS BAKING POWDER

1/2 TEASPOON SALT (OPTIONAL)

1/2 CUP SUGAR

2 EGGS

1/2 CUP MILK

1 TEASPOON VANILLA OR ALMOND EXTRACT

1/4 CUP OIL

2 CUPS FRESH OR FROZEN BLUEBERRIES

❧ Preheat oven to 400°. Combine flour, baking powder, salt, and sugar in medium-sized bowl. In another bowl, beat eggs; stir in milk, flavoring, and oil. Add all at once to flour mixture, stirring just until moistened. Fold in blueberries. Bake in greased muffin tins approximately 25–30 minutes until lightly golden or toothpick inserted in center comes out clean.

Variations:

- *Apple:* Prepare as above, but add 1/2 teaspoon cinnamon with flour. Add 1 apple, coarsely chopped, with egg mixture. Sprinkle cinnamon and sugar over muffins before baking.
- *Raspberry:* Prepare as above, but add 1 cup fresh raspberries with egg mixture. Fill greased muffin tins 1/3 full of batter. Drop a teaspoon of raspberry jam in center of each and cover with remaining batter.

Blueberry Muffins II

Makes 1 dozen

1 EGG

1/2 CUP MILK

1/4 CUP COOKING OIL

1 1/2 CUPS FLOUR

1/3 CUP SUGAR

2 TEASPOONS BAKING POWDER

1/2 TEASPOON SALT

1 CUP FRESH OR FROZEN BLUEBERRIES

❧ In a small bowl, beat together egg, milk, and oil. Set aside. In large mixing bowl, sift flour, sugar, baking powder, and salt. Make a well in center of dry ingredients. Add milk, egg, and oil mixture. Fold in blueberries. Spoon batter into greased muffin cups and fill 2/3 full. Bake in a 400° oven for 20–25 minutes.

Date Muffins

Makes 1 dozen muffins

1 CUP DATES

1 CUP BOILING WATER

1/4 CUP MELTED BUTTER

1 EGG

1 CUP SUGAR

1 TEASPOON VANILLA

1 3/4 CUPS FLOUR

1/2 TEASPOON BAKING SODA

1/2 TEASPOON SALT

3/4 CUP CHOPPED WALNUTS

❧ Cut up dates; add water and butter and let stand 15 minutes. Combine egg, sugar, and vanilla. Sift together flour, soda, and salt. Add flour mixture alternately with date mixture to egg mixture. Add nuts. Spoon into greased muffin tins and bake at 425° for 15–20 minutes. May also be baked in 9" × 5" × 3" loaf pan at 350° for 1–1 1/4 hours.

Oatmeal Muffins

Makes 12 muffins

1 EGG, WELL BEATEN

1/2 CUP OIL

1/2 CUP BROWN SUGAR

1 CUP SOUR MILK

1 CUP OATMEAL

1 CUP FLOUR

1 TEASPOON BAKING POWDER

1 TEASPOON SALT

1 TEASPOON BAKING SODA

1 TEASPOON CINNAMON

1 CUP RAISINS

❧ Mix egg, oil, and sugar. Add sour milk, oatmeal, flour, baking powder, salt, baking soda, and cinnamon. Add raisins. Mix well and pour into 12 greased muffin tins. Bake at 375° for 25–30 minutes.

Molasses Doughnuts

Makes 2–2½ dozen

⅔ CUP SUGAR

⅔ CUP MOLASSES

2 EGGS, BEATEN SLIGHTLY

2 TABLESPOONS BUTTER, MELTED

1½ TEASPOONS BAKING SODA

1½ CUPS SOUR MILK OR BUTTERMILK

2–3 CUPS FLOUR

1 TEASPOON CINNAMON

1 TEASPOON GINGER

๛ Add sugar and molasses to beaten eggs. Add butter and mix. Add soda to sour milk and add to mixture. Sift 2 cups flour, cinnamon, and ginger and stir in. Add additional flour (up to 1 cup) as needed to make a soft dough, stiff enough to handle. If dough is too soft, add up to 1 more cup of flour. Roll out to ¼" thickness, cut, and fry in deep fat. Handle dough as little as possible.

Scotch Scones

Makes 8 large or 12 small scones

2 CUPS FLOUR

3 TEASPOONS BAKING POWDER

1 TEASPOON SALT

¼ CUP SUGAR

⅓ CUP SHORTENING

2 EGGS

½ CUP MILK

¼ CUP CURRANTS, RAISINS, OR DRIED CRANBERRIES

๛ Sift dry ingredients together in bowl; cut in shortening. Add 1 egg and 1 egg yolk (reserve 1 egg white for topping). Add milk and currants, raisins, or cranberries. Mix with a fork until all flour is moistened. Use a little more milk if necessary. Turn onto floured board and knead gently a few seconds. Roll in a circle ½" thick and cut into desired shapes. Brush lightly with the slightly beaten egg white and sprinkle with sugar. Bake at 425° for 12–15 minutes.

Sour Cream Coffee Cake I

Serves 12

1 cup soft margarine
2 cups sugar
2 eggs, beaten
1 cup dairy sour cream
1½ teaspoons vanilla
2 cups sifted flour
¼ teaspoon salt
1 teaspoon baking powder
½ teaspoon cinnamon
2 tablespoons brown sugar
Nuts (optional)

Cream margarine, sugar, eggs, sour cream, and vanilla. Gradually add flour, salt, and baking powder to creamed mixture. Mix well. Grease and flour an 8¼" × 3¼" tube pan and pour in about ⅓ of batter. Mix together cinnamon and brown sugar and sprinkle over batter. Nuts may be added if desired. Add another ⅓ batter and more cinnamon and sugar. Finish with last ⅓ of batter. Bake at 350° for 1 hour.

Sour Cream Coffee Cake II

Serves 15–18

1 cup sugar
1 cup margarine
3 eggs
1½ teaspoons vanilla
16 ounces sour cream
3 cups flour
½ teaspoon salt
½ teaspoon baking soda
3 teaspoons baking powder
½ cup sugar
1 teaspoon cinnamon
½ cup walnuts

This makes a very heavy batter. Have margarine, eggs, and sour cream at room temperature. Cream 1 cup sugar and margarine. Add eggs and beat. Add vanilla and sour cream. Mix well. Sift and add flour, salt, baking soda, and baking powder. Mix well. Spoon ½ of batter into greased 10" round tube pan or Bundt pan. (This is a large cake.) Mix together ½ cup sugar, 1 teaspoon cinnamon, and the nuts. Top batter with ½ of this mixture. Pour rest of batter into the pan and cover with remainder of topping. Bake at 350° for about 1 hour. Let stand in pan 20 minutes before removing.

Cream Cheese Coffee Cake

Makes 18 servings—each 3" × 2"

1 CUP BUTTER

8 OUNCES CREAM CHEESE, SOFTENED

1¼ CUPS SUGAR

2 EGGS

1 TEASPOON VANILLA

1⅓ CUPS FLOUR

1 TEASPOON BAKING POWDER

½ TEASPOON BAKING SODA

¼ TEASPOON SALT

¼ CUP MILK

Topping:

½ TEASPOON CINNAMON

2 TABLESPOONS BUTTER

⅓ CUP FLOUR

⅓ CUP BROWN SUGAR

🍴 Cream butter, cream cheese, and sugar. Add eggs and vanilla. Mix well. Sift together dry ingredients and add alternately with milk. Mix well and spread in greased 9" × 13" pan. Mix together topping ingredients and spread over batter. Bake at 350° for 40 minutes.

German Coffee Cake

Serves 10–12 slices

½ CUP SHORTENING

1 CUP SUGAR

2 EGGS

1 CUP SOUR CREAM

1 TEASPOON VANILLA

2 CUPS FLOUR

1 TEASPOON BAKING POWDER

1 TEASPOON BAKING SODA

Topping:

½ CUP CHOPPED NUTS

½ CUP BROWN SUGAR

1 TEASPOON CINNAMON

🍴 Cream shortening, sugar, and eggs. Add rest of ingredients and beat well. Place ½ of the batter in a greased 10" tube pan, and sprinkle ½ of the topping over batter. Add the rest of the batter and the remainder of the topping. Bake at 350° for 40 minutes.

Chapter Five

Food for the Family in Crisis

According to *Webster's New World Dictionary,* a crisis is a "decisive or crucial time, stage, or event." There are many ways in which our brothers and sisters may experience a crisis. A helping hand may be needed and appreciated. Sometimes the opportunity to help may be as simple as providing a meal or meals until the need passes. In these brief thoughts we shall consider meals for the family in crisis.

Meals brought to people in their time of need always represent much more than food. The additional dividend is knowing that people care, and seeing the friendly faces of those who deliver the meal. Sometimes, a brief conversation is an important bonus, giving a boost to the spirit. Two hearts are warmed—the one who receives and, just as importantly, the one who gives!

Sometimes, a single meal is all that is necessary, while at other times a series of meals is needed over an extended period. If this is the case, organization is called for so that many people have an opportunity to help and no one becomes overburdened. Perhaps an individual or a church committee will take the lead, and volunteer cooks can choose the day on which they will provide the meal. In that way, the family does not receive two dinners on one evening, and none the next!

Some tips: Keep in mind the size of the family for whom you are providing. Tons of food are not really necessary. For one or two people, simply cook a little extra of what you are preparing for your own family, and bring that to your "guests." Although pretty dishes are nice, I prefer to bring food in disposable containers when possible, so that there is very little cleanup for the family, and dishes will not have to be returned.

People who are able to eat only a very little food usually enjoy a baked custard. It's kind of a joke in this house that Mother thinks everything is cured with baked custard. Some people believe it's chicken soup! It's all good nourishment! Many people have told me they especially appreciated the custard because it is very easy to eat. Custard has protein, calories, and flavor. You will find the recipe later in the chapter.

Our American communities, large and small, are places where people care deeply about each other. The caring that is shown when food is shared goes far beyond the feeding of the body, and it is that caring that really sustains us as we journey together through life.

Following is a collection of recipes that may be used in bringing food to families. However, do refer to any of the other sections in the book. You will find many, many possibilities. ❤

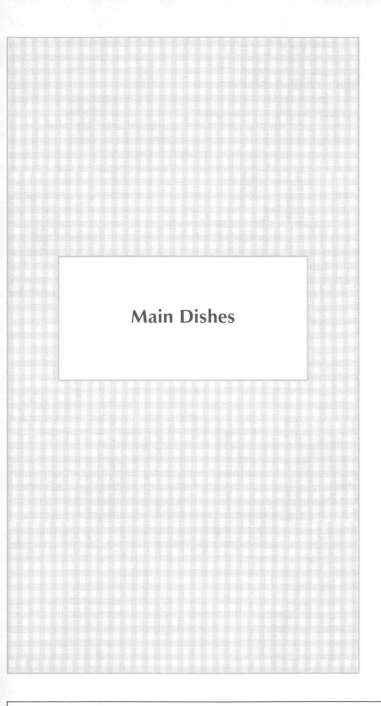

Main Dishes

Flank Steak with Dressing

Serves 4

1 FLANK STEAK, ABOUT 1½ POUNDS
1 TEASPOON SALT
⅛ TEASPOON PAPRIKA
⅛ TEASPOON GINGER
¼ CUP BUTTER OR MARGARINE
2 TABLESPOONS CHOPPED ONION
1 CUP BREADCRUMBS
¼ TEASPOON SALT
DASH OF PAPRIKA
2 TABLESPOONS CHOPPED PARSLEY
3 TABLESPOONS CHOPPED CELERY
1 EGG, SLIGHTLY BEATEN
3 TABLESPOONS OIL
2 TABLESPOONS FLOUR
1 CUP WATER OR STOCK
1 CUP TOMATO JUICE OR WHITE WINE
½ TEASPOON SALT

❧ Rub flank steak with salt, paprika, and ginger. Set aside. Melt butter or margarine and sauté onion until brown. Add breadcrumbs, salt, paprika, parsley, celery, and egg. Spread this dressing over flank steak, roll it loosely, and tie it. Heat oil in skillet and brown steak roll on all sides. Place steak in a casserole dish. Mix together flour, water or stock, tomato juice or white wine, and salt. Pour over the steak and cover casserole dish tightly. Bake it slowly for 1½ hours at 250°.

Teriyaki Steak

Serves 6

2 POUNDS SIRLOIN STEAK OR TENDERIZED ROUND STEAK
    THINLY SLICED

2 TEASPOONS POWDERED GINGER

2 CLOVES GARLIC, MINCED

1 MEDIUM-SIZED ONION, FINELY CHOPPED

2 TABLESPOONS SUGAR

1/2 CUP SOY SAUCE

1/4 CUP WATER

Cut steak into portion-sized pieces. In a saucepan, combine ginger, garlic, onion, sugar, soy sauce, and water. Stir over low heat until sugar dissolves. Pour over meat. Let marinate for 2 hours. Drain. Broil for 3–5 minutes on each side.

Easy Chuck Roast

Serves 4–6

1 1/2 POUNDS CHUCK STEAK

1 ONION, SLICED

1 GREEN PEPPER, SLICED

1 CAN TOMATO SOUP

Cut steak into serving-size pieces. Brown in heavy fry pan. Put meat in roaster or baking dish. Lightly brown the sliced onion and sliced green pepper. Place on top of meat. Rinse fry pan with small amount of water and pour over meat. Pour tomato soup over all. Cover and bake for 3 hours at 250°. This will make its own gravy. Even less tender cuts of meat come out tender.

Sauerbraten Dish

Serves 8

4 POUNDS RUMP BEEF OR MOOSE (YES, *MOOSE*!)

SALT, PEPPER, AND FLOUR

WATER

2 ONIONS, SLICED

1/2 CUP VINEGAR

2 TABLESPOONS LEMON JUICE

2 BAY LEAVES

2 WHOLE CLOVES

2 TABLESPOONS CATSUP

2 TEASPOONS SALT

1/4 TEASPOON PEPPER

8 GINGERSNAPS

❧ In a large pot, dredge the meat well with flour, salt, and pepper and brown on all sides in oil. When nicely browned, add water to cover or nearly cover meat. Add onions, vinegar, lemon juice, bay leaves, cloves, catsup, salt, and pepper. Bring to a slight boil and then simmer for at least 4–5 hours. When meat is done and serving time is near, crush 8 gingersnaps and add to broth. This makes a most delicious gravy. When cooking moose, the gravy will have almost no fat. With mashed potatoes, vegetables, and salad, this will make at least 8 servings. If there are leftovers, moose hash and beef hash are both delicious!

Note: Before serving, remove bay leaf and whole cloves.

Dinner-in-a-Dish

Serves 4 to 5

4 TABLESPOONS BUTTER OR MARGARINE

1 GREEN PEPPER, CHOPPED

1 MEDIUM ONION, CHOPPED

1 POUND GROUND BEEF

SALT AND PEPPER TO TASTE

1 EGG, LIGHTLY BEATEN

2 CUPS WHOLE KERNEL CORN, DRAINED, OR CUT FRESH FROM THE COB

2 TOMATOES, SLICED, OR 1/2 CUP STEWED TOMATOES

1/2 CUP DRY BREADCRUMBS

❧ Heat 3 tablespoons butter or margarine (or olive oil) in a heavy skillet and lightly brown green pepper and onion. Add ground beef and cook over medium heat. Remove from heat and stir in egg. Layer 1/2 the corn, 1/2 the meat mixture, and 1/2 of the tomatoes in a greased casserole. Repeat layers; dot with remaining tablespoon butter and breadcrumbs. Bake in a moderate oven, 350°, for 35–40 minutes. Easily doubled.

Ann's Beans and Beef

Serves 6–8

1 POUND GROUND BEEF
6 STRIPS BACON (OPTIONAL)
1 SMALL ONION
2 1-POUND CANS OF BOSTON-TYPE BAKED BEANS (MOLASSES, NO TOMATO)
1/2 CUP KETCHUP
1/2 CUP MOLASSES
DASH WORCESTERSHIRE

❧ Brown and drain beef. Sauté onion. Combine all ingredients. Bake uncovered at 350° for 45 minutes.

Barbecued Muffins

Serves 8–10

1 10-OUNCE CAN REFRIGERATED BUTTERMILK BISCUITS
1 POUND GROUND BEEF
1/2 CUP KETCHUP
3 TABLESPOONS BROWN SUGAR
1 TABLESPOON CIDER VINEGAR
1/2 TEASPOON CHILI POWDER
1 CUP SHREDDED CHEDDAR CHEESE

❧ Separate dough into 10 biscuits and flatten each into a 5" circle. Press each circle into bottom and up the sides of a greased muffin tin. Set aside. Brown and drain ground beef.

In small bowl, stir together ketchup, brown sugar, vinegar, and chili powder, mixing well. Add to meat and mix well. Divide mixture among biscuit-lined muffin cups and sprinkle with cheese. Bake at 375° for 18–20 minutes or until golden brown. Let cool 5 minutes before serving.

Sweet and Sour Meatballs

Serves 6–8

²/₃ CUP EVAPORATED MILK, UNDILUTED
1¹/₂ POUNDS GROUND BEEF
¹/₂ CUP CHOPPED ONION
²/₃ CUP BREADCRUMBS
1 TEASPOON SALT

❧ Combine evaporated milk, ground beef, chopped onion, breadcrumbs, and salt. Form into small meatballs and brown in skillet in a little butter or margarine. Make the sauce as follows:

1 13¹/₂-OUNCE CAN PINEAPPLE CHUNKS
2 TABLESPOONS CORNSTARCH
¹/₄ CUP VINEGAR
¹/₄ CUP BROWN SUGAR
2 TABLESPOONS SOY SAUCE
1 CUP COARSELY CHOPPED GREEN PEPPER

Drain the pineapple chunks and save the syrup. Add enough water to the syrup to make 1 cup. Mix the syrup with cornstarch, vinegar, brown sugar, and soy sauce. Heat this mixture until thickened and clear. Add pineapple chunks and green pepper. Pour over meatballs and continue to simmer until meatballs are fully cooked.

Sweet and Sour Meat Loaf

Serves 6–8 easily

1 8-OUNCE CAN TOMATO SAUCE
¹/₄ CUP BROWN SUGAR
¹/₄ CUP VINEGAR
1 TEASPOON PREPARED MUSTARD
1 EGG
1 SMALL ONION, MINCED
2 SLICES BREAD, IN CRUMBS
2 POUNDS GROUND BEEF
1 TEASPOON SALT
¹/₄ TEASPOON PEPPER

❧ Heat oven to 400°. Mix tomato sauce with brown sugar, vinegar, and mustard. Stir until sugar is dissolved. Beat egg, and add onion, breadcrumbs, meat, salt, pepper, and ¹/₂ cup of the tomato sauce mixture. Mix together well. Line a shallow pan with foil and shape the meatloaf on the foil. Make holes in top of meat loaf and pour the remainder of the tomato mixture over top. Good hot or cold. Tasty with potatoes and vegetables or with baked beans and potato salad. Leftovers make great sandwiches. This is a nice dish to take to a family because of its versatility.

American Chop Suey

Serves 6

1 POUND LEAN GROUND BEEF
1 MEDIUM ONION, CHOPPED
1 MEDIUM GREEN PEPPER, CHOPPED
2–3 STALKS CELERY, CHOPPED
2 15-OUNCE CANS STEWED TOMATOES
8 OUNCES ELBOW MACARONI, COOKED

❧ Sauté ground beef and drain well. Set aside. Sauté onion, green pepper, and celery in a kettle or large frying pan. When vegetables are sautéed, add beef, stewed tomatoes, and cooked macaroni. Serve with nice bread or biscuits and a salad.

Baked Custard

So simple!

Serves 5–6

3 EGGS, SLIGHTLY BEATEN
2 CUPS MILK
1/3 CUP SUGAR
1 TEASPOON VANILLA
NUTMEG

❧ Beat eggs slightly and add milk, sugar, and vanilla. Beat some more but not too much. Pour into buttered custard cups or a casserole dish. If taking to a sick person, use a buttered foil layer cake pan. The disposable pan holds the custard nicely, and the recipient can just discard the foil pan. Sprinkle top of custard mixture with nutmeg. Bake at 325° for about an hour in a water bath. The dish you use will usually fit into a 9" × 13" pan. Pour about 1/2"–1" of hot water into the pan and put in oven.

To test for doneness, put a knife in the center. If it comes out clean, the custard is done. When removing from the oven, put custard dish on a rack to cool. Let cool a rather short time and then refrigerate. Milk and eggs should not sit out too long.

Quiche Lorraine

Makes 6 main-dish servings or 12 hors d'oeuvres

9" UNBAKED PIE SHELL

½ POUND SLICED BACON, OPTIONAL*

1½ CUPS (6-OUNCES) GRATED NATURAL SWISS CHEESE

3 EGGS

1½ CUPS LIGHT CREAM (MAY USE HALF-AND-HALF)

¾ TEASPOON SALT

DASH NUTMEG

DASH PEPPER

1. Prepare pie shell and refrigerate until ready to use. Heat oven to 375°. If using bacon, fry until crisp and drain well. Crumble into bits. Spread bacon over bottom of pie shell.

2. Sprinkle grated cheese over bacon. Beat eggs with cream, salt, and spices until well combined but *not* frothy. Pour over cheese in pie shell. Bake 35–40 minutes or until top is golden and center seems firm when gently shaken.

*I rarely use bacon anymore. It is delicious without it.

Cranberry Chicken

Serves 6

6 BONELESS, SKINLESS CHICKEN BREASTS

1 PACKAGE DRY ONION SOUP MIX

1 8-OUNCE BOTTLE FAT-FREE DRESSING WITH TOMATO
    AS MAIN INGREDIENT

1 CAN JELLIED OR WHOLE BERRY CRANBERRY SAUCE

❧ Line a 9" × 13" pan with foil. Place the chicken breasts on the foil. Mix together the rest of the ingredients in a bowl and pour over chicken. Bake at 350° for 35–40 minutes or until done. Very delicious and easy! If the breasts are large, cut them and you may be able to serve another person or two. Great warmed up.

Curried Chicken

Serves 4–6

3 LARGE ONIONS

3 WHOLE CHICKEN BREASTS (MAY BE CUT INTO SMALLER PIECES FOR EASE OF SERVING)

BUTTER OR OIL

1 TABLESPOON EACH CURRY POWDER AND GINGER (OR TO TASTE)

SALT AND PEPPER TO TASTE

1 PINT CHICKEN STOCK

1 FRESH LEMON

1/2 PINT HEAVY CREAM

❧ Chop the onions coarsely and sauté with the chicken in butter or oil. Place chicken, onions, spices, and stock in heavy pot and stew very gently until tender. When tender add juice of 1 fresh lemon. Just before serving, add 1/2 pint of heavy cream and simmer gently to reduce sauce.

Lemon Chicken

Serves 6

1/2 TEASPOON SALT

PEPPER

6 BONELESS, SKINLESS CHICKEN BREAST HALVES

1 STICK BUTTER

2 TABLESPOONS DRY SHERRY (NOT COOKING SHERRY)

2 TABLESPOONS GRATED LEMON RIND

2 TABLESPOONS FRESH LEMON JUICE

2 TEASPOONS CORNSTARCH

1 CUP HALF-AND-HALF (FOR LOW FAT, USE 2/3 CUP CHICKEN BROTH AND 1/3 CUP LOW-FAT SOUR CREAM)

2 TABLESPOONS PARMESAN CHEESE

❧ Lightly salt and pepper chicken. Sauté in melted butter for 8–10 minutes. Place chicken in a 9" × 13" dish. To butter in skillet, add sherry, lemon peel, and juice. Stir cornstarch in half-and-half or combined chicken broth and sour cream. Slowly add to mixture in skillet. Heat until thickened, stirring constantly. Pour 1/3 cup sauce over each piece of chicken. Sprinkle with Parmesan cheese. Bake, uncovered, at 350° for 30–35 minutes.

Simple and Delicious
Baked Chicken with Rice

Canned green beans or peas can be added to rice mixture to make a complete meal. When this meal is shared with a family, it is brought uncooked with the recipe and instructions for baking it.

Serves 4

1 CUP RICE, UNCOOKED

1 CAN CREAM OF MUSHROOM SOUP, UNDILUTED

1/4 CUP WATER

1 CUP ORANGE JUICE

1 BROILER CHICKEN, CUT UP, OR SEVERAL CHICKEN BREASTS AND/OR LEGS

1 PACKAGE DRY ONION SOUP MIX

❧ Spread rice on bottom of casserole with cover. Mix mushroom soup, water, and orange juice. Pour mixture over rice. Coat chicken pieces with onion soup mix. Place chicken on top of rice and liquid. Cover snugly. Bake at 325° for 1 1/2 hours.

Chicken with Rice

Serves 8–10

1 1/4 CUPS RAW RICE, UNCOOKED

1 CAN EACH KIND OF SOUP: CREAM OF MUSHROOM, CELERY, AND CHICKEN

1/4 CUP BUTTER, MELTED

1/4 CUP DRY SHERRY

10 PIECES OF CHICKEN

1/3 CUP GRATED PARMESAN CHEESE

❧ Put rice in a 3-quart casserole. In bowl, combine soups, butter, and sherry. Spread 1 1/2 cups soup mixture over rice. Place chicken, skin side up, in single layer. (May use skinless chicken, too.) Cover chicken with remainder of soup mixture. Sprinkle with Parmesan cheese. Cover well. Bake at 350° for 2 hours.

Chicken Divan

Serves 6–8

2 PACKAGES COOKED BROCCOLI

2 CANS CREAM OF CHICKEN SOUP

1 CUP MAYONNAISE

1 TEASPOON LEMON JUICE

2 OR 3 CHICKEN BREASTS, COOKED AND BONED

PARMESAN OR CHEDDAR CHEESE, GRATED

BREADCRUMBS

◦◦ Butter large oblong casserole and put broccoli in bottom. Combine soup with mayonnaise and lemon juice. Pour $1/2$ of this mixture over broccoli. Add cut-up chicken and rest of sauce. Sprinkle with grated cheese and breadcrumbs. (Herb dressing also makes a tasty topping instead of breadcrumbs.) Bake at 350° for 30 minutes.

Baked Chicken Breasts

Serves 4

2 CUPS PREPARED HERB DRESSING, MIXED ACCORDING TO PACKAGE DIRECTIONS

4 BONELESS, SKINLESS CHICKEN BREASTS

SLICES OF SWISS LORRAINE CHEESE (ENOUGH TO COVER CHICKEN)

1 CUP CONDENSED MUSHROOM SOUP

$1/2$ CUP WHITE WINE OR MILK

◦◦ Place dressing divided into 4 servings in small serving dish. Cover each with 1 chicken breast. Put cheese slices over chicken. Pour soup mixed with wine or milk over all. Bake at 325° for $1^1/2$ hours. This recipe is easily doubled.

Apricot Chicken

Serves 4

1 TABLESPOON EACH MARGARINE AND OLIVE OIL

1/4 CUP FLOUR

SALT TO TASTE

4 BONELESS, SKINLESS CHICKEN BREASTS

1/4 CUP APRICOT JAM

1/4 CUP NO-FAT SOUR CREAM

1 1/2 TEASPOONS DIJON-TYPE MUSTARD

1 TABLESPOON SLIVERED ALMONDS

❧ Heat oven to 375°. Put margarine and olive oil in foil-lined pie plate or baking pan and put into oven to melt. Watch carefully and remove when margarine is melted. Put flour and salt in plastic bag and add chicken. Shake well to coat. Place chicken in prepared pan and bake for 25 minutes. Meanwhile, combine apricot jam, sour cream, and mustard. After 25 minutes, remove chicken from oven and coat each piece with this mixture. Return to oven and bake 30 more minutes. Last 10 minutes, sprinkle with almonds. Easily doubled.

Bug Juice Chicken

Serves 4

1 CUT-UP FRYER (MAY USE BONELESS, SKINLESS PIECES INSTEAD OF CUTTING UP A FRYER)

1/3 CUP SOY SAUCE

2 TABLESPOONS LEMON JUICE

1/4 TEASPOON GARLIC POWDER

1/4 TEASPOON ONION POWDER

1/4 TEASPOON GINGER

NOODLES, 4 SERVINGS

❧ Cut fryer into serving-size pieces, or use boneless, skinless pieces, and put skin side down in baking pan. Mix together in a measuring cup soy sauce, lemon juice, garlic powder, onion powder, and ginger. Pour mixture over chicken, and if chicken pieces have skin, turn to skin side up. Bake at 375° for 75 minutes, basting twice. Cook enough noodles for 4 people. When chicken is done, remove to platter. Pour noodles into sauce in baking pan, mix well, and put into serving dish. Serve with Chinese pea pods.

Taco Chicken Wings

Serves 4–6 as main dish; as appetizer
a few more, maybe 8

1/2 CUP FLOUR

1 ENVELOPE TACO SEASONING MIX

3 POUNDS CHICKEN WINGS, TIPS REMOVED

6 TABLESPOONS BUTTER OR MARGARINE

1 CUP CRUSHED CORN CHIPS

❧ Combine flour and taco mix in plastic bag. Coat 2 or 3
pieces of chicken at a time. Melt butter in baking pan; place
chicken in pan and turn once to butter surface. Roll in corn
chips and return to pan. Bake at 350° for 40–45 minutes.

Pork Chop Casserole

Serves 6

6 PORK CHOPS

4 MEDIUM POTATOES, SLICED

SALT AND PEPPER TO TASTE

1 MEDIUM ONION

1 CAN CREAM OF CHICKEN SOUP

❧ Brown chops. Place sliced potatoes into 11/2-quart
baking dish. Salt and pepper to taste. Arrange chops on top
of potatoes. Slice onion on top of chops. Pour soup over all
and cover dish. Bake at 350° for 11/2 hours.

Tuna Bake

Serves 8–9

12 OUNCES MACARONI, UNCOOKED

1 8-OUNCE PACKAGE CREAM CHEESE

2 CANS MUSHROOM SOUP

2 TABLESPOONS CHOPPED ONION

2 TABLESPOONS PREPARED MUSTARD

1 SMALL JAR PIMIENTOS

2 7-OUNCE CANS TUNA

1 CUP PREPARED DRY HERB DRESSING

2 TABLESPOONS BUTTER, MELTED

❧ Cook and drain macaroni. Combine next 5 ingredients. Stir in tuna. In another bowl, combine stuffing mix and butter. In a casserole, alternate layers of macaroni, sauce, and stuffing until casserole is full. Sprinkle topping over all. Bake at 375° for 20–25 minutes.

Tuna Scallop

Serves 2–3

1 CAN MUSHROOM SOUP

1 CUP MILK

4 TABLESPOONS BUTTER OR MARGARINE

3 TABLESPOONS FLOUR

3/4 TEASPOON SALT

3/4 TEASPOON SUGAR

1/4 TEASPOON PEPPER

MINCED ONION TO TASTE

1 6-OUNCE CAN TUNA, FLAKED

1 CUP COOKED NOODLES

❧ Combine all ingredients and pour into buttered casserole. Put buttered crumbs on top. Bake for 30 minutes at 350°. Easily doubled.

Grilled Salmon Oriental

Serves 6

1 1/2 POUNDS SALMON STEAKS OR FILLETS
1 6-OUNCE CAN UNSWEETENED PINEAPPLE JUICE
1 TABLESPOON LIGHT SOY SAUCE
1 TEASPOON HOT PEPPER OIL
1 TABLESPOON VEGETABLE OIL
2 CLOVES GARLIC, MINCED
1/2 CUP ONION, FINELY CHOPPED
1 TABLESPOON FRESH GINGER, GRATED
1/2 TEASPOON LIME RIND, GRATED
2 TABLESPOONS FRESH LIME JUICE
VEGETABLE OIL SPRAY

❧ Rinse fish and pat dry. Arrange fish in a rectangular glass baking dish. Combine all ingredients in a small bowl, stir well, and pour over steaks. Turn to coat steaks evenly. Cover and refrigerate overnight. Preheat grill or broiler. Lightly spray grill top or broiler with oil. Remove steaks from marinade and place steaks over hot coals or under broiler, 4"–5" from heat. Grill 5–7 minutes on each side or until fish flakes easily with a fork.

Zucchini Casserole

Makes 6–8 servings

1–2 CARROTS, GRATED
1–2 ONIONS, SLICED THIN
BUTTER OR MARGARINE
2 OR 3 CUPS CUT-UP ZUCCHINI
1 CUP SOUR CREAM
1 CAN CREAM OF MUSHROOM SOUP
3–4 TABLESPOONS BUTTER OR MARGARINE
1 8-OUNCE PACKAGE DRY HERB STUFFING MIX

❧ Sauté carrots and onions in butter or margarine. Cook zucchini in salted water, 6–8 minutes. Stir together sour cream and soup and add zucchini, carrots, and onions. Pour into casserole dish. Melt margarine and toss with dressing. Top the casserole with dressing. Bake 30 minutes at 300°.

Deluxe Broccoli Casserole

Serves 6–8

1 POUND FRESH BROCCOLI OR 2 10-OUNCE FROZEN PACKAGES

1 PINT SMALL ONIONS OR FROZEN EQUIVALENT

1/4 CUP BUTTER OR MARGARINE

2 TABLESPOONS FLOUR

1/4 TEASPOON SALT

DASH PEPPER

1 CUP MILK

1/2 CUP CONDENSED MUSHROOM SOUP

1 3-OUNCE PACKAGE CREAM CHEESE

1/2 CUP PARMESAN CHEESE

1/2 CUP SHREDDED SHARP CHEDDAR CHEESE

1 SMALL CAN MUSHROOMS

1 CUP STUFFING MIX

ﹾ Cook broccoli until tender along with onions. Melt 1/2 the butter; blend in flour, salt, and pepper. Add milk and cook until thickened. Reduce heat and add mushroom soup and cream cheese. Blend until smooth. Add Parmesan cheese and 1/2 of sharp cheese. Place vegetables in 1 1/2-quart casserole, adding 1/2 of stuffing mix. Pour sauce over top and mix slightly. Top with remainder of sharp cheese and rest of stuffing mix, which has been tossed with rest of melted butter. Sprinkle on top. Bake at 350° for 40–45 minutes.

Corn Pudding and Cheese

Makes 10–12 side servings

3 TABLESPOONS BUTTER OR MARGARINE

2 TABLESPOONS SUGAR

2 TABLESPOONS FLOUR

1 TEASPOON SALT

3 WHOLE EGGS

2 CUPS CANNED OR FRESH CORN

1 LARGE OR 2 MEDIUM ONIONS, DICED OR SLICED

1 3/4 CUPS MILK

CHOPPED PIMIENTO, OPTIONAL

1 CUP SHREDDED CHEESE, SWISS, CHEDDAR

ﹾ Blend butter, sugar, flour, and salt. Add eggs, beating well. Stir in corn, onions, milk, and pimiento. Pour ingredients into buttered casserole and bake at 325° for about 45 minutes. Halfway through cooking (after 20 minutes) add 1 cup shredded cheese and stir. When done, a knife inserted will come out clean.

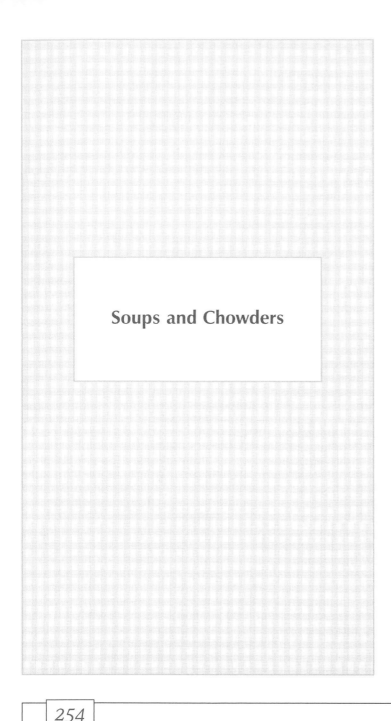

Soups and Chowders

Slow Cooker Beef Stew

Serves 6

3 CARROTS, CUT UP

3 POTATOES, CUT UP

2 POUNDS BEEF CHUCK OR STEW MEAT, CUT INTO 1$\frac{1}{2}$" CUBES

1 CUP BEEF STOCK, INSTANT, CANNED, OR HOMEMADE

1 TEASPOON WORCESTERSHIRE SAUCE

2 TABLESPOONS KETCHUP

1 CLOVE GARLIC

$\frac{1}{2}$ CUP BURGUNDY WINE (OPTIONAL)

1 BAY LEAF

$\frac{1}{2}$ TEASPOON PAPRIKA

3 ONIONS, QUARTERED

1 STALK CELERY, CUT UP

❧ Put all ingredients in slow cooker in order listed. Stir just enough to mix spices. Cover and turn heat to high for 5 to 6 hours.

Note: This stew may be cooked in a conventional oven. If using a conventional oven, cook everything except carrots, potatoes, and onions at 350° for 1 hour. Add potatoes, carrots, and onions, and cook for another 1 hour and 15 minutes. Stew may be thickened if you wish.

German Beef Stew

Serves 4

1½ POUNDS STEW BEEF, CUT IN 1" CUBES

2 TABLESPOONS COOKING OIL

1 LARGE APPLE, PARED AND SHREDDED

1 MEDIUM CARROT

½ ONION, SLICED

½ CUP WATER

⅓ CUP RED WINE

½ TEASPOON ANCHOVY PASTE

1 CLOVE GARLIC, MINCED

⅛ TEASPOON DRIED THYME

1 SMALL BAY LEAF

2 BEEF BOUILLON CUBES

4 CUPS NOODLES COOKED AND DRAINED

Brown meat in kettle in 2 tablespoons cooking oil (olive or canola). Add all other ingredients except noodles. Cover and cook over low heat for 1 hour or until tender. (A longer slow cooking time would enhance flavor.) When done, remove bay leaf and serve over hot noodles.

Flavorful Tomato Bouillon

Makes 6 1-cup servings

1 46-OUNCE CAN NO-SALT-ADDED TOMATO JUICE

2 CUPS HOMEMADE BEEF BROTH OR 1 14.5-OUNCE CAN
    LOW-SODIUM VARIETY

2 BAY LEAVES

6 WHOLE CLOVES

2–3 TABLESPOONS FRESH DILL WEED, MINCED

½ TEASPOON DRIED SWEET BASIL

½ TEASPOON DRIED MARJORAM

½ TEASPOON DRIED OREGANO

½ TEASPOON SUGAR

¼–½ TEASPOON BLACK PEPPER, FRESHLY GROUND

1 LEMON, THINLY SLICED FOR GARNISH

Mix tomato juice and beef broth in a large glass bowl or jar. Add remaining ingredients, except lemon. Stir to blend. Cover and chill in refrigerator overnight. Next day, pour soup into a heavy saucepan and bring to a boil. Reduce heat and simmer for 30 minutes. Remove bay leaves and whole cloves. Tip: Cloves can be difficult to retrieve from soup. Try using a tea ball by putting cloves in the ball and hanging ball on side of kettle with ball in the soup. When ready to serve, ladle into soup bowls or mugs and top each with a slice of lemon.

Microwave method: Remove soup from refrigerator and place the ingredients in a 3-quart microwave-safe dish. Cover and place in microwave. Bring to a boil on high power. When boiling, reduce power to low or simmer, and cook 7–8 minutes. Let soup rest 5 minutes and then serve hot with a slice of lemon.

Old-Fashioned Corn Chowder

Serves 5–6

4 SLICES BACON

2 MEDIUM ONIONS, CHOPPED

4 MEDIUM POTATOES, PEELED
    AND DICED

1/2 CUP WATER

1 1-POUND CAN CREAM-STYLE
    CORN

1 1-POUND CAN WHOLE
    KERNEL CORN

1 3-OUNCE CAN
    EVAPORATED MILK

2 1/2 CUPS WHOLE MILK

1 TABLESPOON BUTTER

2 TEASPOONS SALT

1/8 TEASPOON PEPPER

❧ Cook bacon in large kettle until crisp. Remove bacon and set aside. Add onions to bacon drippings and cook until transparent. Add potatoes and water. Simmer 5 minutes. Add corn and simmer 5 minutes longer. Stir in milks, butter, salt, and pepper. Heat, being careful not to boil. Crumble bacon and sprinkle over servings of chowder. This is an excellent meal for a cold winter night when served with old-fashioned Johnny Cake and homemade pickles.

Note: Who doesn't love the bacon flavor in chowders and the rich milk? For some of us, there comes a time when we have to modify our dietary habits in order to stay away from lots of medication or severe health problems. From experience, let me suggest if you must do away with the bacon and the rich milk, you do not have to do away with corn chowder, fish chowder, and any number of other favorites. Sauté the onions in olive oil and use a lower-fat milk and a little less salt. You may be surprised at how you adjust to a slightly different flavor.

Lobster Stew

Serves 4

1 1/2 POUNDS LOBSTER TAIL MEAT

1/4–1/2 CUP BUTTER

1 1/2 QUARTS MILK

1/2 CUP CREAM

❧ Sauté lobster in butter. Add milk and cream. Heat through, but do not boil.

Oven Fish Chowder

Serves 6–8

2 POUNDS HADDOCK

4 POTATOES, PEELED AND SLICED

1 BAY LEAF

2 1/2 TEASPOONS SALT

4 WHOLE CLOVES

1 CLOVE GARLIC, MINCED

3 ONIONS, SLICED

2 TABLESPOONS BUTTER

1/4 TEASPOON DRIED DILL SEED

1/4 TEASPOON WHITE PEPPER

1/2 CUP DRY WHITE WINE

2 CUPS BOILING WATER

2 CUPS LIGHT CREAM OR
    EVAPORATED MILK

❧ Put all ingredients *except* cream into casserole. Cover; bake at 375° for 30 minutes. Turn down oven to 350° and bake 30 minutes longer. Remove from oven. Add scalded cream. Stir to break up fish. Remove bay leaf and whole cloves.

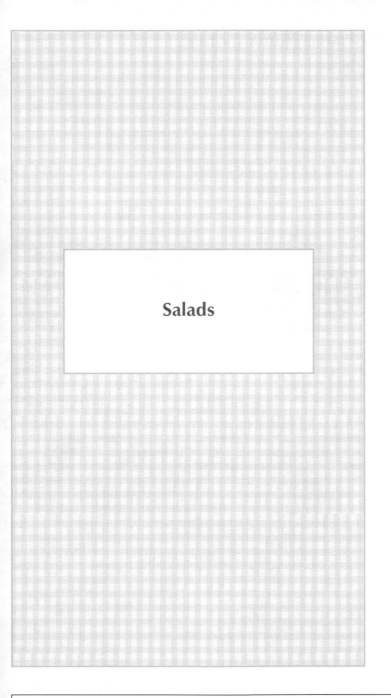

Salads

Spiced Cranberry Ring

Makes 12 side salads

1 6-ounce package raspberry gelatin

1/8 teaspoon cinnamon

Dash cloves

1/4 teaspoon salt

2 cups boiling water

2 8-ounce cans whole berry cranberry sauce

2 tablespoons grated orange rind

1 cup diced orange segments

1 cup chopped apple

❧ Dissolve gelatin, cinnamon, cloves, and salt in boiling water. Add sauce and orange rind. Chill until thickened. Fold in orange and apple. Pour into 6-cup mold and chill.

Note: This salad could be divided in 1/2 if recipe is too large for the family you are helping. Or, maybe your family and the family in need could both have salad.

Fresh Spinach Salad

Serves 6–8

10 OUNCES FRESH SPINACH LEAVES
$1/2$ POUND BACON, COOKED AND CRUMBLED
$1/2$ CUP SLIVERED ALMONDS
1 GRANNY SMITH APPLE, CHOPPED
$1/8$ RED ONION
3 TABLESPOONS CIDER VINEGAR
$1/3$ CUP OIL
$1/4$ CUP SUGAR
$1/4$ TEASPOON SALT

❧ Toss spinach leaves, bacon, almonds, and apple. For the dressing, blend onion, vinegar, oil, sugar, and salt in blender. Toss salad with dressing just before serving.

Mystery Tomato Mold

Serves 4

1 3-OUNCE PACKAGE RASPBERRY GELATIN
6 OUNCES BOILING WATER
$1\frac{1}{2}$ CUPS STEWED TOMATOES, DRAINED
1 DROP TABASCO SAUCE
1/16 TEASPOON WORCESTERSHIRE SAUCE
HORSERADISH AND SOUR CREAM FOR GARNISH

❧ Dissolve gelatin in boiling water. Chop tomatoes in blender or food processor. Add to gelatin. Mix in seasonings and blend well. Chill slightly and ladle into individual molds. Chill until set. Unmold and garnish with horseradish and sour cream mixed to taste.

Garden Slaw

Serves 4–6

2 CUPS COARSELY GRATED CABBAGE

1/2 CUP CHOPPED CELERY WITH TOPS

1 TABLESPOON SUGAR

1/2 TEASPOON SALT

1/4 TEASPOON PEPPER

1/4 CUP SOUR CREAM

1 TABLESPOON VINEGAR

2 MEDIUM-SIZED CARROTS, GRATED

❧ Mix cabbage, celery, sugar, salt, and pepper. Chill 30 minutes before serving. Combine sour cream and vinegar. Toss lightly with cabbage and celery. Spoon into serving bowl. Garnish with grated carrots.

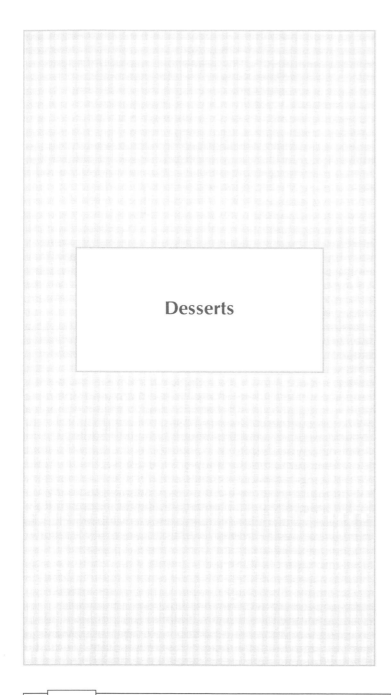

Desserts

Blueberry Crunch

Serves 8

1 PINT BLUEBERRIES, FRESH OR FROZEN

2 TABLESPOONS FLOUR

1/4 TEASPOON SALT

1/2 CUP SUGAR

2 TABLESPOONS LEMON JUICE

1 CUP FLOUR

1 CUP OATMEAL

1/2 CUP BROWN SUGAR

1/2 TEASPOON SALT

1/2 TEASPOON VANILLA

1/2 CUP BUTTER

Combine blueberries, flour, salt, sugar, and lemon juice. Pour this mixture into bottom of buttered pie plate. Combine flour, oatmeal, brown sugar, salt, and vanilla. Cut into this mixture 1/2 cup butter or margarine. Sprinkle this mixture over the berry mixture. Bake at 350° for 30–40 minutes, or until nice and bubbly. May top with whipped cream or ice cream if desired. Wonderful any time of year!

Bread Custard Pudding

Serves 8–10

3 CUPS MILK

3 TABLESPOONS BUTTER OR MARGARINE

4 EGGS, SLIGHTLY BEATEN

1/4 CUP SUGAR

2 SLICES WHITE BREAD (INCLUDING CRUSTS), BROKEN
INTO PIECES

1/2 CUP RAISINS

1 TEASPOON VANILLA

❧ Scald milk with butter. Pour this mixture over slightly beaten eggs and add sugar. Stir. Add bread pieces, raisins, and vanilla. Mix together well. Bake at 350° for 45 minutes or until knife inserted comes out clean.

Mocha Pie

Serves 6–8

4 TOFFEE-TYPE CANDY BARS

1 1/2 TABLESPOONS INSTANT COFFEE

1 TABLESPOON BOILING WATER

1 QUART VANILLA ICE CREAM

1 GRAHAM CRACKER CRUST

❧ Break up candy bars in small plastic bag, very fine. Dissolve coffee in boiling water. Mix above into 1 quart partially softened ice cream. Pour into shell and freeze. (Cover with foil.) Take out of freezer about 15 minutes before serving. Quite rich. Delicious!

Ruth's Wonderful Brownies

Makes 24 2" brownies

1/2 CUP SHORTENING

4 EGGS

1 POUND CONFECTIONERS' SUGAR

4 SQUARES UNSWEETENED CHOCOLATE, MELTED

1 3/4 CUPS FLOUR, SIFTED

1/4 TEASPOON SALT

1 TEASPOON VANILLA

1 CUP CHOPPED NUTS

ॐ Cream shortening, eggs, and sugar together. Add the rest of the ingredients. Pour into a greased 9" × 13" pan and bake in a 350° oven for 30 minutes. These brownies freeze well. Chewy and delicious!

Gail's Molasses Cookies

Makes about 4 dozen

3/4 CUP CANOLA OIL

1 CUP SUGAR

1/4 CUP MOLASSES

1 EGG

2 TEASPOONS BAKING SODA

2 CUPS FLOUR

1/2 TEASPOON CLOVES

1/2 TEASPOON GINGER

1 TEASPOON CINNAMON

1/2 TEASPOON SALT

ॐ To canola oil, add sugar, molasses, egg, and baking soda. Beat well. Sift together flour, cloves, ginger, cinnamon, and salt. Add this to the sugar mixture. Mix well. Place parchment paper on cookie sheet, or grease the cookie sheet. Drop dough by tablespoon or cookie scoop on cookie sheet. Press down gently with a fork or fingers and sprinkle with sugar. Bake at 350° for 8–10 minutes.

Oatmeal–Chocolate Chip Bars or Cookies

Makes about 4 dozen cookies or about 35 2" squares

1 CUP BUTTER OR MARGARINE

3/4 CUP BROWN SUGAR

3/4 CUP WHITE SUGAR

2 EGGS

1 TEASPOON VANILLA

1 1/2 CUPS FLOUR

1 TEASPOON SALT

1 TEASPOON BAKING SODA

1/2 TEASPOON WATER

2 CUPS OATS

12-OUNCE PACKAGE CHOCOLATE CHIPS

❧ Cream butter and sugars. Add eggs and vanilla. Mix in flour, salt, soda, and water. Stir in oats and chocolate chips. Drop on greased cookie sheet and bake at 375° for 10–12 minutes. You may also spread batter into a jelly roll pan and bake at 350° for 25 minutes. Batter will be thick. Cool before cutting. Squares are quicker, easier, and very tasty.

Note: When making cookies, using parchment paper instead of greasing pans does save time and effort. Also, when making cookies, a cookie dough scoop or small ice-cream scoop is a handy tool.

Chapter Six

The Church Family Picnic

Soon after the celebration of Easter and Mother's Day (or Festival of the Christian Home), our thoughts turn to summer and the wonderful, carefree occasions we enjoy during that time of year. High on the list is the annual Church Family Picnic. It's a happy day with children running in all directions. Think balloon bouquets, only Mylar, of course, for safety reasons. Balloons say that something exciting and fun is happening. They "kick it up a notch," if you will. You may see a kite or two, a few fishing poles, croquet set(s), badminton, and lots of tasty food treats. The young and the more mature gather to enjoy the sharing of a fun day. Those whose children are grown and whose grandchildren live far away enjoy the children of the church. The children's enthusiasm may be even further enhanced by the presence of a special attraction like pony rides or some celebrated children's entertainer from within your greater community.

Of course, church picnics can be enjoyed by the various individual groups within the church (choir, bell choir, ladies circles, adult study class, etc.) as well as by the whole church family.

There are many options to consider when planning the picnic for the church family. Where will it be held? Do you want to have it close to your church community, or do you want to travel? Will there be a lake, pond, or ocean for swimming, fishing, et cetera? Will you be going to an amusement park? Does someone in your church family have a home or summer spot where they might be willing to host such an event? Church picnics can happen in a variety of different settings.

The planning must also include how the food is going to handled. Most often in my experience, families bring whatever meat they wish to grill and a dish to share. Grills are brought and set up at the site the day before the event, if possible. Therefore, meat recipes are not included in the recipe section of this chapter.

The planning committee should provide paper plates, napkins, flatware, and hot and cold drinking cups. Even though the event will, hopefully, be outdoors, a long serving table (maybe a couple of picnic tables) needs to be set with a paper tablecloth and the above-mentioned utensils. Coffee and cold drinks can be provided as well.

Appetizers and munchies can be put out on the table for people to enjoy before getting serious about the meal. Then hot dishes and salads. An alternative to having people bring desserts, is to offer hot fudge sundaes, provided by the church or someone who just wishes to donate them. Adults as well as children seem to enjoy dessert sundaes at a picnic. Chocolate syrup can be squeezed out of a container for this, but included in the recipe section is a recipe for a quickie hot fudge sauce. Before the picnic begins, pour the sauce into a slow cooker and warm it up. Ladle the sauce onto the sundaes from the slow cooker. An easy serving cup for the sundaes is a plastic punch cup. If you wish to be more elaborate, make a sundae buffet. However, the sundaes dipped up and served simply are quite sufficient and a big hit! Cans of whipped cream, a bowl of chopped nuts, and cherries complete the dessert.

Another form of a church picnic can be the all-church family camping trip. Families that enjoy camping can take an overnight or two at a family-type campground. When our children were young, we would do this with a number of families in the church. The kids and the adults had a great time. If Sunday came during the camping trip, worship would be held by the lake or around the campfire. A couple of the more spirited men would take the sash from their bathrobe and wear it for a necktie, which brought plenty of attention and laughter. The meals were potluck, with everyone contributing to the meal. These were memorable events. Recipes appropriate for this kind of trip can be found throughout this book. ❦

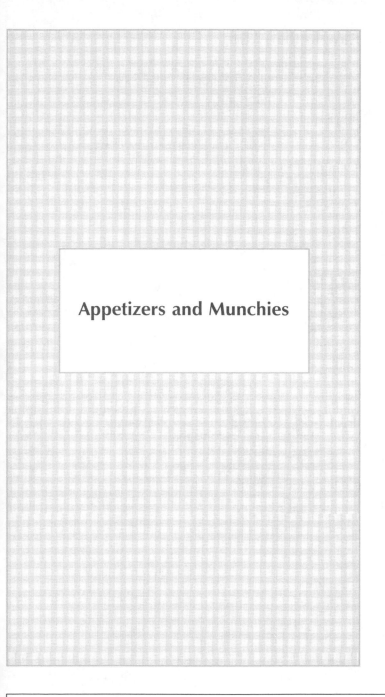

Appetizers and Munchies

Leza's Southwest Salsa

Makes 9–10 cups salsa

2 28-ounce cans tomatoes, drained
6–10 cloves garlic
1 jalapeño pepper
1 tablespoon chipotle flakes
1–2 serrano peppers (optional)
Juice from 2 limes
1/2–1 onion
1 sweet pepper
1/4–1/2 cup fresh cilantro
Salt and pepper to taste

❧ Either chop ingredients by hand or blend all ingredients in blender. Chill and enjoy with your favorite chips.

Plum and Walnut Baked Brie

Serves 12–14

2 TABLESPOONS (1 OUNCE) PLUM PRESERVES
2 TEASPOONS WATER
1 15-OUNCE WHEEL OF RIPE BRIE, WELL-CHILLED AND RIND
    LEFT ON*
1 FIRM RIPE RED PLUM, THINLY SLICED**
1–2 TABLESPOONS WALNUTS, CHOPPED

ஃ Preheat oven to 350°. Melt preserves and water in small pan over low heat. Place Brie on foil-lined baking sheet with lip. Brush melted preserves over top and sides of well-chilled Brie. Brush fruit slices with additional melted preserves and arrange on top of Brie. Sprinkle walnuts over all. Bake 10–15 minutes in center of oven until heated through. Remove from oven and let sit for 2 or 3 minutes. Using a large spatula, carefully move Brie to a serving platter. Delicious with nice breads and crackers.

*You may use any size wheel of Brie. Adjust fruit amounts and heating times accordingly.
**You can substitute whatever fruit appeals to you or is in season.

Raw Radish Dip

Prepare 2–4 hours ahead of serving time.

Makes 2 cups

1 8-OUNCE PACKAGE CREAM CHEESE, SOFTENED
1 TABLESPOON LEMON JUICE
1/4 TEASPOON DRIED DILL WEED
1 TEASPOON SALT
1 CLOVE GARLIC, MASHED
1 CUP CHOPPED RADISHES

ஃ In a small bowl, blend together cream cheese, lemon juice, dill weed, salt, and garlic. Add chopped radishes and stir until blended. Cover; refrigerate for at least 2 hours. Garnish with a radish rose and parsley. Serve with corn chips, or other sturdy chips or crackers.

Onion-Dill Dip

Prepare 1 hour to 1 day ahead.

Makes about 3 cups

2½ cups regular or low-fat yogurt
1 package (amount for 4 servings) dry onion soup mix
1 tablespoon minced parsley
¼ teaspoon onion powder
1 teaspoon dried dill weed
Dash pepper

❧ Combine all ingredients. Chill at least 1 hour to blend flavors. Serve with cherry tomatoes and pieces of crisp vegetables such as carrots, radishes, cauliflower, green beans, zucchini, turnips, or asparagus.

Party Salad Tray

Use your imagination with this one! I will list some items for the tray, but do use your imagination and fill a tray with colorful, tasty, even healthy treats for a picnic appetizer.

Lettuce—Colorful
Sliced bananas, sprinkled with lemon juice
Grapefruit sections, especially red grapefruit
Pear slices
Apple slices, unpeeled
Watermelon
Honeydew melon
Cantaloupe
Fresh strawberries
Fresh blueberries
Fresh mint leaves, sprinkled over all

❧ Enjoy! This would make an attractive centerpiece for your table. Don't forget a flower or two.

Frosted Braunschweiger Roll

18–20 servings

1 POUND BRAUNSCHWEIGER
1/2 CUP CATSUP
1 TEASPOON WORCESTERSHIRE SAUCE
1 3-OUNCE PACKAGE CREAM CHEESE, SOFTENED
PARSLEY, SNIPPED
PAPRIKA

❧ Skin braunschweiger and mash well with fork. Beat in catsup and Worcestershire sauce. Place on waxed paper and shape into 9"-long roll. Refrigerate until firm. Remove paper and place on plate or tray. Thin cream cheese with 1/2 teaspoon or more of milk to make it like thick frosting. Frost roll. Decorate with parsley and paprika. Serve with crackers.

Sweet and Sour Franks

Serves 20–25 as appetizer

3/4 CUP DIJON-TYPE MUSTARD
1 CUP CURRANT JELLY
2 POUNDS FRANKFURTERS OR 2 POUNDS SUMMER SAUSAGE

❧ Place mustard and jelly over hot water in double boiler. This could be done in the microwave, but watch very carefully. Slice the franks or summer sausage into 1/2" slices and add to sauce. Put in slow cooker and let cook for several hours before serving. Serve from the slow cooker with toothpicks.

Deviled Eggs

What's a picnic without deviled eggs?

Makes 1 dozen

6 HARD-BOILED EGGS

1/4 CUP MAYONNAISE OR SALAD DRESSING

SCANT 1/4 CUP PICKLE RELISH

2 TABLESPOONS FINELY CHOPPED CHIVES OR GREEN ONIONS

1 TEASPOON FLAVORFUL MUSTARD

DASH SALT

PAPRIKA

Cut cooked eggs in 1/2 lengthwise and remove yolks. Set aside the whites. Mash the yolks and add the rest of ingredients. You may adjust the amounts of the ingredients to your taste. Spread the mixture over the egg whites and sprinkle with paprika. Serve on tray or in basket on lettuce garnished with parsley. Be sure to keep well refrigerated until serving time. For a large group, boil a dozen eggs and double the filling amounts.

Honey-Roasted Munchies

Makes 18–20 cups

14 CUPS OF YOUR FAVORITE CORN/RICE CEREAL

2 CUPS TINY PRETZELS

2 CUPS PEANUTS (IF ALLERGIC TO PEANUTS, ANY NUT WILL DO)

1 STICK PLUS 2 2/3 TABLESPOONS BUTTER OR MARGARINE

1/2 CUP HONEY

1 1/2 CUPS BROWN SUGAR

2 TABLESPOONS VANILLA

Mix together first 3 ingredients and put in large roasting pan or 2 9" × 13" pans. In a saucepan, put butter or margarine, honey, and brown sugar. Bring to boiling and boil for 5 minutes, stirring constantly. Remove from heat and add vanilla. Pour this mixture over cereal, pretzels, and nuts. Bake in a 225° oven for 1 hour. Stir about every 15 minutes. Bake until crisp. It may take more than an hour. Store in airtight container(s). You probably won't bring much home from the picnic!

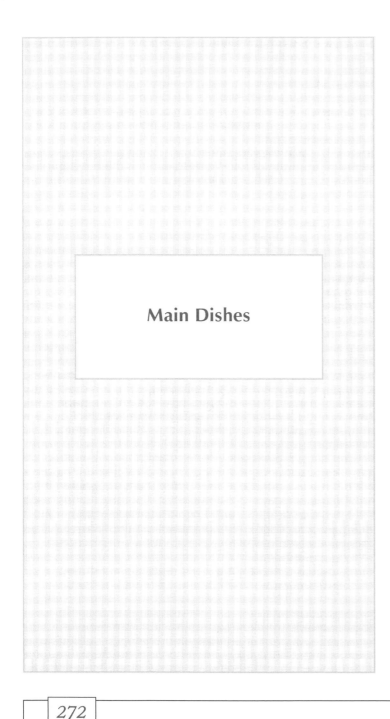

Main Dishes

Sheila's Beans

Beans can be wonderful, even when not started from scratch.

Serves 6

1 28-ounce can baked beans

4 tablespoons ketchup

2 tablespoons molasses

2 tablespoons brown sugar

Onion, celery, and green pepper, minced

Salt to taste

3 drops Tabasco or a few grains of red pepper

Bacon or franks, sliced or whole

❧ Mix all ingredients together except bacon and franks. Place mixture in a shallow ovenproof dish. Cover with bacon or franks. (If desired, you may sauté bacon beforehand and add later.) Bake at 375° for about 30 minutes. These are great served with fresh bread and butter or margarine. Easily doubled.

"Scratch" Beans

Serves 10

2 POUNDS DRY BEANS, YOUR CHOICE	1 CUP MOLASSES
2 QUARTS WATER	1 TEASPOON DRY MUSTARD
1/2 POUND LEAN SALT PORK	1 TEASPOON GINGER
1 ONION, QUARTERED	2 TEASPOONS SALT
	2 TABLESPOONS BROWN SUGAR

1. Pick over beans; discard any bad or broken beans and wash thoroughly in a colander. Put in large pot and cover well with water. Soak overnight.

2. In the morning, drain beans and cover with fresh water. Bring to a good boil. Take a few beans on a spoon and blow on them. When the skins "pop" when blown on, they are ready to be drained and put into the beanpot for baking.

3. While beans are coming to a boil, if you are using salt pork, put in a dish and cover with boiling water. Drain after 2 or 3 minutes and cut slices into the salt pork down to the rind. Put a couple of onion quarters and some salt pork in bottom of beanpot and then put beans into the pot. Wedge the rest of the pork and onion down through the beans.

4. In a small bowl, mix the molasses, dry mustard, ginger, salt, and brown sugar. Mix a little of the hot bean water in the bowl and stir to dissolve molasses and brown sugar. Pour the mixture over the beans and mix through as well as you can. Cover the beans. Bake at 250–300° for 6–8 hours. Add hot water to beans while they cook so that they are always covered with water while cooking. You do not want them to dry out. Smelling them cook is worth the effort!

Janson's (Jansson's) Temptation

Serves 6–8

2 MEDIUM ONIONS, CHOPPED

2–3 TABLESPOONS BUTTER OR MARGARINE

6 RAW POTATOES, PEELED AND CUT INTO STRIPS

18 ANCHOVY FILLETS, RESERVE BRINE

1 CUP CREAM

Sauté onions in 1/2 of the butter. Butter a shallow baking pan. Layer potatoes, onions, and anchovies, making sure there is a layer of potatoes on top. Pour anchovy brine over and dot with the other 1/2 of the butter. Pour over 1/2 cup cream. Bake at 400° for 45 minutes. After 15 minutes add other 1/2 of cream.

Bean Casserole

Serves 18–20 as a side dish

1 15-ounce can baby lima beans

1 15-ounce can kidney beans

1 15-ounce can butter beans

1 1-pound, 13-ounce can pork and beans

1 cup brown sugar

1/2 cup vinegar

1 teaspoon garlic salt (may use garlic powder)

1 teaspoon dry mustard

2 large onions, chopped

1 pound bacon

❧ Combine all ingredients, except bacon, and mix together well. Fry bacon to "wilt" stage and add to bean mixture. Do *not* drain juice from beans. Pour into large buttered casserole and bake uncovered at 325° for 3 hours.

Chicken Wings

Serves 18–20 as an appetizer or part of a picnic buffet

1/4 cup soy sauce

2 tablespoons white corn syrup or honey

1 tablespoon brown sugar

1 teaspoon salt

1/2 teaspoon pepper

1/2 teaspoon ginger

1/2 teaspoon garlic

1/2 ounce brandy

5 pounds chicken wings

❧ Combine all ingredients except chicken wings. Dip each chicken wing in the mixture and put into large baking pan. Pour sauce over chicken wings. Bake at 350° for 1 1/2–2 hours.

Baby Carrots with Ripe Olives

Serves 6–8

2 POUNDS FRESH BABY CARROTS

2 TABLESPOONS OLIVE OIL OR COOKING OIL

1/2 TEASPOON DRIED THYME, CRUSHED

DASH PEPPER

1/3 CUP RIPE OLIVES, PITTED AND FINELY CHOPPED

❧ Cook carrots until just tender, about 15–20 minutes. Drain well. In a large skillet, heat oil; add carrots, thyme, and pepper. Cook until lightly browned, about 8–10 minutes, stirring frequently. Stir in olives and heat through. Turn mixture into a serving bowl.

Sweet Vidalia Onion Pie

Serves 6 as a main dish and 12 as an appetizer

1 STICK BUTTER OR MARGARINE

2 POUNDS VIDALIA ONIONS, THINLY SLICED

1 CUP SOUR CREAM

3 EGGS, BEATEN

1/4 TEASPOON SALT

1/2 TEASPOON PEPPER

DASH OR 2 OF HOT PEPPER SAUCE

UNBAKED 9" OR 10" PIE SHELL

1/4 CUP GRATED PARMESAN CHEESE

❧ Heat butter in large skillet over medium heat until bubbling; add onions and cook until nice and tender. Combine sour cream, eggs, salt, pepper, and pepper sauce. Stir into onions. Pour into shell and sprinkle with Parmesan cheese. Bake at 450° for 20 minutes. Reduce heat to 325° and continue baking for another 20 minutes. Let stand a few minutes before serving.

Salads

German Potato Salad

Serves 8–10

8 BOILED POTATOES, PEELED AND CUBED

1 STALK CELERY, DICED

2 HARD-BOILED EGGS

1 ONION, CHOPPED

1 TABLESPOON PARSLEY, CHOPPED

4 SLICES BACON

2 EGGS, WELL BEATEN

1 CUP SUGAR

¼ TEASPOON DRY MUSTARD

½ TEASPOON SALT

¼ TEASPOON PEPPER

½ CUP VINEGAR

½ CUP COLD WATER

Mix potatoes, celery, hard-boiled eggs, onion, and parsley. Fry bacon in skillet until crisp and brown. Drain, reserving fat, and dice. Beat eggs; add sugar, spices, vinegar, and water. Mix well and pour into hot bacon fat. Before adding egg mixture, spoon off fat, leaving just 2–3 table-spoons. (If on special diet, cook mixture in olive oil.) Stir mixture until it thickens, about 10 minutes. Pour over the potato mixture and mix lightly. Chill for several hours before serving.

Nana's Potato Salad

Serves 10

10 MEDIUM POTATOES, BOILED WITH SKINS ON
FRENCH DRESSING (SEE FOLLOWING RECIPE)
1 ONION, MINCED
1/2 CUP MINCED CELERY
1/2 CUP MAYONNAISE
LETTUCE
PAPRIKA
GARNISHES: SLICED OLIVES, TOMATOES, RADISHES, AND A
    HARD-BOILED EGG

❧ Boil potatoes until tender; peel and cut into cubes. Marinate in French Dressing overnight, stirring occasionally. Near serving time, add onion, celery, and mayonnaise and mix together well. Serve on a bed of lettuce and garnish with paprika and slices of hard-boiled egg, olives, tomatoes, and radishes.

Nana's French Dressing:

2/3 CUP VEGETABLE OIL
1/4 CUP VINEGAR
1 TEASPOON SALT
1/4 TEASPOON PEPPER
1 TEASPOON CELERY SALT
1/2 TEASPOON PAPRIKA

❧ Beat together well with mixer.

Summer Salad

Serves 10

1 1/2 POUNDS BROCCOLI
1 HEAD CAULIFLOWER
2 SMALL ZUCCHINI
2 BASKETS CHERRY TOMATOES
1/2 POUND MUSHROOMS
2 BUNCHES GREEN ONIONS
1 CUP DICED CELERY
2 8-OUNCE CANS WATER CHESTNUTS
1 6-OUNCE CAN PITTED RIPE OLIVES
2 CUPS DICED SWISS CHEESE
LETTUCE

❧ Mix all but lettuce in a large bowl.

Dressing:

1/2 CUP HONEY
1/4 CUP MUSTARD
1 1/2 CUPS SALAD OIL
2 CUPS MAYONNAISE
1/4 CUP CIDER VINEGAR
1/8 CUP CHOPPED ONIONS
DASH WORCESTERSHIRE
PINCH SALT

❧ Blend together the above ingredients in food processor or blender. Cover platter with lettuce and arrange salad on lettuce. Could be divided in 1/2 for a smaller group.

Apple, Nut, and Feta Salad

Serves 8–10

Step I: Peppered Walnuts (or pecans)

3 TABLESPOONS BUTTER

1 CUP WALNUTS OR PECANS

1/2 CUP SUGAR

1 TABLESPOON FRESHLY GROUND BLACK PEPPER

❧ Melt butter in an ovenproof pan. Add nuts and roast in 350° oven for 15 minutes, stirring every 5 minutes. Remove from oven. In a large bowl, toss roasted nuts with sugar and pepper. Set aside.

Step II: Vinaigrette

1/2 TEASPOON SUGAR

1/4 TEASPOON OREGANO

2 TABLESPOONS MINCED ONION

2 TABLESPOONS VINEGAR (MAY USE BALSAMIC VINEGAR OR WHITE WINE VINEGAR)

1 CLOVE GARLIC, MINCED

1/2 TABLESPOON DIJON MUSTARD

3/4 CUP OLIVE OIL

❧ Combine all ingredients in a food processor until emulsified.

Step III: Salad

1 LARGE OR 2 SMALL HEADS OF LETTUCE OR YOUR FAVORITE MIXED GREENS (ROMAINE IS ESPECIALLY GOOD)

2 APPLES, CORED AND SLICED, UNPEELED (TART IS GOOD)

1/2 CUP CRUMBLED FETA CHEESE

❧ Combine lettuce, sliced apples, and feta cheese. Toss with vinaigrette to coat. Top with peppered nuts and toss lightly.

Note: This salad would also be tasty and attractive with the addition of dried cranberries.

Three Bean Salad

Serves 12–15

1 15-ounce can kidney beans

1 15-ounce can wax beans

1 15-ounce can green beans

1 15-ounce can chickpeas

1 onion, sliced

1/2 cup vinegar

1/2 cup oil

1/8 cup sugar

1 teaspoon salt

❧ Drain and rinse all beans and peas. Place in glass or china bowl and add onion. Pour vinegar, oil, sugar, and salt over all. Cover and refrigerate overnight.

Layered Spinach Salad

Serves 8–10

1 pound spinach, chopped fine

1/2 pound bacon, cooked and crumbled

6 hard-boiled eggs, chopped

1 head lettuce, or greens of your choice, chopped

1 10-ounce box frozen petite peas, cooked and cooled

1 red onion, thinly sliced

Mayonnaise, thin layer (may use fat-free)

1/2 pound Swiss cheese, shredded (may use Cheddar or Parmesan)

❧ In a clear large bowl, layer ingredients in order. Sprinkle spinach layer with salt, pepper, and sugar. Sprinkle lettuce layer with salt, pepper, and sugar. Do *not* mix anything, just leave in layers. Can be made the night before.

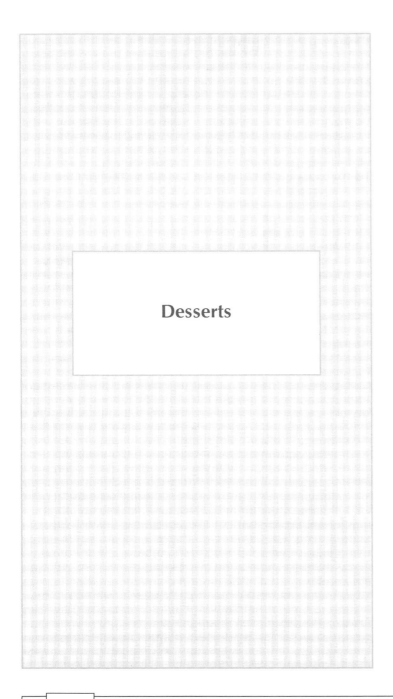

Desserts

Best "Quickie" Chocolate Sauce

Approximately 6–8 servings

1 6-OUNCE PACKAGE SEMISWEET CHOCOLATE CHIPS

1 5½-OUNCE CAN EVAPORATED MILK

2 TABLESPOONS HOT WATER

ɔ Put ingredients in small saucepan. Cook, stirring constantly, until chocolate is melted and sauce smooth. Serve hot or cold. Makes 1¼ cups. Easily multiplied to serve lots of people. Store tightly covered in refrigerator. May be frozen.

Candy Bar Delight

Makes 9–12 servings

1 LARGE ANGEL FOOD CAKE
1/4 CUP BUTTER OR MARGARINE
2 CUPS POWDERED SUGAR
2 TEASPOONS VANILLA
1 PINT WHIPPING CREAM, WHIPPED
3 LARGE "PEANUTBUTTERY, GRAINY" CANDY BARS
1 CUP PECANS OR WALNUTS

❧ Break up angel food cake into small pieces and put 1/2 in a greased 9" × 13" pan. In mixer, blend butter, powdered sugar, and vanilla until fluffy. Fold in whipped cream. Spoon 1/2 mixture over cake pieces. Crush candy bars and put 1/2 over filling, along with 1/2 the nuts. Repeat with cake, filling, candy, and nuts. Press down a little with a spoon or fork. Chill.

Chocolate Celebration Cake

Makes 18–20 good-sized pieces; makes 24 2" squares

2 1/3 CUPS FLOUR
1 4-OUNCE PACKAGE CHOCOLATE PUDDING MIX (NOT INSTANT)
1 TEASPOON SALT
1 TEASPOON BAKING SODA
1 1/2 CUPS PACKED BROWN SUGAR
2/3 CUP BUTTER OR MARGARINE
1 CUP BUTTERMILK
3 EGGS
1 TEASPOON VANILLA
1/4 CUP CHOPPED NUTS
1 6-OUNCE PACKAGE CHOCOLATE CHIPS

❧ Sift flour, pudding mix, salt, and soda together in mixing bowl. Add brown sugar, butter, and buttermilk. Beat 1 1/2 minutes on low speed. Add eggs and vanilla. Beat 1 1/2 minutes on medium speed. Pour into greased 9" × 13" pan. Sprinkle with nuts and chocolate chips. Bake at 350° for 30–35 minutes.

Chewy Blond Brownies

Makes 24 2" bars

1/2 CUP BUTTER OR MARGARINE
1 1/4 CUPS BROWN SUGAR, FIRMLY PACKED
1 1/3 CUPS FLOUR
2 EGGS
1/2 CUP SEMISWEET CHOCOLATE CHIPS
1/2 CUP NUTS, CHOPPED
2 TEASPOONS VANILLA
3/4 TEASPOON SALT
3/4 TEASPOON BAKING SODA
1 1/3 CUPS OATMEAL, UNCOOKED

❧ Beat together butter and brown sugar until well blended. Add flour, eggs, chocolate chips, nuts, vanilla, salt, baking soda, and uncooked oatmeal. Mix well. Spread into a greased 9" × 13" baking pan. Bake at 350° for 25 minutes or until golden brown. Cool and cut into bars. Instead of chocolate chips, you may use butterscotch or peanut butter–flavored chips.

Tiramisu Toffee Pie

Serves 8

1–2 TABLESPOONS COFFEE BRANDY
1 1/2 TABLESPOONS INSTANT COFFEE GRANULES
3/4 CUP WARM WATER
1 FROZEN POUND CAKE, THAWED
1 8-OUNCE PACKAGE CREAM CHEESE
1/2 CUP POWDERED SUGAR
1/2 CUP CHOCOLATE SYRUP
2 1/2 CUPS FROZEN WHIPPED TOPPING
1 TOFFEE CANDY BAR, CRUSHED

❧ Stir coffee brandy and coffee granules into water and cool. Cut cake into 14 slices; halve each slice. Place slices in a 9" pie plate. Drizzle coffee mixture over cake. Beat cheese, sugar, and chocolate syrup until smooth. Add whipped topping and beat until fluffy. Spread mixture evenly over cake. Sprinkle with candy. Chill 8 hours. Very rich.

Easy Cheesy Bars

Makes 24 2" squares

2 PACKAGES CRESCENT ROLL DOUGH
2 8-OUNCE PACKAGES CREAM CHEESE
1 CUP SUGAR
1 EGG
1 TEASPOON VANILLA

Cover bottom of a 9" × 13" pan with 1 package of crescent rolls. Soften cream cheese and beat with sugar, egg, and vanilla until creamy. Pour over base and cover with other package of crescent rolls. Sprinkle with cinnamon and sugar. Bake 30 minutes at 350°.

Punch Bowl Banana Pudding

Serves 20–25

3 POUNDS BANANAS
2 QUARTS VANILLA PUDDING
6 OUNCES WHIPPED TOPPING
1 CUP SOUR CREAM
1 BOX VANILLA WAFERS

Slice bananas and make pudding. Mix pudding, whipped topping, and sour cream together. Layer pudding mixture, vanilla wafers, bananas, and pudding. Continue to layer, ending with pudding. If this recipe is doubled, assemble in a punch bowl.

Blueberry Citrus Cake

Serves 10–12

1 18.25-OUNCE PACKAGE WHITE CAKE MIX
1/2 CUP ORANGE JUICE
1/2 CUP WATER
1/3 CUP OIL
3 EGGS
1 1/2 CUPS FROZEN BLUEBERRIES
1 TABLESPOON ORANGE PEEL, FINELY SHREDDED
1 TABLESPOON LEMON PEEL, FINELY SHREDDED
FROSTING, RECIPE FOLLOWS

In large mixing bowl, combine mix and next 4 ingredients. Beat on low 30 seconds. Turn to medium speed and beat 2 minutes. With wooden spoon, gently fold in berries and peels. Pour batter into 2 greased and floured 9" cake pans. Bake at 350° for 35–40 minutes or until toothpick comes out clean. Cool on rack in pans for 10 minutes. Remove from pans and finish cooling on racks. Frost with Citrus Frosting and refrigerate.

Citrus Frosting:

1 8-OUNCE PACKAGE CREAM CHEESE, SOFTENED
1 STICK BUTTER, SOFTENED
1 TABLESPOON EACH LEMON AND ORANGE PEEL
5 CUPS CONFECTIONERS' SUGAR
HALF-AND-HALF

Cream together cream cheese and butter. Beat in orange and lemon peel, confectioners' sugar, and enough half-and-half for spreading consistency.

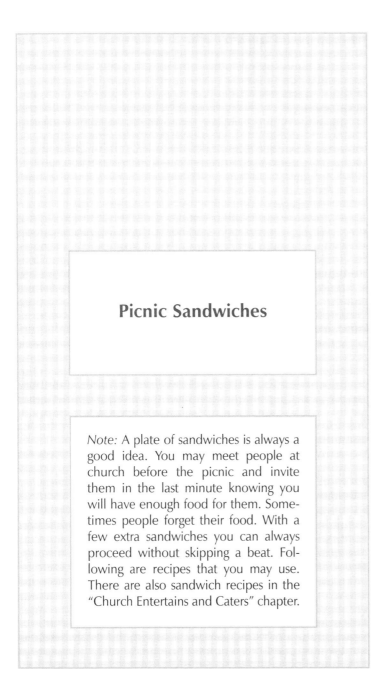

Picnic Sandwiches

Note: A plate of sandwiches is always a good idea. You may meet people at church before the picnic and invite them in the last minute knowing you will have enough food for them. Sometimes people forget their food. With a few extra sandwiches you can always proceed without skipping a beat. Following are recipes that you may use. There are also sandwich recipes in the "Church Entertains and Caters" chapter.

Simple Egg Salad Sandwiches

This recipe will make about 24 sandwiches

2 DOZEN EGGS, HARD-BOILED
1½ TEASPOONS PREPARED MUSTARD
SALT AND PEPPER TO TASTE
LIGHT MAYONNAISE

After boiling eggs, cool and peel them. To make a smooth spread, grate the eggs using the finest side of the grater. Put grated eggs into a large bowl. Mix in mustard, salt, and pepper to taste and enough light mayonnaise to make a spreadable consistency. It would be easily multiplied or divided.

Pimiento Cheese Spread

Makes about 25 sandwiches

28 OUNCES MILD CHEESE
3½ OUNCES PIMIENTO, FINELY MINCED
2 CUPS LIGHT SALAD DRESSING
SALT AND PEPPER TO TASTE

❧ Grate the cheese on the finest side of the grater. In a large bowl, mix the cheese, pimiento, and salad dressing. Season with salt and pepper to taste. Mix to a good spreadable consistency.

Luncheon Meat Sandwich Spread

Will make about 25 sandwiches

¼ MEDIUM ONION
2 12-OUNCE CANS LUNCHEON MEAT
1 DOZEN EGGS, HARD-BOILED
½ CUP PICKLE RELISH
BLACK PEPPER TO TASTE
2 CUPS MAYONNAISE

❧ Put onion in food processor to chop. Add meat, chop, but do not allow to become mushy. Chop eggs and add to meat mixture. Add pickle relish and black pepper. Do not add salt. Mix with enough mayonnaise to make the mixture spreadable.

~

*C*hurch picnics can be wonderful, and they are especially memorable in an outdoor setting. We recall the stories of Jesus feeding 5,000 people one evening in the countryside, and sharing with his disciples the fish and bread cooked one morning over a charcoal fire on the shore of the Sea of Galilee. When we "break bread" in fellowship with each other, with the vast sky overhead and the green grass or beach sand beneath our feet, truly there is a dimension to the experience we can call "blessed."

Index

Index